An Introduction to
Neural Computing

Remembering Bettina
1912 – 1989

An Introduction to Neural Computing

Igor Aleksander
Professor of Neural Systems
Head of Department of Electrical Engineering
Imperial College
London

and

Helen Morton
Lecturer
Department of Human Sciences
Brunel University
Middlesex

CHAPMAN AND HALL
LONDON•NEW YORK•TOKYO•MELBOURNE•MADRAS

UK	Chapman and Hall, 11 New Fetter Lane, London EC4P 4EE
USA	Chapman and Hall, 29 West 35th Street, New York NY10001
JAPAN	Chapman and Hall Japan, Thomson Publishing Japan, Hirakawacho Nemoto Building, 7F, 1-7-11 Hirakawa-cho, Chiyoda-ku, Tokyo 102
AUSTRALIA	Chapman and Hall Australia, Thomas Nelson Australia, 480 La Trobe Street, PO Box 4725, Melbourne 3000
INDIA	Chapman and Hall India, R. Sheshadri, 32 Second Main Road, CIT East, Madras 600 035

First edition

© 1990 Igor Aleksander and Helen Morton

Typeset in Great Britain by
KEYTEC, Bridport, Dorset
Printed in Great Britain by
T. J. Press (Padstow) Ltd, Padstow, Cornwall

ISBN 0 412 37780 2

British Library Cataloguing in Publication Data

Aleksander, Igor, 1937–
    An introduction to neural computing.
    1. Artificial intelligence
    I. Title   II. Morton, Helen
    006.3

    ISBN 0-412-37780-2

Library of Congress Cataloging-in-Publication Data available

Contents

A software package simulating many of the neural networks described in this book is available from Unistat Ltd, PO Box 383, Highgate, London N6 5UP and in North America from Adhoc Reading Systems Inc, 28 Brunswick Woods Dr, East Brunswick, NJ 08816, USA, Tel: 201-254 7300, Fax: 201-254 7310, who will be happy to supply further information and quote prices for supplying the software on floppy disk and issuing site licences for its use.

Introduction
Why the fuss?

The late 1980s will be remembered among computer scientists as the time when an area of study called *connectionism* or *neural networks* or *parallel distributed processing* suddenly came to the fore not only as a topic for research but also as an area for commercial development. All the above names are synonyms: they refer to machines that, unlike conventional computers, have a structure that, at some level, reflects what is known of the structure of the brain.

As we shall show, this is not entirely a new field: indeed its past stretches back beyond that of conventional computing. What is new, however, is a concern with well-founded analysis and a deepening understanding.

In this introduction we briefly review some of the history of the connectionist way of doing things and give reasons for the revival of interest and, consequently, the reasons for writing this book. Ultimately the rationale for connectionism has to do with the fact that mechanisms do matter and, in order to design machines that work well, mechanisms need to be understood. We also preview the plan for the rest of the book: simple aspects of neural system analysis and design.

IS THERE A FUSS?

In 1987 the American Institute of Electrical and Electronic Engineering called the first conference on neural nets. It took place at San Diego, California where 200 authors presented their papers to 2000 delegates. It was described as 'the dawn of a new era'; the scientists were talking of a kind of computing that is inspired by the cellular networks of living brains. The following year saw even bigger events: more papers and more delegates. So, as far as most computer scientists were concerned, something new was going on.

The next two years saw a considerable influx of research funding, which at the time of writing, is still on the increase. Major learned societies have been set up world-wide, and the subject has now been embraced by most research centres in computing and electrical engineering and by some centres in the natural, life and human sciences.

The subject has an interdisciplinary flavour not known in technology since the 1960s when 'cybernetics' (the study of information and control in man and machine) held some researchers' attention. Neural computing, however, has fired the imagination of a larger community. It is normal at conferences on neural computing for as many contributions to come from physicists, biologists, neuropsychologists and statisticians as come from computer scientists. This reflects the character of this science: it defines an interdisciplinary culture which is based on brain-like learning, as opposed to traditional computing which is based on programming. The fuss is about the discovery of a new form of computing which is distinct from the traditional variety, and which seems likely to open up a host of new possibilities.

THE CONVENTIONAL COMPUTING CULTURE: ALGORITHMS

Computers have become so much a part of our lives that we forget that their structure is based on just one person's view of the way in which a computational process can be organized. We are referring to John von Neumann's incredibly far-sighted view of the way a computer worked. The computing is done by a single arithmetic/logic unit that operates on data held in memory. A series of instructions, also held in memory, controls where the data is obtained by this unit, what is to be done with it, and where the result is to be directed in the memory (von Neumann, 1947). No matter how sophisticated the task performed by a computer, the machinery is eventually called upon to execute long lists of elementary instructions. The strength of the technique lies in the scope for packing groups of instructions together to create more elaborate instructions. For example, a computer might execute the instruction to multiply two numbers together as a series of simpler, addition instructions. $A \times B$ means adding A to itself B times. Computer languages such as Pascal or PROLOG consist of so-called 'high-level' instructions which are made up of complexes of simpler instructions. Loading such a language into a computer involves providing the machine with a 'compiler' or an 'interpreter' for that language. These are series of instructions that translate the high-level commands into low-level ones that the machine can execute. (A compiler does the translation on complete programs, while an interpreter does it line-by-line.)

Artificial intelligence (AI) makes use of the highest levels of this packaging in order to get a computer to do things which if done by humans would be said to require intelligence. For example, a computer that plays chess merely executes a massive series of instructions, such as 'if the board state is A, then find all the possible next moves which can be made from state *A* . . .'. The rules for doing this are arranged in an ordered series of levels. For example, the above instruction is at a 'high' level, and needs to be broken up into simpler steps at lower levels. At the next level down are rules which test a given move, to see whether it is applicable to that particular board state or not. At an even lower level there are rules that determine the legality of the applicable rules within the conventions of the game of chess, and so on.

The concept that is used at each of these levels is the *algorithm*. An algorithm is a 'series of steps that achieves a desired aim'. Multiplying *A* by *B* may require the algorithm: 'to achieve $A \times B$ add *A* to itself *B* times.' Similarly, to make a chess-playing program work, the computer needs algorithms such as: 'for board state *A*, test for all applicable rules' and: 'for each applicable rule and for each board piece to which it applies, apply the rule and store the resulting board state.' To choose the best move, the program must also be given a way of evaluating the listed board states: this too is a series of algorithms.

The central question here is, where do these algorithms come from? The answer is simple: they are representations of human knowledge. The humble repetition of additions to achieve multiplication is a representation of the basic arithmetic that we learn as children at school. The algorithms that go into an AI chess-playing or problem-solving program are representations of human knowledge of the rules and strategies for chess or for solving problems. The art of the programmer is that of turning algorithms into code that the computer can understand through the use of a suitable computer language, while the art of the AI scientist is to find algorithms for the forms of computer behaviour he or she is trying to achieve. Complicated hierarchies and interactions between algorithms are what make a computer work, whether it is crunching numbers or playing chess. All of these algorithms must be invented and implemented by a human being to give a computer a semblance of intelligence.

The sobering implication of this is that the range of things that can be done with a conventional computer is limited to those tasks for which a human can find algorithms. This simple fact distinguishes information processing in conventional computers from human information processing: humans are capable of developing their behaviour through 'learning' while computers have to wait for some human to feed them the algorithms required to accomplish the desired task.

THE NEURAL COMPUTING CULTURE: EXPERIENCE ACQUISITION

While living creatures are endowed with some predispositions when they are born, they mostly become viable through a process of gathering 'experience' about the environment in which they live. This occurs through a process of exploration or through interaction with other living creatures, for humans have developed sophisticated languages whereby they can interchange experience. However, the point which is being stressed is that the difference between this style of becoming a competent 'mechanism' and the way in which a computer acquires its competence by being programmed is quite enormous.

Programming a computer involves spelling out to it every step of a process. A human being relates his or her conversations to experience. A child who is told 'be gentle with the new kitten' may or may not obey the command, depending on a whole variety of previous events that the child may have experienced. The child may not know what the word 'gentle' means; he or she may have been scratched by a cat and not wish to approach the kitten at all; or he or she may have previously been rough with a cat which then hissed and ran away. The way that a kitten responds to a child may also be determined by its previous experience of children. So, stored experience is the basis from which the interaction with the world is interpreted by living creatures.

In many ways, if one's aim is to build machines that work well, doing it by conventional programming seems a more direct and controlled way of doing things. Experience seems to be too closely related to the makeup of an individual and, if this mode were to exist in machines, it might lead to individualistic and enigmatic devices. Their control might become expensive and unreliable. But neural computing is not about building humanoid machines: it is about discovering how machines might store and use experience, should this be necessary to the design of devices with skills that cannot be achieved by programming. Are there such skills?

WHERE EXPERIENCE SCORES OVER PROGRAMMING

The period between the mid-1960s and the mid-1980s was a time of great euphoria and confidence among those working in artificial intelligence laboratories. The style of step-by-step design of programming algorithms seemed set to conquer a vast variety of tasks which 'if done by humans would be said to require intelligence' (as defined earlier). Programming rules were being discovered that could allow a machine to look for good moves at chess rather than exhaustively looking at all possible moves; general methods of solving clearly stated problems were being developed; robot planning programs were shown to be feasible and algorithms were being developed that would extract meaning from sentences input into the computer in something that resembled natural language.

The first warning signs were sounded in the UK in 1973 in a review by Sir James Lighthill (Lighthill, 1973). He pointed out that most of these methods relied on getting the computer to sift through vast amounts of data and that the techniques were being tested on highly restricted 'toy-like' problems. He foresaw that if the methods were to be applied to real problems the power and speed of computers would have to grow at a rate which was greater than that which was conceivable: he called this problem the 'combinatorial explosion'. It is this graphic notion of the computer having slavishly to search through myriads of possibilities that begins to point to the limitations of the programming approach. When a person sees an old friend he or she does not search a database of stored images of all the people he or she knows. The recognition, if it happens at all, is almost instantaneous. So the brain does not succumb to the combinatorial explosion. In any case, a search through stored images may well be a totally fruitless algorithm. The face might be older, distorted by a grimace or partly obscured by hair – how then does one effect a match with similar faces stored in memory?

In recent years, much work in artificial intelligence has been tidied up under the heading of 'expert systems'. An expert system is an algorithmic method for trying to capture experience by using two standard components: a memorized list of rules (such as: 'if X is a child of A and Y is a child of A then X and Y are siblings') and ways of inferring conclusions from these rules and some supplied facts in order to answer a question. For example, the facts might be: 'Mary is the child of Joan' and: 'Fred is the child of Jack': using the rule quoted earlier, the machine would say 'no' to the question: 'are Mary and Fred siblings?' unless there is another rule that deals with the possibility of Joan and Jack being married.

With reference to vision tasks such as face recognition, the key point is that there are no obvious rule sets that can equal the performance of the brain in important tasks such as recognizing a friend, or reacting rapidly to a dangerous situation while driving. A typical example of a task that has unfortunately proved a stumbling block for the application of expert systems is the provision of guidance to unmanned vehicles from the image 'seen' by a computer through a television camera. Such vehicles might be important in the exploration of dangerous or remote areas. Is the image in fig. 0.1(a) a road or a tree? Notice how once little clues are added in fig. 0.1(b) and 0.1(c), it is easier to decide that 0.1(b) is a tree, and 0.1(c) is a road. Of course, rules could be developed to distinguish between these images, but the occurrence of each slightly different distinguishing clue would require the addition of yet another rule. Thus a seemingly endless explosion of rules seems to be inevitable whenever the algorithmic approach is applied to this type of input,

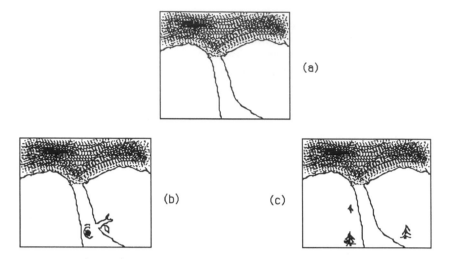

Fig. 0.1 (a) Tree or road? (b) clue for tree (c) clue for road.

making the understanding of images and speech the veritable Achilles' heel of algorithmic, rule-based methods.

Human beings find these tasks easy, and all they have to go on is their experience stored in a network of interconnected brain cells (neurons). The 'computing' that these devices perform is clearly different in kind from the algorithmic, rule-based method. So the quest for investigators of neural nets is to identify how it is that these networks are capable of storing and using experience.

TURING, OTHERS AND BRAINS

Many will be aware of the fact that in 1936 Alan Turing, a British mathematician, laid down the principles for defining what is and what is not computable. He reduced a computation machine to a reading head armed with simple rules for reading symbols on a tape, printing new symbols, and moving to another point in the tape. These rules, which Turing showed would exist for any task that could be said to be computable, are the first manifestations of the concept of an algorithm. But not so many will be aware of the fact that Turing was highly conscious of the fact that brains do their computations in ways that do not depend on algorithms (Turing, 1936). He wrote of the way in which the brain did its computations through cycles of activity in neural nets. He rejected this as a way of thinking about computing machines solely because it did not help with theorizing about computable numbers, which was the subject that motivated his personal interest in theoretical computing machines at that time.

Indeed, John von Neumann, another mathematician, and a giant in the history of the design of computing machines and hence a contributor to the algorithmic way of computing (von Neumann, 1947), also talked of neural nets, seeing them as providing a way of doing computations that emerges from the structure of the net itself. Notable is his concept of 'self-reproducing automata' (Burks and von Neumann, 1966), where neural structures are analysed for their ability to transfer a behaviour that takes place in one part of a net to another part of the net.

Working at the Massachusetts Institute of Technology, Norbert Wiener, whose name is associated with the definition of cybernetics, saw the interplay of logic and network structure as being fundamental to a mathematical understanding of computation in both brains and machines (Wiener, 1947).

Therefore it seems that the algorithmic method has always been seen as the well-behaved, predictable kind of computing, while the neural mode has always been seen as the less predictable, but nonetheless powerful, way of carrying out computations. Indeed, it has always been recognized that neural networks, unlike conventional computers, have properties that emerge from the structure of the hardware, a topic that is only now being properly discussed.

So how is it that the algorithmic methodology has shot ahead so fast, and neural work lain largely dormant for so long? The rest of this book traces the development of neural methodology in a chronological fashion so as to show why there was a collapse of interest in the late 1960s followed by a revival in the 1980s. In Chapter 1 the basic principle is explained in a general way how a neural net does its computations. We show that a net can retrieve stored knowledge by reconstructing learnt patterns of activity from partial clues. This is the 'autoassociative' mode. It is contrasted with the 'associative' style in which a net learns to associate an output with a given input and to produce roughly the right output even if the input is slightly distorted. These two properties are human-like and lead to high hopes that such systems may extend artificial intelligence out of the domain limited by discoverable rules, and allow for fast retrieval of data and the better understanding of living brains.

YEARS OF DEFINITION: 1943–1969

The starting point for most who have studied neural networks has been a model of the fundamental cell of the living brain: the neuron. The recognized US pioneers who first suggested such a model were the neurophysiologist Warren McCulloch and the logician Walter Pitts. In 1943, much in the spirit of cybernetics, they developed a simple model of variable resistors and summing amplifiers that represents the variable synaptic connections or weights which link neurons together and the operation of the neuron body (soma), respectively. In Chapter 2 the behaviour of this highly influential model is analysed fully, which was not only adopted by the pioneers of neural computing but also provides the basis of most nets that are being discussed today. Another important idea was put forward in 1949 when the seeds of a model of dynamic memory were sown by a neuropsychologist, Donald Hebb, who suggested that a group of neurons could reverberate in different patterns, each of these patterns relating to the recall of a different experience (Hebb, 1949). In Chapter 1 (section 1.5) it is shown how the learning mechanisms embedded in simplified models control these groups of reverberating neurons.

Probably the 'buzz-word' that was most heard in cybernetic circles in the 1960s was 'perceptron'. It was coined in 1962 by Frank Rosenblatt who used the word to refer to a system which recognized images using the McCulloch and Pitts model in conjunction with some non-learning 'feature extractors' of an image. To some extent this modelled what was known of the early stages of primate vision (Rosenblatt, 1962). This is another influential model that is very much part of contemporary discussion, and Chapter 2 deals with those elements of perceptron design that have survived to the present day.

ANALYSIS AND IMPLEMENTATION

The early work done in the mid-1960s led to an understanding of the capabilities of the nets in so far as they could be simulated on contemporary computers. But this empirical approach was severely challenged in 1969 in a seminal book written by Marvin Minsky and Seymour Papert (Minsky and Papert, 1969). In Chapter 3 the nature of their objection is explained which lies in the inability of some neural nets to learn to perform tasks that require 'internal representations' not explicitly specified by the training data. For example, a neural net that has learnt to distinguish between images of cars and bicycles may have, within it, a net which has learnt to recognize the presence of two wheels, and another which recognizes four wheels. These are what one calls internal or 'hidden' representations. Because the net must somehow work out these representations for itself, training turns out to be a difficult task. This issue is very much part of current debate and most modern learning algorithms and net structures are being designed with the possibility of solving this difficulty in mind.

Once most of the theoretical basis has been put in perspective, one can then ask how a neural computer could ever be made. In Chapter 4 the issues involved in implementing neural nets are introduced. Most nets are currently being studied as programs running on serial computers or on special fast cards that plug into conventional computers. But the future of this subject turns upon the ability of engineers to make systems which are physically parallel, and in Chapter 4 we consider the questions that arise from the implementation of neurons as silicon chips: should these be analog, digital, mixtures of the two or something different altogether? Should machines have the ability to learn or should the learning be off-line, with the neural net coming into play only when it is required to solve a problem? We also introduce the notion that random access memories (RAMs) might be used to model neurons. Such memory devices have been developed and perfected for conventional computers and have the advantage that they are already being mass produced and are thus readily available for use in neural nets. In a very broad principle, they perform the function of the neuron – they vary their behaviour on demand – but it is important to face the central question of what is lost and gained by this approach.

In Chapter 5, with the above in mind, we describe the WISARD (**WI**kie, **S**tonham's and **A**leksander's **R**ecognition **D**evice), first built in 1981, which demonstrated that a large machine based on neural principles could be built. The device learns to recognize patterns of about 250 000 picture points in 1/25th of a second. The principles of this machine and ways of understanding its performance are discussed.

THE REVIVAL

There is little doubt that it was John Hopfield of the California Institute of Technology who was responsible for a revival of interest in the analysis of neural nets (Hopfield, 1982). But what was the basis of this breakthrough? Interestingly, his orientation was very practical: he saw the stable reverberations mentioned above as being a good way of making advanced computer memories. However, in retrospect, it was his analysis of such systems, which was closely related to the analysis of systems of physical particles, that impressed the scientific community. This is the subject of Chapter 6.

But Hopfield's analysis did not tackle the problems of 'hard learning' which still cast a large shadow over the future of neural nets as devices that could actually be used to carry out useful computations. Many also realized that the net could get stuck in the wrong reverberations. It was Geoffrey Hinton (then at Carnegie Mellon University in Pittsburgh) who suggested a way of overcoming these problems through what he called 'the Boltzmann machine', named after the Austrian physicist Ludwig Boltzmann (Hinton, Sejnowski and Ackley, 1984). Boltzmann added much to physics by studying the effect of heat on the agitation of molecules. In Chapter 7 it will be shown that it is the similarity between systems of physical particles and neural nets which enabled Hinton to use the electronic equivalent of heat (which is electronic 'noise') to avoid false reverberations and deal with the hard learning problem.

No sooner had they defined the Boltzmann machine, than Hinton and his colleagues started asking important questions about whether there was a real need for a close analogy with physical systems. They concluded that 'feed-forward' networks which do not reverberate required investigation (Rumelhard, Hinton and Williams, 1986). These serve to take a pattern at the input of the net and feed it forward to the output where it is translated into another pattern – this can lead to the association of input patterns, such as a written word, with output patterns, which might control a voice synthesizer so that it utters the appropriately related sounds. We discuss this technique in Chapter 8.

MATHEMATICS

The work of Hopfield, Hinton and others who have followed in their wake is grounded in mathematics. We have not avoided the use of mathematical notation altogether. This is not only because it provides a useful and compact language for representing the principles that govern the behaviour of nets, but also because anyone wishing to delve more deeply into the literature of the subject will need to be able to decipher this mode of expression.

We have tried to tread a narrow path between too much and too little mathematics. So that the reader should not be put off by such notation, we have provided some guidance on parts of explanations which could be skipped by those not interested in mathematical detail, and have tried to give numerical examples of the meaning and use of symbols wherever possible.

VARIATIONS

Hopfield and Hinton, though clearly very influential, are by no means the only contributors to the development of neural computing techniques. In Chapter 9 the well-established work of Teuvo Kohonen of Helsinki University is reported upon, which goes under the heading of 'unsupervised learning'. In this mode, the net discovers hidden patterns in the input data which even the designer of the net may not be aware of. The chapter also considers the applications of such systems to speech recognition and looks at ways in which special neuron models help in the recognition of rotated images.

Continuing with the theme of variations, in Chapter 10 descendants of the WISARD species of neural nets are described. In common with the WISARD these systems are distinguished by being 'weightless' and dependent on conventional RAM devices. It is shown that what can be achieved with weight-based systems such as Hopfield and Boltzmann models, can also be achieved by RAM-based systems that perform in 'logical' ways. It is shown that this approach forms a basis for the design of highly implementable nets. The object of the chapter is to give the reader the means for designing such nets with specific tasks in mind.

APPLICATIONS

The field of neural nets is very much in its infancy. This means that the numerous researchers who are giving their attention to the new science are applying neural nets to simplified problems to test their ideas rather than solving problems on a realistic scale. In the final sections of this book we therefore concentrate on the principles which will guide the use of neural nets for practical and useful tasks. After all, neural computing will only have 'made it' when computing engineers will begin to use the technique, as one of several tools available to them, in their quest to achieve specific computing tasks. So we try to answer the question, 'what are these tools?'

Because of the closeness of the technique to ideas that come from the structure of the brain, many of the applications that have been studied to date not only attempt to solve engineering problems, but also have an element of trying to explain 'how the brain does it'. It is argued that finding out how the brain does things may lead to the discovery of some efficient engineering principles. After all, the brain does useful things with rather unreliable components and in areas such as speech and vision the brain still seems to set a standard of competence which computers find very hard to equal.

The first application area tackled in Chapter 11 is one of the most successful and proven demonstrations of the ability of neural nets. The task is to take symbolic representation of words as letters and generate phoneme (sound segment) codes that may be used to drive a voice synthesizer. This is the opposite problem to Kohonen's work on speech recognition (Chapter 9) where phonemes were turned into recognized words (Kohonen, 1984, 1988). The chapter continues with a description of the way that a neural net could be made to follow conversations about simple scenes and paraphrase simple stories.

Probably the major application of neural nets lies in the recognition of visual patterns. This is an area where the brain reigns supreme and this chapter is concluded by describing the approaches taken by those who have based the design of vision machines on what is known of vision in the brain. The work of a leading Japanese contributor, Kunihiko Fukushima is reviewed, who has devised and partially built a machine called the 'Neocognitron' which, because it is able to attend selectively to sections of the image, can recognize images from their features (e.g. corners, straight lines, etc.) (Fukushima, 1988).

THE FUTURE OF NEURAL COMPUTING: HYBRID SYSTEMS

Ultimately the property which distinguishes neural computing from the conventional kind is the ability to learn from example. But the word 'learning' must be used with great care. Does a slipper that becomes more comfortable with wear 'learn' to adapt to one's foot? Is a net that 'learns' to respond in one way to the image of a smiling face and in another when the face is frowning displaying the same mechanisms as those employed by a schoolchild learning to do arithmetic? Are these differences of degree or of kind? More pertinently perhaps, how could neural nets be organized so as to perform the more complex tasks that, in living creatures, are central to the learning activity? How could learning in a neural computing machine best be enmeshed with conventional computing methods?

These are the questions that occupy the last chapter of the book. In Chapter 12 a paper design for a comprehensive tripartite computing architecture is proposed where the aim is to enhance a machine's ability to interact with human users. After all, the main payoff from neural nets will not come from the fanciful creation of humanoid machines, but from machines which, by being capable of processing the same information as their users, will be more amenable to being understood and used.

The proposed architecture contains, first, a conventional computing section that controls the rest and performs algorithmic tasks; second, a learning neural net which performs cognitive (knowledge-dependent) tasks combining, say, speech and vision; and, third, a sensory neural net which does not learn, but which processes visual and auditory signals to make them available in an appropriate form for the cognitive net. The need for this last component leads us to review the work of Carver Mead (1989) who is leading the way in the design of analog silicon chips for the processing of sensory information.

The chapter, and the book, end with suggestions for research into important unsolved problems, and a scenario of future applications which would benefit from neural computing.

EXERCISES FOR THE READER

The questions posed below are designed merely to raise some general debating points about the distinction between 'algorithmic' and 'experiental' (or neural) forms of computing. They assume a minimal knowledge of conventional computing. The reader who is not equipped with such knowledge can easily skip to the next chapter and the rest of the book where no such assumptions will be made.

1. Discuss the different ways in which the word 'memory' is used when referring to a conventional computer and a human being.
2. The recognition of a human face is generally considered to be a difficult task for a computer and an easy one for a human being. Why might this be so?
3. The Turing principle that a conventional computer can compute anything for which an algorithm can be found is generally accepted. At the end of the day, a neural computation is just another algorithm. So why should there be a field known as neural computing, and why should one build special machines?
4. Logic programming takes pride in being able to explain exactly how the solution to a problem in artificial intelligence is solved. This is not necessarily true of neural computers. Is this not a major disadvantage?

Suggestions for appropriate discussions may be found on pp 220–1.

1

Principles and promises

To introduce the principles of neural nets, the principles that lead to the promises, we take a 'black box' approach to the description of a neural node. This means that we concern ourselves with the essential features of what constitutes a neural node without worrying about the details of how such features are physically created.

We explain what is meant by 'adaptation' in such a node and discuss a property which helps the neuron to react correctly even if its stimulus is not the same as that to which it has adapted. This property is called 'generalization', and results from the specification of a 'firing rule'.

Two types of network are discussed: one associates outputs with inputs, another learns to stabilize on patterns that resemble those used during a period of training. The way in which such nets can be said to store knowledge is discussed through the use of simple examples which are also used to illustrate the potential of the neural computing technique.

1.1 A GENERAL DEFINITION

Newcomers to neural computing may be somewhat puzzled by the variety of terms used to describe what appears to be the same thing. We happen to have chosen the words 'neural computing' to describe the field. But what of 'neural networks', 'connectionism', 'parallel distributed processing' and 'connection science'? These are all synonymous defining as they do a mode of computing which, in contrast with the classical school of artificial intelligence, seeks to *include* the style of computing of the brain. The distinction between algorithmic and experiential modes of computing has been discussed in the Introduction, so here we seek a way of defining the experiential mode. For the purposes of this book, we shall continue to use the phrase 'neural computing', assuring the reader that the phrase is totally interchangeable with any of the others.

> **Definition:** Neural computing is the study of networks of adaptable nodes which, through a process of learning from task examples, store experiential knowledge and make it available for use.

This definition is such that the neural nets of the living brain are included in the field of study. The nodes of the brain are adaptable, they acquire knowledge through changes in the function of the node by being exposed to examples. Admittedly, very little is known of the details of how all this happens, but the above definition deliberately provides room for a consideration of biological findings. Of course, it must be understood that an explanation of the way the brain works is only one possible benefit of neural computing. The way in which the science may be used to design useful artificial computing artefacts is also a major concern and is the focus of this book.

In this chapter we shall first concentrate on explaining, in the most general terms, *how* adaptable nodes can be organized to store experiential knowledge. The expectations that arise from this form of computing are then briefly discussed.

1.2 A SIMPLE ADAPTABLE NODE

Here we invent the simplest possible node which will help us to explain the notion of storing experiential knowledge. We are not concerned with whether this node bears any resemblance to a neuron or whether it is a sensible component for making systems. It is merely a device for explaining what any adaptable node has to do. We call our device the Toy Adaptive Node or TAN.

Figure 1.1 is a diagram of the TAN which shows it as some sort of electronic component. We take the step, which is conventional when giving descriptions of computing circuits, of ignoring the actual values of voltages or currents in this circuit and simply assuming that each

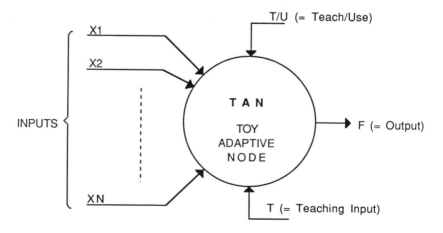

Fig. 1.1 The Toy Adaptive Node (TAN).

connection can be in one of two states: 0 and 1. We leave it to the engineer to decide what these two symbols mean in electronic terms. He or she may choose to specify something like: 1 is the presence of 10 volts, and 0 is the absence of any voltage (assuming that voltages other than 10 and 0 are impossible). Interestingly, it is not necessary to know this specification to discuss the logical function of the node.

There are N *inputs* labelled X1, X2, . . ., XN, and one output F. The actual 0 and 1 values present at the input will often be referred to as an *input bit pattern* since the 1s and 0s can be thought of as binary digits or bits, as in conventional computing. The inputs of one node are connected either to the *outputs* of other nodes or to some external source. The *function* of the node is a list showing what F will be for each of the possible patterns of 0s and 1s that can occur at the inputs. The function may be shown as a truth table. For example, the function of a 3-input node which responds with a 1 when the input pattern contains one 1 and no more than one 1 has the following truth table:

X1:	0	0	0	0	1	1	1	1
X2:	0	0	1	1	0	0	1	1
X3:	0	1	0	1	0	1	0	1
F:	0	1	1	0	1	0	0	0

The table is a simple means of showing that:

when X1 = 0, X2 = 0 and X3 = 0 ('000'), then F = 0
when X1 = 0, X2 = 0 and X3 = 1 ('001'), then F = 1,
and so on . . .

The node may operate in two modes: it can be taught (during which time its function can change) or used (during which time it cannot change). Which of these modes it operates in is determined by setting the T/U terminal to 1 for teaching or to 0 for using. While teaching, the node associates whatever is present (i.e. 0 or 1) at the teaching input T with whatever pattern is present at the X1, X2, . . . terminals. This means that whenever that particular input pattern occurs again in a subsequent using phase, the learnt or associated output symbol (i.e. 0 or 1) is at F.

In this node we shall also define an 'undefined' output '0/1'. For such a condition the node outputs a 0 or a 1 chosen at random. This condition exists either if the particular input has not been taught at all, or if there is some sort of confusion about the desired output for a particular input. For example, if the node is taught to output a 1 in response to a particular input pattern and is then taught to output a 0 in response to the same pattern the output will be undefined. Similarly, a node that has been only taught to output a 0 for the 000 input and a 1 for the 111 input will have undefined outputs for all other input patterns. Its truth table is shown below:

X1:	0	0	0	0	1	1	1	1
X2:	0	0	1	1	0	0	1	1
X3:	0	1	0	1	0	1	0	1
F:	0	0/1	0/1	0/1	0/1	0/1	0/1	1

1.3 SOME DEFINITIONS OF NETWORK SHAPE

A *feed-forward* (or *associative*) net is one in which there are no closed loops. Some examples of what are and are not feed-forward nets are shown in fig. 1.2. Of the nets shown, (a), (b), and (c) are feed-forward

(i) A single-layer, feed-forward net

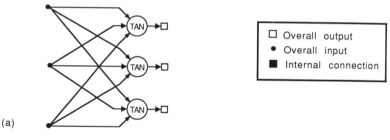

(a)

ii) Feed-forward nets

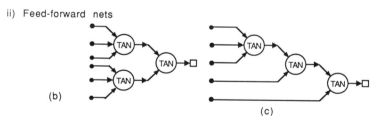

(b)

(c)

iii) Feedback nets

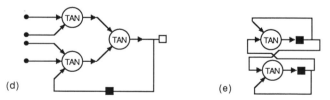

(d)

(e)

Fig. 1.2 Network structures.

In descriptions of networks from here on, the T and T/U terminals will not necessarily be shown, the fact that they are there and being used as described is merely assumed.

nets while (d) and (e) are not. Feed-forward nets act between a set of *overall input* terminals and a set of *overall output* terminals by learning to associate patterns at the former with patterns at the latter. Net (a) has additional properties: it is what is known as a *single-layer*, feed-forward net. That is, it has only one node between any overall input and overall output. It is also *fully connected* which means that every output node is connected to every overall input terminal. Single layer nets of the kind shown in (a) present few problems in training. Their input is known and so is their desired output. This desired output may be fed directly to the teaching inputs (not shown) of the TANs.

The other feed-forward nets (b) and (c) are not of the single-layer kind: they have nodes that are not directly connected to the output and these are called *hidden* nodes. It will be seen in Chapter 3 that these hidden nodes cause problems during training. The training information, consisting only of bit patterns of inputs and their corresponding outputs, does not contain a specification of what should be fed to the teaching inputs of these hidden units. But there is no hope of achieving the appropriate links between inputs and outputs if they are allowed to act at random. This will be discussed fully in Chapter 3 where this difficulty is given the name of the *hard learning problem*.

A *feedback* net is one where information can find its way around a loop from the output back to the input. In fig. 1.2, (d) has one such loop while (e) has two. Each node output that is in such a loop is said to be an *internal* output. These are marked with black rectangles in fig. 1.2. It is seen in Chapter 3 that such internal outputs can be *visible* or *hidden*, depending on whether the data they require during training is known or not known.

Finally, the type of feedback net shown in (e) is said to be *autoassociative* because training takes place so as to use a selected pattern on internal connections as data both for inputs and desired outputs of the nodes. Instead of associating a pattern at an overall input with a pattern at the overall output (as occurs in (a) to (d)), the net in (e) associates the training pattern with itself. To be precise, the net in (d) is also partly autoassociative *via* the loop containing the black rectangular internal connection. It also has four overall inputs and one overall output (which happens to be the same as the internal connection). In contrast, (e) has no overall inputs as the output of the TANs constitutes their inputs. So (e) is said to be 'fully' autoassociative, while (d) is autoassociative 'with controlling inputs'.

Autoassociation is assured by training. Assuming that all nodes in the feedback nets above are visible, during training 0 or 1 values are fed to the internal connections and used both for fixing the related inputs and the desired outputs. If some of this material seems a little complicated at this point, it may be because we have had to go beyond the need to define *shape* properties for nets and are beginning to anticipate some of the problems of using them. The question of what is done with such shapes and how it is done will be revisited in some detail in the rest of this book. For example it will be seen later in this chapter that autoassociation has powerful properties on which many of the hopes for neural nets are pinned.

1.4 FIRING RULES

The word *firing* comes from the language of the biologist interested in the real neurons of the brain. A neuron is said to fire when it emits a buzz of electrical pulses at the rate of about 100 per second. In general, brain scientists are interested primarily in whether neurons fire or not and are not too concerned with the possible intermediate conditions. So we can agree that, in the simple TAN model we have seen so far, we can relate the 1 state of node outputs to firing and the 0 to the absence of firing. (Exactly the opposite could have been agreed as the relationship is arbitrary. The way we have done it is just easier to remember.)

A *firing rule* determines how one calculates whether the node should fire for any input pattern. It relates to all input patterns, not only the ones on which the node was trained. In the basic models that we will discuss in the next chapter, it will be seen that these firing rules are couched in terms of some 'strength' (or 'weight') associated with each connection in the net. Here, as an example, a firing rule is introduced into the TAN model so as to be able to proceed with the aim of describing the way in which nets store experiential knowledge. The rule goes as follows.

> Take a collection of training patterns for a node, some of which cause it to fire (the 1-taught set of patterns) and others which prevent it from so doing (the 0-taught set). Then the patterns not in the collection cause the node to fire if, on comparison, they have more input elements in common with the 'nearest' pattern in the 1-taught set than with the 'nearest' pattern in the 0-taught set. If there is a tie, then the pattern remains in the undefined state

This needs a bit of unravelling by means of an example. For a three-input node, say that the 1-taught set is (X1 X2 X3:), 111, 101 and the 0-taught set, 000, 001. Then, before applying the firing rule, the truth table is:

X1: 0   0   0   0   1   1   1   1
X2: 0   0   1   1   0   0   1   1

X3:	0	1	0	1	0	1	0	1
F:	0	0	0/1	0/1	0/1	1	0/1	1

As an example of the way the firing rule is applied, take pattern 010. It differs from 000 only in the second element, from 001 in the second and third elements, from 101 in all three elements and from 111 in the first and third element. Therefore the 'nearest' pattern in the two taught sets is 000 which belongs to the 0-taught set. Therefore the firing rule would require that the node should not fire for 010. On the other hand, 011 is equally near to the two taught patterns, differing by one element from 001 in the 0-taught set, and also by one element from 111 in the 1-taught set. Therefore 011 remains classified as 0/1.

(As an aside, the distance between two binary patterns in terms of the number of elements in which they differ, is called the *Hamming distance*, after the US engineer R. W. Hamming, who in the 1950s used this measure to develop error-correcting codes.)

After application of the firing rule, the new truth table can now be stated:

X1:	0	0	0	0	1	1	1	1
X2:	0	0	1	1	0	0	1	1
X3:	0	1	0	1	0	1	0	1
F:	0	0	0	0/1	0/1	1	1	1

The difference between the truth table before and after application of the firing rule is called the *generalization of the node* due to the firing rule. In other words, the firing rule gives the node a sense of the 'similarity' between input patterns and enables it to respond with a measure of success to patterns not seen during training. It is this ability to respond to patterns *similar*, but not identical, to those seen in training which gives rise to some of the most exciting aspects of neural net behaviour.

1.5 A FEED-FORWARD (ASSOCIATIVE) NET

Figure 1.3 shows an example of a simple net that illustrates the associative property of a feed-forward network. It consists of three TANs (T1, T2, T3).

It is intended to train it to recognize a T-shaped pattern at a matrix of inputs X11 (i.e. the first input to TAN1) to X33 (the third input to TAN3) by causing the three TANs to fire at their outputs, F1, F2 and F3. Also, an H-shaped input pattern is used to train the net *not* to fire at F1, F2 and F3. After applying the firing rule discussed above, the truth tables for the three TANs may be derived.

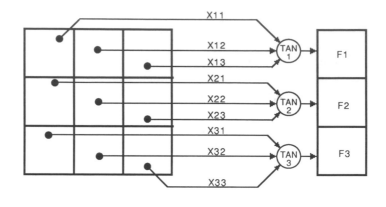

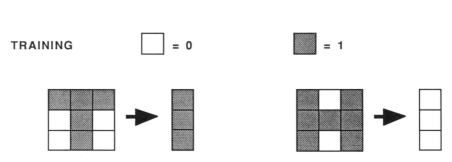

TRAINING

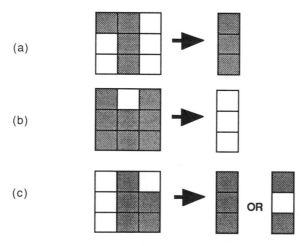

Fig. 1.3 An associative TAN net.

					'H'		'T'	
X11:	0	0	0	0	1	1	1	1
X12:	0	0	1	1	0	0	1	1
X13:	0	1	0	1	0	1	0	1
F1:	0	0	1	1	0	0	1	1

				'T'				'H'
X21:	0	0	0	0	1	1	1	1
X22:	0	0	1	1	0	0	1	1
X23:	0	1	0	1	0	1	0	1
F2:	1	0/1	1	0/1	0/1	0	0/1	0

				'T'		'H'		
X31:	0	0	0	0	1	1	1	1
X32:	0	0	1	1	0	0	1	1
X33:	0	1	0	1	0	1	0	1
F3:	1	0	1	1	0	0	1	0

In order to predict the output pattern for any given input patterns, these truth tables are applied in a purely mechanical fashion. Some of these results are shown in fig. 1.3. For example, test pattern (a) supplies inputs 110, to TAN1, generating 1 at F1, while F2 and F3 are the same as for the 'T' training pattern, hence the output classifies (a) in exactly the same way as a 'T'. Similarly (b) is seen as an 'H' pattern. On the other hand (c) produces 101 or 111. How the net signifies an output of 101 *or* 111 depends on how the electronics of $0/1$ is tackled: it could, for example, be made to produce 0 and 1 alternately. Metaphorically, the net is 'saying' that, if pressed, it suggests that pattern (c) is more like T than H, but the alternation of F2 may be taken as an indication of uncertainty.

1.6 DISTRIBUTED OR LOCALIZED?

Another fundamental parameter of neural nets worth mentioning at this stage is whether output (or internal) representations of information should be *distributed* or *localized*. Before considering this question, the term 'representation' needs to be clarified. Say that the numbers from 0 to 10 are to be 'represented' by binary patterns. This could be done by four binary digits encoded in the usual way (e.g. 0000 representing decimal 0, 0001 representing decimal 1 . . . 0101 representing decimal 5, and so on). This is called a distributed representation because the '1's in the pattern appear in all four binary positions depending on the chosen code. Alternatively, ten binary digits could be chosen to represent the same numbers by placing the 1 in the *n*th place from the left (say) for the *n*th number. So decimal 0 is represented as 0000000000, decimal 1 as 1000000000, . . . decimal 5 as 0000100000, and so on. This is called a localized representation because the coding uses the location of the '1' to represent the data.

In fact, the 'H' and 'T' patterns (fig. 1.3) in the previous example are a distributed representation because the output data that is used for deciding whether the input is an 'H' or a 'T' is distributed across the three nodes of the net.

A localized representation could now be obtained with the system shown in fig. 1.4. The additional net layer containing TAN4 and TAN5 can be trained so that when F1, F2 and F3 are 111 (that is, a 'T'-pattern is present at the input) TAN4 fires (setting F4 to 1), while when F1, F2 and F3 are 000 (that is, an 'H'-pattern is present at the input) TAN5 fires (setting F5 to 1). The decision has now been localized in the output of the net.

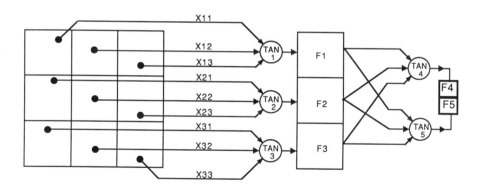

Fig. 1.4 A localized representation.

1.7 WHERE IS THE KNOWLEDGE STORED?

Very loosely speaking, the nets discussed so far have learnt not only to distinguish between a prototype 'T' and an 'H', but also to provide an opinion of the 'T-ness' or 'H-ness' of similar patterns. This could easily be done in conventional computing by programming a simple algorithm such as:

Store the prototype 'T' and 'H' patterns. When an unknown pattern is found calculate its Hamming distance from the prototypes and classify it according to the lower distance.

SMILING   SERIOUS   ?????

Fig. 1.5 A classification problem.

Indeed, this way of doing things is known as *template matching*. The difficulty with this technique occurs when the images are large (in terms of the number of picture points they contain) and when the definition of classes is rather vague. The task could be something like 'differentiate between smiling and serious faces'. In this case endless examples would have to be stored and, in fact, there would be no guarantee that the Hamming distance measurement would give the right answer. The reason for this may be illustrated with the example in fig. 1.5.

Say that a smiling bald-headed man was in the stored data and as well as a serious-looking man with hair. Then a smiling man with hair may well be classified as serious not because of difference in the pattern of the mouth but purely on the basis of hairiness. In other words applying the Hamming distance rule to the whole pattern is far too rough and inaccurate a method.

But if the problem is broken up into many decisions (one per neuron) the net will build up many little rules that are stored in the neurons themselves. It is the fact that the net simultaneously takes an opinion from all these neurons in order to arrive at a decision that gives it its flexibility. In other words, the Hamming distance firing rule used over and over again for small chunks of the image is flexible, whereas trying to apply it to a whole image in one go leads to a lack of flexibility. This is a theme that will be developed in some detail as we progress through the book. It is so fundamental to neural computing that it occurs in most of the discussions from here on. For the time being, the essential point to grasp is that the knowledge in the feed-forward net has been stored as many local rules which are derived from examples and then aided by some kind of firing rule that is the same for all the nodes.

1.8 AN AUTOASSOCIATIVE NET

A net containing nine TANs, each with four inputs, is shown in fig. 1.6. The TANs receive inputs from their 'nearest neighbours' in an array

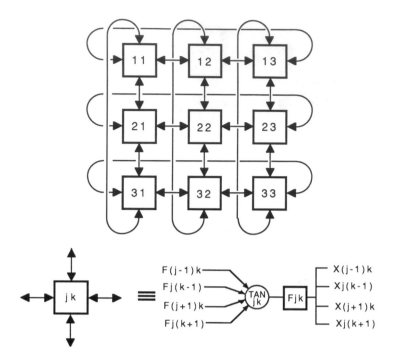

Fig. 1.6 An autoassociative network.

(note that the net is also assumed to be connected bottom edge to top edge and left edge to right edge, as indicated in the figure) and return their decisions to the same nearest neighbours. The whole system possesses a careful method of timing which ensures that the processing by the nodes is done under the control of a clock. When the clock emits a pulse, each node reads its inputs and computes its output; the neighbouring nodes can only read this output as a new input at the arrival of the next clock pulse.

During training, the states of all the elements are selected by the trainer. So each node is trained to produce a selected output, F_{jk}, using the outputs of the four nearest-neighbour nodes as inputs. During use, a firing rule is used as discussed for feed-forward nets. Additionally the user can choose whether to start with a selected pattern on all F_{jk}'s and observe how the pattern of F_{jk}'s develops with each clock pulse, or to *clamp* some of the F_{jk} values by not allowing them to change as the clock pulses arrive. The interest is in the way that the activity of the nodes develops as the clock pulses arrive. If some nodes are clamped, it is the activity of the unclamped nodes which is important.

A *state* being a snapshot of all the F_{jk} values at some instant of time, there are precisely 2^9 (= 512) possible binary states for a net with nine nodes (or 2^k for a net with k nodes). This set of states includes the 'T' and 'H' pattern. Whatever are the current functions of the nodes, any state defines precisely just one next state. As clock pulses are applied, states will follow one another until a state which has already occurred, occurs again. Then the states between these occurrences repeat over and over again, forming a *cycle* of states. In much of neural computing, cycles of only one state are of interest. This is called a *stable* state.

Assume again that the net is trained on the 'T'-shaped pattern and the 'H'-shaped pattern. But this time the output is simply the training pattern itself.

So, TAN11 is trained to output 1 (that is, the value of F11 selected by the trainer) both for 'T' and 'H', because that part of the pattern is black for the two patterns.

Similarly, TAN12 is trained to output 1 for 'T' and 0 for 'H', because F12 selected by the trainer is black for 'T' and white for 'H'.

TAN13 is trained to output 1 for 'T' and 1 for 'H', and so on . . ..

It is now important to concentrate on the input that each node receives while it is being trained on the above outputs. TAN22 is probably easier to understand because it is not affected by the way that the net is 'wrapped' around its edges. So TAN22 receives inputs from F21 (its 'west' input), F12 (its 'north' input), F23 (its 'east' input) and F32 (its 'south' input). TAN23 is a little harder to understand as its 'east' input comes from F21 at the other end of the array.

We shall now look at the content of TAN truth tables which result from training. Because there are four inputs per node, there now are 16 columns in these truth tables. We track below the content of the 23 node (centre of the right-hand column) resulting from this training ($ is shorthand for 0/1).

Before applying the firing rule we have:

									'T'					'H'		
F22:	0	0	0	0	0	0	0	1	1	1	1	1	1	1	1
F13:	0	0	0	0	1	1	1	1	0	0	0	0	1	1	1	1
F21:	0	0	1	1	0	0	1	1	0	0	1	1	0	0	1	1
F33:	0	1	0	1	0	1	0	1	0	1	0	1	0	1	0	1
TAN23 OUTPUT:	$	$	$	$	$	$	$	$	$	$	$	$	0	$	$	1

After applying the firing rule (see p. 6) we have:

									'T'					'H'		
F22:	0	0	0	0	0	0	0	1	1	1	1	1	1	1	1
F13:	0	0	0	0	1	1	1	1	0	0	0	0	1	1	1	1
F21:	0	0	1	1	0	0	1	1	0	0	1	1	0	0	1	1
F33:	0	1	0	1	0	1	0	1	0	1	0	1	0	1	0	1
TAN23 OUTPUT:	0	$	$	1	0	$	$	1	0	$	$	1	0	$	$	1

It is possible to show the output of all the nodes. Conveniently the top four lines of each truth table are the same and can be labelled in terms of their west, north, east and south inputs:

(Input for each cell W: 0 0 0 0 0 0 0 0 1 1 1 1 1 1 1 1
from its neighbours) N: 0 0 0 0 1 1 1 1 0 0 0 0 1 1 1 1
                    E: 0 0 1 1 0 0 1 1 0 0 1 1 0 0 1 1
                    S: 0 1 0 1 0 1 0 1 0 1 0 1 0 1 0 1

OUTPUT OF TAN11: 1 1 1 1 1 1 1 1 1 1 1 1 1 1 1 1
                                (always on for both 'T' and 'H')
OUTPUT OF TAN12: 0 0 0 0 1 1 1 1 0 0 0 0 1 1 1 1
OUTPUT OF TAN13: 1 1 1 1 1 1 1 1 1 1 1 1 1 1 1 1
                                (always on for both 'T' and 'H')
OUTPUT OF TAN21: 0 $ 0 $ 0 $ 0 $ $ 1 $ 1 $ 1 $ 1
OUTPUT OF TAN22: 1 1 1 1 1 1 1 1 1 1 1 1 1 1 1 1
                                (always on for both 'T' and 'H')
OUTPUT OF TAN23: 0 $ $ 1 0 $ $ 1 0 $ $ 1 0 $ $ 1
OUTPUT OF TAN31: 0 0 0 0 1 1 0 0 1 1 0 0 1 1 1 1
OUTPUT OF TAN32: 1 1 0 1 1 1 0 1 0 1 0 0 0 1 0 0
OUTPUT OF TAN33: 0 0 1 1 1 1 1 1 0 0 0 0 0 0 1 1

The above statement of what each TAN will do for each input is called the *long-term memory state* of the net (LTM state) as it represents what has been learnt. This, however, does not give a clear indication of how the system behaves. Nevertheless it can be used to work out the way in which the state of the net changes with time. Let us start by assuming that all the TANs are set to output 0. This 0-state, and all the other states that the net passes through with successive pulses of the clock, are called the *short-term memory states* (STM states) as they represent the transitory states which change with time. Clearly, in the 0-state the current inputs to all the TANs are 0 and the output of all the nodes in their next STM state can be read off the left-hand column of the LTM state. Clearly, the resulting next state is different from the current 0-state.

The changes in the short term memory state of our example are shown below:

0	0	0		1	0	1
0	0	0		0	1	0
0	0	0		0	1	0

         Starting   Second
        STM state   STM state
      (the 0-state)

The second STM state shown above, now produces new inputs for us to look up in the LTM state which, of course, produces new outputs. We say that the STM state *addresses* the LTM state. For example TAN12 in the array receives inputs 1111 from the first STM state and will generate an output of 1 which causes F12 to become 1 in the third STM state. Below, the way the whole LTM state as addressed by the second STM state is shown (the parts of the truth table that are addressed are in bold type).

```
        a b c d e f g h i j k l m n o p
W:      0 0 0 0 0 0 0 0 1 1 1 1 1 1 1 1
N:      0 0 0 0 1 1 1 1 0 0 0 0 1 1 1 1
E:      0 0 1 1 0 0 1 1 0 0 1 1 0 0 1 1
S:      0 1 0 1 0 1 0 1 0 1 0 1 0 1 0 1
```

The boldface means

OUTPUT OF TAN11:
  1 1 1 1 1 1 1 1 **1** 1 1 1 1 1 1 1   TAN12 input is in column i
OUTPUT OF TAN12:
  0 0 0 0 1 1 1 1 0 0 0 0 1 1 1 **1**   TAN13 input is in column p
OUTPUT OF TAN13:
  1 1 **1** 1 1 1 1 1 1 1 1 1 1 1 1 1   TAN14 input is in column c
OUTPUT OF TAN21:
  0 $ 0 $ 0 $ **0** $ $ 1 $ 1 $ 1 $ 1   TAN21 input is in column g
OUTPUT OF TAN22:
  1 **1** 1 1 1 1 1 1 1 1 1 1 1 1 1 1   TAN22 input is in column b
OUTPUT OF TAN23:
  0 $ $ 1 0 $ $ 1 0 $ $ 1 **0** $ $ 1   TAN23 input is in column m
OUTPUT OF TAN31:
  0 0 0 **0** 1 1 0 0 1 1 0 0 1 1 1 1   TAN31 input is in column d
OUTPUT OF TAN32:
  1 1 0 1 **1** 1 0 1 0 1 0 0 0 1 0 0   TAN32 input is in column e
OUTPUT OF TAN33:
  0 0 1 1 1 1 1 1 0 **0** 0 0 0 0 1 1   TAN33 input is in column j

From this the third STM state can be read off giving us the sequence:

0	0	0		1	0	1		1	1	1
0	0	0		0	1	0		0	1	0
0	0	0		0	1	0		0	1	0

Starting	Second	Third
STM state	STM state	STM state
(the 0-state)		

It may be seen with a little effort that the third STM state addresses the LTM state so as to make the fourth STM state the same as the third. In fact it is the taught T-pattern. This means that the net *stablilizes on one of the taught patterns* (the T-pattern). In a similar way it can be shown that, if the net starts with the all-1 pattern, it will now stabilize on the H-pattern at the third STM state. In general, this points to the idea that the net stabilizes on the taught state that is nearest in terms of Hamming distance to the starting state. This idea will be discussed in other parts of the book.

1.9 WHERE IS THE KNOWLEDGE IN THE AUTOASSOCIATIVE NET?

It is of some interest to look at the way in which the LTM and the sequences of STM states work together. Clearly the LTM tables contain a complete record of the training procedure. However, it would be hard to infer what has been learnt just by looking at the LTM. On the other hand, it is the sequences of STM states that say something of the training information in the following sense. Above it has just been shown that given a starting state which is closer (in Hamming distance) to one of the taught patterns than the other, the net can be expected to create another pattern which is even closer to the taught prototype, and so on until the prototype itself is reached. The object of the teaching procedure is to make these prototypes self-sustaining. In short, the net will associate states similar to the taught prototypes with the prototypes themselves. A couple of additional examples can serve to show some characteristics of this form of knowledge storage. Take the STM state below, which is equidistant in Hamming distance from both the 'T' and 'H' differing in three cells from each of the prototypes:

```
1   1   1
1   1   1
0   1   1
```

Figure 1.7(a) shows the STM state changes which follow. The fact that two states could follow the initial one is due to the fact that the initial state really leads to:

```
1   1   1
$   1   1
1   1   0
```

The $ is interpreted as giving rise to 0 and 1 arbitrarily but with equal probability. However, following through the rest of the diagram, using the LTM table on p. 14 as before, we can see that eventually the net

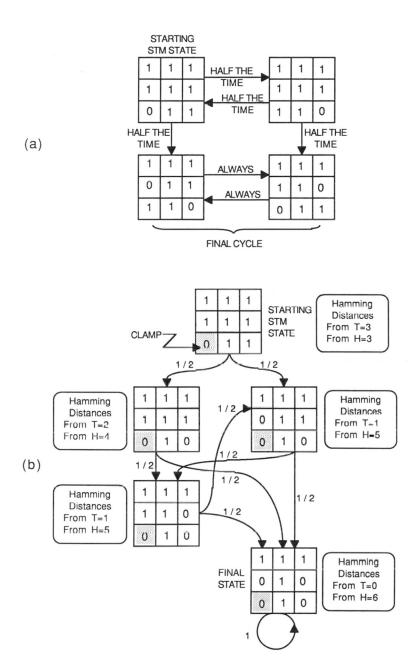

Fig. 1.7 Behaviour of an autoassociative net (a) unclamped (b) clamped.

will end up in a *cycle* where it alternates between two states:

$$
\begin{matrix}
1 & 1 & 1 & \rightarrow & 1 & 1 & 1 \\
0 & 1 & 1 & & 1 & 1 & 0 \\
1 & 1 & 0 & \leftarrow & 0 & 1 & 1
\end{matrix}
$$

It could be said that this is a way in which the net can say: 'I don't know.'

The knowledge stored in the net can also be tapped by a process of *clamping* some of the nodes, that is setting them to some value and preventing them from changing as the net states develop. If we take the bottom left node (TAN31) it would be 0 for the T-pattern and 1 for the H-pattern. This is called a *distinguishing feature* because it distinguishes between the 'T' and the 'H' patterns. In fig. 1.7(b) it is shown that clamping this node to 0 eventually retrieves the pattern related to this distinguishing feature, even if the starting pattern is equidistant from the two prototypes. This process is called *pattern completion* and is a powerful property that is fundamental to autoassociative nets, and is at the root of much of the interest in neural nets.

1.10 PROMISES OF THIS APPROACH

From the discussion so far it would be easy to form the (wrong) impression that neural nets are merely a scheme for performing pattern recognition or pattern reconstruction tasks. There is a far greater expectation of nets than this and it is again based on their associative and autoassociative properties.

First, it could be argued that much of what requires intelligence in human beings is based on the human's ability to associate events and to anticipate events. The relationship between the starting STM state and the final one in a computation is a form of anticipation. The net could be used for anticipating, say, a dangerous event from a current STM state that represented a situation on a road. It could even be argued that a human's ability to do arithmetic is a result of the associative properties of the brain. Filling in the unknowns in $(6 \times 8 = ?)$ or $(5 \times ? = 35)$ is a process of association (although it would be quite perverse in electronic systems to do this with a neural net, since specialized circuits do this sort of work so well). A child balancing a broom on the tip of her hand does so by anticipation and association; to perform the same task a computer has to solve a long series of complex differential equations. But in many other tasks such as the recognition of a known face in a crowd, following 'hunches' when buying and selling shares on the stock market, the recognition of rough roads for automatic guided vehicles, we do not have appropriate rules and equations. In such situations neural nets can give computing equipment a new lease of life.

Association also 'gets into' territory classically held by conventional rule-based methods. For example a logical database that needs to store something like:

JOHN IS THE FATHER OF MARY

could be interrogated as:

? IS THE FATHER OF MARY

where the answer 'JOHN' is found by net autoassociation. These ideas will be developed in subsequent chapters.

From a technical point of view, perhaps the greatest promise of neural computing is that it may enable us to overcome some of the limitations of artificial intelligence. It has been seen in this chapter that the strongest feature to emerge from neural nets is their ability to accept examples and generalize from them. So the major examples of applications of nets to areas of 'intelligent' computing come from pattern recognition where the patterns are human speech, human language and images important to living beings.

Of course not all nets behave as well as the ones shown here. The rest of this book concerns itself, first, with the details of the way real nodes may be created to behave a little like the idealized ones seen here, and then with methods of analysis. The latter are directed towards establishing in which situations training leads to appropriate stabilizations and how the processes of both designing and training nets may be understood and controlled.

EXERCISES FOR THE READER

1. It is the firing rule which causes some of the generalization seen in the above examples. For the same training set as used in fig. 1.3, predict the behaviour of the associative net for truth tables which have *not* been subjected to the firing rule. Compare this to the results in fig. 1.3 itself.
2. Using the firing rule, carry out more tests on the feed-forward net of fig. 1.3 and plot a graph with the Hamming distance of the test pattern from 'T' *less* the Hamming distance of the test pattern from 'H' on the x (variable) axis, putting the difference of the related *output* distances (from the all-1 and the all-0 patterns) on the other axis. This should be a pictorial representation of the generalization of system. If patience persists, or a computer simulation is handy, repeat this without the firing rule and compare the result.
3. For the autoassociative net shown in fig. 1.6, carry out non-clamped

'experiments' with starting patterns to try to provide a general statement of what the net is doing (in terms of the Hamming distance of the starting patterns from the prototype patterns).

4. For the clamped method used on the circuit in fig. 1.6 see how the net behaves if the central node (i.e. TAN22) is clamped first to 0 and then to 1. The first (F22 = 0) is in neither training set and the second (F22 = 1) is in both and is therefore ambiguous.

5. If you have some familiarity with the way rule-based knowledge is stored in a conventional computer, compare and contrast this to the way it has been handled in the above examples.

2

The McCulloch and Pitts legacy

The building brick of any neural computing system is some sort of representation of the fundamental cell of the brain: the neuron. This was first modelled by McCulloch and Pitts in 1943, and it is the influence of their model that sets the mathematical tone of what is being done today. Here the model is described, analysed and used in simple tasks.

Of particular interest is the 'delta rule' which is the means whereby this model converges on a desired function. This is the basis for more sophisticated rules which are discussed in other chapters. Here it is illustrated in use.

The perceptron, which was the focus of thinking in neural computing in the 1960s, has a McCulloch and Pitts model at its heart. This device is described, not primarily for historical interest but because it is now one of the many schemes that constitute the neural computing scientist's armoury of components.

2.1 THE NEURON

The adaptive node of the brain is the *neuron*. An 'artist's impression' of this element is shown in fig. 2.1. There are 10^{11} of these in the average human brain. They are organized in recognizable and complex structures. A simplified view of the neuron has the following features. The cell usually has a well defined output fibre called the *axon*. Electrical activity in the shape of short pulses has been observed at the axon which can be said to be firing or not. When firing (as seen in the last chapter) the pulses occur about 100 times a second. The axon often divides up, forming several endings each of which makes contact with another neuron.

The contact is made at a button-like terminal called the *synapse*. A neuron can receive from 5000 to 15000 inputs from the axons of other neurons. Most neurons have jagged surfaces with carrot-like protuberances (*dendrites*) that are the sites for their synapses. Synapses are

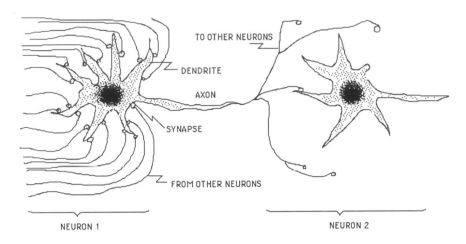

Fig. 2.1 Neurons.

known to be either *excitatory*, in which case their firing aids the firing of the neuron, or *inhibitory* in which case it discourages the neuron from firing.

2.2 THE McCULLOCH AND PITTS MODEL

The precise, electrochemical way in which the brain's neurons work is beyond the scope of this book. Indeed, much has still to be discovered by biologists. Nevertheless, one aspect of the function of a neuron is fundamental: the effect of the synapses is variable, and it is this variability that gives the neuron its adaptability. Very early explanations saw the process of synaptic change as one of growth, and proposed that new synaptic connections could be made (grown) between neurons while, at other times, existing connections could be broken. But in 1943 the neurophysiologist Warren McCulloch and the logician Walter Pitts proposed a model in which synaptic changes are continuous and it is their model that is the basis of neural net calculations in contemporary neural computing.

In this model (which we shall call MCP, for McCulloch and Pitts) the adaptability comes from representing the synaptic action by a variable weight which determines the degree to which a neuron should 'take notice' of firing signals that take place at the synapse concerned. The neuron is thought to take firing signals at all its synapses into account by summing their effects, both excitatory and inhibitory, and thereby determining whether it should or should not fire. In the MCP model it is assumed that firing at the *axon* of a neuron may be represented by the number 1 and no firing at the axon by the number 0. When it is not known what this number is, the state of the axon of the neuron is given the label X. The effect of a synapse is represented by a weight W, which can (somewhat arbitrarily) take values in the range between −1 and +1. The effect on a neuron of any particular synapse is then the product: XW.

The negative values of W represent inhibitory synapses. As there are many synapses another label j must be attached to each of these numbers. So X_j and W_j are the input and weight of the jth synapse. To account for all the synapses, MCP merely adds these effects and compares them to some threshold T. If the total sum exceeds this threshold then the neuron fires. What we have just described is the firing rule for an MCP node. This is usually stated in simple mathematical form as follows:

The neuron fires (i.e. its output F = 1) if the following inequality is true:

$$X_1W_1 + X_2W_2 \ldots X_jW_j \ldots X_nW_n > T$$

or, in more compact form:

$$\sum_{j=1}^{n} X_jW_j > T$$

2.3 AN ENGINEERING INTERPRETATION

(Those not interested in implementation may skip to the next section)

McCulloch and Pitts put this model forward as something that an electrical engineer could build. This idea is shown in fig. 2.2.

The summing device (*summing amplifier* in engineering jargon) provides the necessary summation (an output voltage proportional to the sum of X_jW_j for all values of j) where the X_j values are voltages

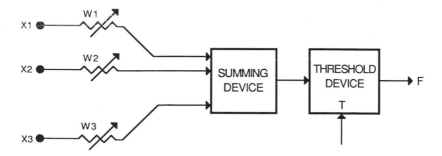

Fig. 2.2 The McCulloch and Pitts model.

selected from two values (one for firing and one for not) and W_j is a value set by a resistor (its reciprocal value, to be precise). The threshold device is some form of voltage comparator which generates a voltage corresponding to 1 if the output voltage of the summing device exceeds another voltage of value T.

There are several problems with this circuit. First, it is not possible to represent inhibition by having negative weights. This problem can be overcome by a trick of inverting the input (this will best be justified after some of the analysis has been done in the next section). Perhaps the more worrying problem for the engineer is the implementation of the variable weight. This may come as a surprise, as even those with little knowledge of electronics will know that the volume control of a radio set is a variable resistor. The subtlety of the difficulty is brought home by asking the question: 'During a learning operation, when the weights have to be changed in order to achieve a specific function, who is going to be turning the knobs on the variable resistors?'

This operation must be done by the machine itself according to some scheme called the learning rule (this will be discussed later). In one well-known implementation in the late 1950s (Taylor, 1959) the variable resistors were attached to motors which were activated appropriately during the learning process. Although these could be driven by the machine itself, any reasonably sized machine would require thousands, if not millions, of little motors. Now, of course, it is possible to make the weights digitally and this will be discussed in Chapter 4.

2.4 SOME ALGEBRA

The simple way in which the firing rule of the MCP model is stated makes it amenable to some easy algebra from which we may understand what is happening. For example, it is possible to answer the question: 'Given a desired truth table, what values must the weights and threshold be given in order to achieve it?'

To make things simple, but without sacrificing any of the character of this analysis, we take an MCP with only two inputs: X_1 and X_2. A desired truth table is shown below:

$$X_1: \quad 0 \quad 0 \quad 1 \quad 1$$
$$X_2: \quad 0 \quad 1 \quad 0 \quad 1$$

$$F: \quad 0 \quad 1 \quad 1 \quad 1$$

The general form of the firing rule for a 2-input MCP becomes:

$$F = 1 \text{ if } X_1W_1 + X_2W_2 > T$$

The truth table provides values for X_1, X_2 and F that can be inserted into this inequality as follows:

For the right-hand column of the truth table we have $X_1 = 1$, $X_2 = 1$ while $F = 1$ indicates that the threshold must be exceeded, hence:

$$1 \times W_1 + 1 \times W_2 > T$$

or, more cleanly,

$$W_1 + W_2 > T \tag{2.1}$$

Similarly, working from right to left across the columns of the truth tables we get another three inequalities:

$$W_1 > T \tag{2.2}$$

$$W_2 > T \tag{2.3}$$

$$0 < T \tag{2.4}$$

The last of these (2.4), is obtained from knowing that both X_1 and X_2 are 0 but that the left side of the inequality must be less than T so as to make $F = 0$. We recall that W_1 and W_2 must be in the range between -1 and $+1$ (as suggested in the original MCP formulation), and deduce that consequently, T must be in the range between -2 and $+2$ (to accommodate $W_1 + W_2$ irrespective of the values of W_1 and W_2 within their allowed range).

Now, the desired function, through the above inequalities further constrains these values as follows: (2.4) restricts T to the range between $0+$ and 2 ($0+$ reads: just over 0); (2.1) and (2.2) both require that T be less than $1-$ (just less than 1), then restricting W_1 and W_2 to the range between $T+$ and 1. So a suitable set of values for all three unknowns may be obtained by selecting some value for T between 0 and $1-$, say 0.5, then selecting W_1 and W_2 in the range $0.5+$ to 1, say 0.7. It is left for the reader to go back to the overall inequality and check that it generates the desired truth table.

Several insights may be gleaned from this way of describing the MCP node. First, it is clear that if (2.2) and (2.3) are satisfied, this implies that (2.1) will be automatically satisfied. This leads to a second conclusion. Had the truth table for the right-hand column been: $X_1 = 1$, $X_2 = 1$ and $F = 0$, with all the other columns being as they are, the function just could not have been achieved at all. In fact, for a 2-input MCP node only 14 of the 16 possible truth tables can be achieved. Things get worse as the number of inputs, n, increases, with the number of achievable functions becoming only a small fraction of the possible ways of constructing a truth table.

The algebra can also throw some light on the need for negative weights. First, it is worth looking at a function that requires negative weights:

$$X_1: \quad 0 \quad 0 \quad 1 \quad 1$$
$$X_2: \quad 0 \quad 1 \quad 0 \quad 1$$

$$F: \quad 1 \quad 0 \quad 1 \quad 1$$

In the usual way, inequalities may be generated from this:

$$W_1 + W_2 > T$$
$$W_1 > T$$
$$W_2 < T$$
$$0 > T$$

The last of these implies that T is negative and the second last inequality implies that W_2, having to be less than T, must also be negative. (As a matter of interest, $T = -0.2$, $W_2 = -0.3$ and $W_1 = 0.5$ would satisfy the inequalities.)

The intuitive notion is that inverting (replacing 0 by 1 and *vice versa*) the line leading to the negative weight returns the weight to being positive. In terms of our example, this causes the inversion of the second line of the truth table, giving:

$$X_1: \quad 0 \quad 0 \quad 1 \quad 1$$
$$X_2: \quad 1 \quad 0 \quad 1 \quad 0$$

$$F: \quad 1 \quad 0 \quad 1 \quad 1$$

This is now the same as our first example (but written in a different sequence) which requires only positive weights. This confirms the intuition.

2.5 GEOMETRICAL VISUALIZATION

As with many algebraic descriptions, the above inequalities have a geometrical interpretation. This is particularly useful in creating a visual model of MCP behaviour. There are two ingredients: the space in which the firing rule is placed (called the *input space*), and the representation of the firing rule itself. Initially, we shall use the now familiar 2-input MCP. The space is represented in two dimensions, one for X_1 and the other for X_2. This is just like any graph we may draw of a variable *y*

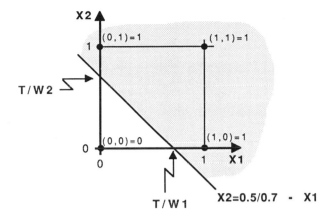

Fig. 2.3 Geometrical representation of a MCP function.

dependent on variable x. This time (arbitrarily) it is X_2 as a function of X_1 as shown in fig. 2.3.

However, as each input can only take on two values (0 and 1), there are only two corresponding points of interest on each axis of the graph. This pinpoints four points in the space corresponding to the four combinations of the input (columns of the truth table): X_1, X_2: (0,0) (0,1) (1,0) (1,1). The firing rule stated as an inequality divides those points in this space for which the MCP node fires from those for which do not. The dividing line will be given by turning the inequality into an equation:

$$X_1W_1 + X_2W_2 = T$$

That is, the > sign has been replaced by = as the dividing line occurs just as T is being overcome, indeed, when it is equalled. For example, we saw in the first evaluation of the last section that the dividing line would be given by:

$$X_1(0.7) + X_2(0.7) = 0.5$$

This can be rewritten into a slightly more familiar form:

$$X_2 = (0.5/0.7) - X_1$$

This indeed, is the equation for a straight line which is shown in fig. 2.3 to divide those points in the truth table that require a 0 output from those that require a 1 output. In general, the equation for this dividing line is:

$$X_2 = T/W_2 - X_1W_1/W_2$$

Again, we ask what insights are gained through this mathematical representation. First, in the case of the 2-input MCP model it is noted that any function can be achieved which is represented by a dividing straight line in the input space. This explains why the function shown below cannot be achieved by an MCP node.

X_1:	0	0	1	1
X_2:	0	1	0	1
F:	0	1	1	0

No single straight line can separate the points as indicated by the truth table. This visualization may be used to come to the conclusion that there are only 14 functions that can be achieved with the scheme. There are only six significantly different ways in which a straight line can cut through the input space. There is also the trivial possibility of leaving the line right outside the four input points (all points giving the same value of F). For each of these seven possibilities, the input points can be labelled in two opposite ways (for example in fig. 2.3 the same line could lead to the truth table):

X_1:	0	0	1	1
X_2:	0	1	0	1
F:	1	0	0	0

which is the opposite of the function for which the line was drawn in the first place. So this gives us:

$7 \times 2 = 14$ possibilities.

But what if the node had more than two inputs? There is no problem in visualizing a 3-input, input space. It must have three dimensions: X_1, X_2, X_3. These can be imagined as in fig. 2.4. It can also be shown that any MCP function for three inputs may be represented as a plane cutting through the input cube as shown in fig. 2.4. Things get difficult to visualize if the number of dimensions rises above three, as pictures of what is happening can no longer be drawn. But this is no hindrance to the mathematician. The rules that apply to 2- and 3-dimensional geometry still apply to higher dimensions. What in three dimensions is called a cube with eight vertices, in n dimensions becomes an n-dimensional *hypercube* with 2^n *vertices*. 10110 is a vertex of a 5-dimensional hypercube, say. Where a vertex of a 3-cube has three

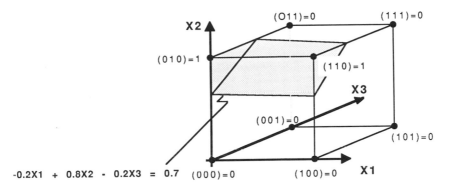

Fig. 2.4 A three-variable MCP function.

neighbouring vertices, the n-dimensional hypercube has n such neigh-bours (these are 00110, 11110, 11010, 10100, 10111 for $n = 5$ and vertex 10110).

The sort of conclusions that can be reached with hypercubes go as follows. In the 2-dimensional case we saw that $W_1 > T$, $W_2 > T$ implies $W_1 + W_2 > T$ – that is, 10 firing ($X_1 = 1$ and $X_2 = 0$), and 01 firing and 00 not firing, imply that 11 must fire. In the n-dimensional case the fact that all the neighbouring vertices of a given vertex fire, while more 'distant' vertices do not, implies that the given vertex must fire.

But the most general thing that can be said about a n-input MCP node is that any function it can perform must be defined by a $(n\text{-}1)$-dimensional *hyperplane* (line for $n = 2$, plane for $n = 3$) which cuts the n-hypercube. This is a most important characteristic of MCP models. It is called the property of *linear separability*. It will often be said in this book that one of the disadvantages of the MCP node is that it can only perform *linearly separable functions*. This is seen as a disadvantage because it cuts out important functions such as 'parity': firing only for patterns that have an odd number of 1s in them.

However, we do not wish to imply that hypercube thinking is central to the understanding of neural nets: it is not. What we have shown is that visualization in two and three dimensions merely illustrates some important characteristics of the behaviour of MCP nodes in general.

2.6 A LEARNING RULE

Much discussion of neural nets focuses on the way in which the weights can be changed to achieve a particular function. The problem is to make sure that the process ends in situations where examples of the task are continuously presented. That is, the adjustment should be such that when weights are altered to deal with one column of the truth table, it should not disrupt what has been done for other columns. This property is called *convergence*, and the procedure for function alteration is the *learning algorithm*.

The biological basis for such learning rules comes from a hypothesis first proposed by Donald Hebb, who suggested that if a neuron is in a network in which one of its synaptic inputs fires consistently at the time that the neuron itself is firing, then the weight for that synapse will be strengthened, see Hebb (1949). The difficulty with this idea is that it seems to leave the responsibility for causing the neuron to fire to some other (already learnt) action of other synapses. Although this technique has been used in some investigations of neural nets, here we shall look at another important rule first suggested by Bernard Widrow in 1962 (Widrow, 1962). This is now widely used and is known as the *Widrow–Hoff rule* or, sometimes, the *delta rule*. (It has recently been best described by Sutton and Barto (1981).)

The rule has the following steps:

1. Select a truth table column.
2. If an error is detected, work out how far the MCP is from the desired firing value.
3. Adjust the weights that are 'live' (have firing inputs) and the threshold to remove a portion '*d*' of the error.
4. Go back to step 1, until none of the columns cause errors.

As an example, consider a 2-input MCP. Its starting parameters are:

$$W_1 = +0.2 \qquad W_2 = -0.5 \qquad T = +0.1$$

The implied truth table is:

$$
\begin{array}{lcccc}
X_1: & 0 & 0 & 1 & 1 \\
X_2: & 0 & 1 & 0 & 1 \\
F: & 0 & 0 & 1 & 0
\end{array}
$$

Say that the target truth table is:

$$
\begin{array}{lcccc}
X_1: & 0 & 0 & 1 & 1 \\
X_2: & 0 & 1 & 0 & 1 \\
F: & 1 & 1 & 0 & 0
\end{array}
$$

In fig. 2.5(a) we show the starting position of the dividing line for the initial value of the weights, and subsequent images show what happens as the learning rule is applied as described below.

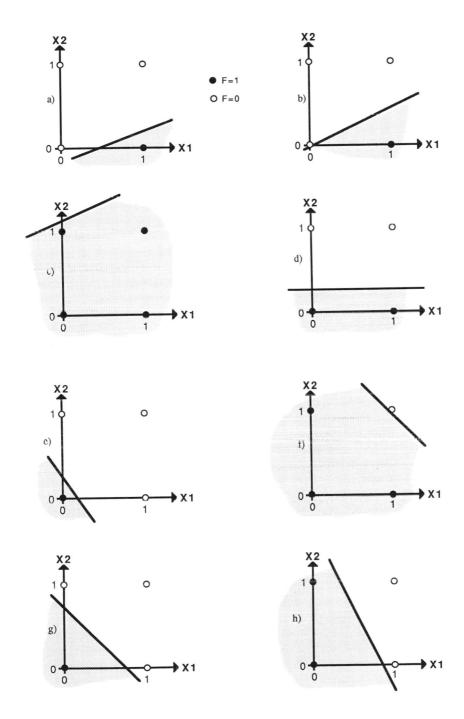

Fig. 2.5 Movement of the discriminant line with training.

Assume that the initial test column is X_1, X_2: 0,0. This has $F = 0$ where it should be $F = 1$. Remembering that the inequality that describes when this MCP fires, is:

$$W_1X_1 + W_2X_2 > T$$

if X_1 and X_2 are zero, as required for this column, the inequality is reduced to:

$$0 > T$$

This pinpoints the need to tidy up the learning rule a little. In the above case no amount of changing of weights will make any difference to the error for this column: it is the threshold T that needs changing.

In practical terms, there is no difference between changing weights or changing the threshold. Indeed the basic inequality may be rewritten as:

$$W_1X_1 + W_2X_2 + W_3X_3 > 0$$

where X_3 is always 1 and $W_3 = -T$.

This simply shows that the rule may be applied equally to the threshold and to the weights. In practical terms, it is also necessary to determine a clear increment by which an error might be corrected and the value of d, the proportion of the error to be removed (see p. 30, step 3). In the present case T is currently $+0.1$ and it is necessary to achieve $0 > T$. To make a positive difference we aim not only to correct the error, but to surpass it by an amount e. The selection of both e and of d is usually a matter of experimentation. Here we let $e = 0.1$ and $d = 0.5$ to illustrate the learning procedure.

So, $0 > T$ is interpreted as requiring a target for T to change from $+0.1$ to $0 - e$, that is to -0.1. The total target change is -0.2 which when multiplied by d (0.5) gives an actual change of -0.1 giving a new value for T, that is, 0. The new function of the MCP is:

$$0.2X_1 - 0.5X_2 > 0$$

and this is shown in fig. 2.5(b).

The rest of the process can be presented in a slightly accelerated fashion in Table 2.1.

Clearly the process stops at (h) as this has achieved the right truth table and no more errors remain to be corrected. The final inequality for the desired function is:

$$-0.225X_1 - 0.0875X_2 > -0.1875$$

It is worth noticing that the positioning of the function line is altered

Table 2.1 The progress of training the MCR node

Next error column X_1, X_2	Error E	Correction factor $(E + e)/2$	New W_1	New W_2	New T	Diagram
0,0	0.1	0.1	—	—	0	(b)
0,1	0.5	0.3	—	−0.2	−0.3	(c)
1,1	0.3	0.2	0	−0.4	−0.1	(d)
1,0	0.1	0.1	−0.1	—	0	(e)
0,1	0.4	0.25	—	−0.15	−0.25	(f)
1,0	0.15	0.125	−0.225	—	−0.125	(g)
0,1	0.025	0.0625	—	−0.0875	−0.1875	(h)

with increasing subtlety. The correction factor becomes smaller and smaller, and it is this property which is called convergence. If any learning rule is to be usable it is important that it should have this convergence property. This was first shown for the delta rule by Rosenblatt in 1962 (Rosenblatt, 1962).

2.7 IMPLEMENTATION OF THE LEARNING

It should be stressed that the success of this learning rule depends on a knowledge of the error between the relative values of the left- and right-hand sides of the inequality which feeds a correction loop for altering the weights. The biological credibility of anything of this kind happening in the neuron still remains to be demonstrated by neurophysiologists. The engineer needs to build these correction mechanisms into the nodes themselves. We return to this topic in Chapter 4 where the implications for implementation of these correction loops are discussed.

2.8 PERCEPTRONS

The most influential work on neural nets in the mid-1960s went under the heading of 'perceptrons' a term coined by Frank Rosenblatt (Rosenblatt, 1962). The simplest form of a perceptron is shown in fig. 2.6. This turns out to be a McCulloch and Pitts node with some additional, fixed, preprocessing. Units labelled $A_1, A_2, \ldots A_j, \ldots A_P$ are called *association units* and their task is to extract specific, localized features from some input image. In fact, perceptrons were presented as pattern recognition devices, although their applications may be as general as those of any neural net. In a sense the perceptron as shown in fig. 2.6 mimics a part of what is known of the mammalian visual system.

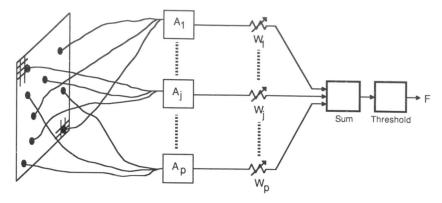

Fig. 2.6 A perceptron.

David Hubel and Torsten Wiesel were responsible in the early 1960s for laying down an explanation of the early stages of vision (based on experiments on the visual cortex of the cat). They identified specific groups of cells which responded in an apparently pre-programmed way to simple events that occur in a limited area of the retina (the receptive field of the eye) (Hubel and Wiesel, 1962). Typical examples are groups of cells that respond to the existence of a line in a specific direction or of an edge. It has also been observed more recently that there are cells which respond to moving edges and not to still ones. This kind of predetermined mechanism was the inspiration behind the association units in the perceptron.

The familiar example of distinguishing T-shapes from H-shapes seen in Chapter 1 is used with the perceptron scheme shown in fig. 2.7. There is a set of three association units, Ah1, Ah2 and Ah3, which have 3-point horizontal receptive fields, and another set of three vertical units, Av1, Av2 and Av3. Each of these units performs a fixed function of firing if two or more of their inputs are black (this is called the *majority* function). The weights related to these association units are H1, H2, H3, V1, V2 and V3. Training of the perceptron may be carried out using the delta rule exactly as used above.

If the maximum score is to be obtained with the T-shape, H1 and V2 will tend to have high positive values as a result of the delta rule (say, +1), while if the minimum score is required for the H-shape, V1, V3, H1, H2 and H3 will have low values (say, −1). Note that H1 is common to both and will therefore end up with a low value (say 0). The total score for the T prototype is +1 and for the H prototype −4. It can easily be shown (as a result of the majority function of the association units) that most of the prototypes with any one of the pattern points changed will generate the same scores as the prototype. This includes (a) in fig. 2.7. But (b) is different: it causes Av2 to be energized which

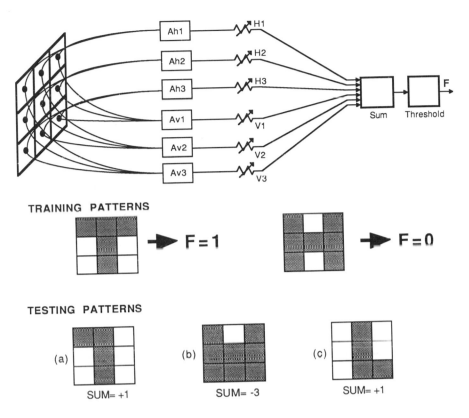

TRAINING PATTERNS

F = 1

F = 0

TESTING PATTERNS

(a) SUM= +1

(b) SUM= -3

(c) SUM= +1

Fig 2.7 Recognition of T and H patterns with the perceptron

makes the total score −3. Nevertheless, a threshold near zero will cause the necessary division with a reasonable amount of generalization. Pattern (c) will score +1 and will be classified as a T.

Many versions of the perceptron were studied in the 1960s. Some of these had several layers, others had feedback connections, while still others had inhibitory connections set between the association units. But the perceptron is not merely a relic of the past. It takes its place among contemporary neural models; for example, see Almeida (1988). It has its own characteristics and properties which will be contrasted to other models as they are met in the rest of this book.

2.9 McCULLOCH AND PITTS IN PERSPECTIVE

Most of what is being discussed in neural computing owes its origins to the work of McCulloch and Pitts and those who have worked with the MCP model. The concept of a variable weight is appealing as it is easily related to the process of 'making and breaking' connections. Also the idea that the body of the neuron performs a simple sum-and-threshold operation is easy to grasp.

But the reader should remain aware that the appeal of this model can be misleading, in that there is much that still needs to be understood about the operation of brains which it does not necessarily encompass. First, the learning rules imply an as yet undiscovered intelligent operation in the neuron itself. Also, in a massive and intricate system such as a living brain, it is not known exactly how error information actually gets to a neuron so that it can adjust its weights. There are broad theories on this topic: it is thought that learning in the brain is controlled by hormonal substances called neurotransmitters which are capable of acting in a global way on synapses, allowing them to alter or inhibiting them from so doing. It may be that until this biochemical function becomes properly understood we will not have a complete model of learning in real neurons.

It is also becoming clear that the function of many neurons may be much more complex than is implied by the MCP, and that such complexity needs eventually to be introduced into some models, see Crick and Asanuma (1986). For example, it may be that the input to the summing part of a neuron is the product of two synaptic activations rather than only the sum allowed by the MCP model.

EXERCISES FOR THE READER

1. For each of the four 3-input truth tables below, work out if the function can be achieved by a 3-input MCP model.

X_1:	0	0	0	0	1	1	1	1
X_2:	0	0	1	1	0	0	1	1
X_3:	0	1	0	1	0	1	0	1
F_1:	1	1	0	0	0	1	0	0
F_2:	1	0	1	1	1	0	1	1
F_3:	1	0	1	0	1	0	1	0
F_4:	1	0	0	0	0	0	1	0

2. Repeat the calculations for the learning example related to fig. 2.5 above, but with $d = 1$. What happens?
3. Do the same again, but this time keep $d = 0.5$ while letting $e = 0$. What happens?
4. It is possible to modify the delta rule slightly to calculate the augmented error as above, by dividing its removal among the 'live' weights and threshold equally. For example if for X_1, $X_2 = 1,1$ the

error augmented by e is 0.6, then each of W_1, W_2 and T are altered by 0.2. If, on the other hand, the augmented error is 0.6 for X_1, $X_2 = 0,0$ then it is all removed from T. What happens?

5. Why is the 3×3 perceptron of fig. 2.7 bad at distinguishing between an X-shape and an O-shape? What modifications are needed to improve things?

3

The hard learning problem

The publication in 1969 of Minsky and Papert's book, '*Perceptrons: An introduction to computational geometry*', was a significant event in the history of neural computing. It drew attention to some tasks which perceptrons (described in the previous chapter) cannot perform. Currently these are no longer seen as impossible in neural computing, but rather are considered to offer a challenge to the neural net designer. While they are hard to achieve (hence hard learning) they can be resolved by network structures which are more sophisticated than the perceptron. In this chapter we concentrate, not on the solutions, but on Minsky and Papert's formulations and proofs that tasks that go under the names of *parity* and *connectedness* are indeed impossible for perceptrons. This provides insight into the tasks themselves which will be used when solutions to the hard learning problem are discussed in subsequent parts of this book.

3.1 WHY 'HARD LEARNING'?

The central question is what can and cannot be done with neural nets? In the wake of the development of perceptron-like systems in the 1960s, Marvin Minsky and Seymour Papert showed that there were some simple image recognition tasks that perceptrons could not perform (Minsky and Papert, 1969). The detection of 'connectedness' and 'parity' are examples of such tasks. To detect connectedness a perceptron must fire if and only if there is just one blob in the image. Parity is similar: the perceptron is required to fire only if the number of blobs in the image is odd (as opposed to even). Figure 3.1 shows examples of images that possess and those that do not possess these properties.

Shortly, we shall show why these tasks are difficult for neural nets, the difficulty being mainly to do with finding the right learning algorithm. First it is important to realize that the necessary distinctions can easily be made with conventional, algorithmic computing. For example, an algorithm that detects connectedness is very simple to design. It is based on the assumption that the pattern is stored in a special system called the *framestore*. This has its storage cells arranged so that they

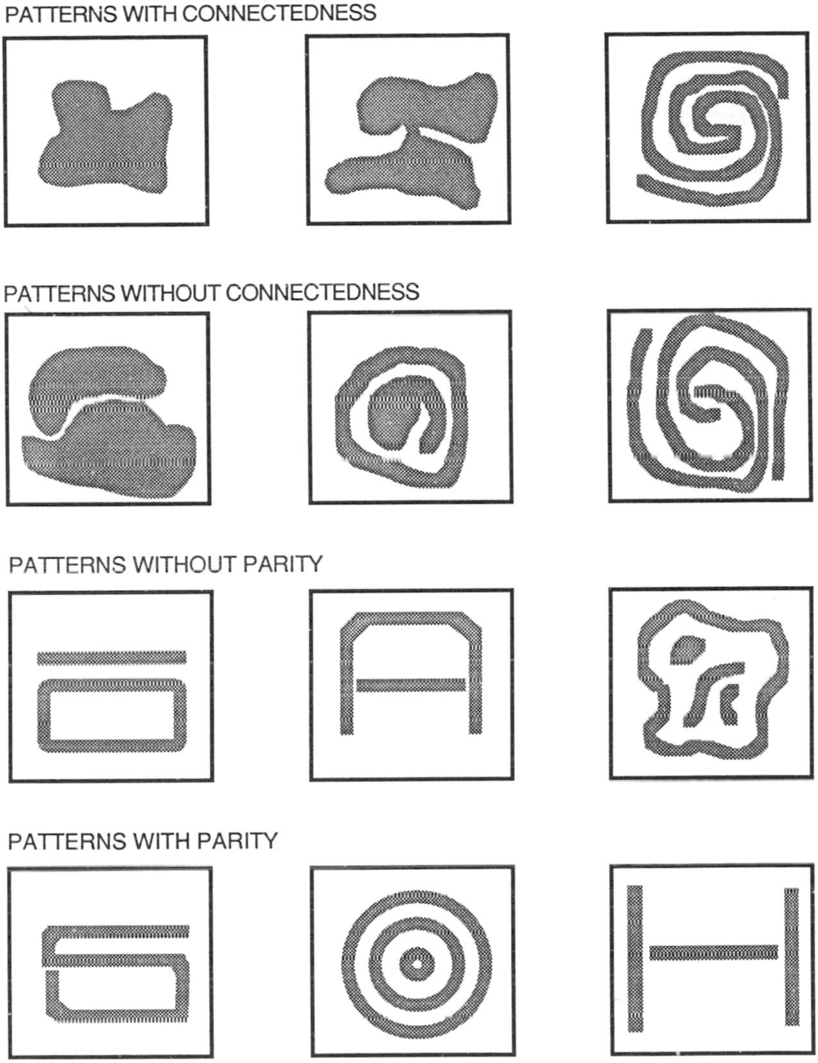

PATTERNS WITH CONNECTEDNESS

PATTERNS WITHOUT CONNECTEDNESS

PATTERNS WITHOUT PARITY

PATTERNS WITH PARITY

Fig. 3.1 Patterns with 'hard' properties.

correspond to the picture points in an image. Therefore one cannot only find the value (black or white, say) of any point in the picture by addressing its horizontal and vertical parameters, but also identify the nearest neighbours of any such picture point. The algorithm goes as follows:

1. Scan the picture points line by line, left to right, starting at the top left-hand corner of the image until the first black square is reached.

(The blobs are assumed to be black on a white background.)
2. Mark this square and find all its black nearest neighbours. Then mark these neighbours and all their nearest black neighbours and so on until no new black elements can be found. (This marks all the elements of a blob.)
3. Remove all the marked elements (by turning them from black to white: this removes the blob).
4. Scan the image again and if any black element is found, the image is not connected.

The parity task is executed just as easily: the scan-and-remove procedure can be used as before, it then becomes merely a question of counting the number of times the blobs have to be cleared. If this number is even, the image possesses parity.

There are many other examples of similar tasks that cause problems which are beyond the scope of this chapter; but one that should perhaps be mentioned is 'symmetry'. This will be explored further in an exercise at the end of this chapter. Take a string of 0s and 1s such as 0010110100. This string is said to be *symmetrical* about the middle (or *axis of symmetry*), in a *reflected* sense. That is, if we take the five bits in the right-hand half of the string and reflect them left to right they will form a string which is identical to the left-hand half. The strings 001000111, 01, 110010 clearly do not possess reflected symmetry, while strings such as 1111, 10000001, etc., do. Detecting the presence or absence of this property is a hard task for neural nets, but is relatively easy for a conventional computer. (It can be achieved by simply storing the whole string and comparing the first digit with the last, the second with the penultimate and so on, working inwards to the centre. If the comparison holds all the way to the middle the string has the property, otherwise it does not.)

In this chapter we shall rehearse the arguments advanced by Minsky and Papert in some detail so as to expose their foundations. This is important as many contemporary neural net structures and, in particular, the methods of training them, are designed to overcome these difficulties. In fact, having seen the difficulties it will also be seen that they are not insurmountable.

3.2 THE 'ORDER' OF A PERCEPTRON

Glancing back at fig. 2.6 (page 34), it will be recalled that the success of a perceptron depends on the local processing that is done by the association units (or A-units, for short) in parallel with one another. The weights-and-sum part of a perceptron simply combines the results of such independent computations. The *order* of a perceptron is said to be the number of inputs of the A-unit with the largest number of inputs. So the order of the perceptron in fig. 2.7 (page 35) is 3; but if any one of its A-units were connected to an additional input point, then its order would become 4.

Minsky and Papert's central argument is that perceptrons are only any good if their order remains constant for a particular problem irrespective of the size of the input 'retina'. This is similar to the requirement that a program in conventional computing, such as a routine for sorting a list of numbers, should be largely invariant to the size of the task. It is accepted that such a program might need to be given the length of the list as input data, but it would be of little use if it had to be rewritten for lists of different lengths.

In the context of perceptrons let us say that the task is: fire if there is one or more black groups of 2×2 adjacent elements in the input image of the retina. This requires as many A-units as there are elements in the retina (say R), each covering a group of 2×2 adjacent points. The function of the A unit is 'fire if all inputs are black' (i.e. the logical AND function). If the weights of the perceptron are then set to unity, and the threshold just below unity, it will fire whenever there is at least one group of 2×2 elements that are black. So the order of the perceptron that can accomplish this task is 4 and the order itself does not depend on the size of the retina, even if the overall size of the perceptron does. The key criticism of perceptrons found in Minsky and Papert's analysis is that the perceptrons required for tasks such as 'parity' and 'connectedness' are not of finite order, their order being dependent on R, and increasing directly with R. Parity is the more fundamental of these, so this shall be explained first and illustrated in fig. 3.1.

3.2.1 Parity

Part of the excellence of Minsky and Papert's arguments lies in the elegance with which they used a wide range of mathematical techniques to prove their points with maximum rigour. We shall not attempt to emulate their rigour here: we shall merely point to some intuitive notions that underlie the proofs. The first property that comes under scrutiny is that of parity. However, to simplify the discussion, rather than dealing with blobs, as discussed above, the aim here is for the perceptron to fire if and only if the number of black elements (that is, picture points on the retina) of R is odd.

To simplify things further, take R = 3. The complete truth table for the function is shown below (r1, r2 and r3 being the elements of the 3-input retina):

Line no.	r1	r2	r3	F
0	0	0	0	0
1	0	0	1	1
2	0	1	0	1
3	0	1	1	0
4	1	0	0	1
5	1	0	1	0
6	1	1	0	0
7	1	1	1	1

Consider first an order-1 perceptron. This would require that the sum-and-threshold part of the perceptron should act directly on the entire input image. That is, the question becomes: can the McCulloch and Pitts model (MCP) as defined in Chapter 2 carry out the parity task? The answer is easy: no. Let weight wj be associated with input rj for all three values of j. Just looking at the top half of the truth table, line 1 implies that w3 > T (using the methods learnt in the last chapter), while line 2 implies that w2 > T. Now, line 3 requires that w2 + w3 < T. The final catch is that line 0 requires that 0 < T, that is that T should be positive hence that w2 and w3 should be even more positive than T, from what has been said.

There is no way in which two positive numbers added together can be less than one of them as is implied by the above requirements. Therefore a parity-detecting perceptron cannot be of order-1. In fact the parity function is the classical task that any MCP node cannot achieve: it is not 'linearly separable'. 'Linear separability' was defined in Chapter 2 (page 29). It may be worked out that the parity function requires a labelling for one set of diagonal points of the geometrical representation shown in fig. 2.3 which is different from the other. This cannot be done by separating the labels with a single line and is therefore not 'linearly separable'.

So now one can ask if an order-2 perceptron can do the job. Initially, there appear to be three possible A-units: one that receives r1 and r2, another for r2 and r3 and another for r1 and r3. However, a proof of whether the perceptron can or cannot do the task must be general and should be based on the perceptron that has the greatest aptitude for doing the task. Such a device is called the *mask perceptron*. Masks and mask perceptrons are explained in what follows, here we *anticipate* the direction of the argument: it will be shown that if a *mask* perceptron of order-2 cannot achieve the task, no other order-2 perceptron can do the job and therefore the order of perceptron to do this task is 3. This, we shall argue, means that the order of the task is the size of the retina (R) itself, in the general case.

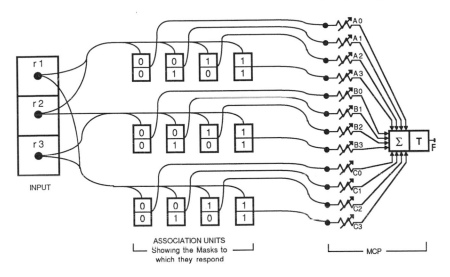

Fig. 3.2 An order-2 mask perceptron and the detection of parity.

An order-2 mask perceptron is shown in fig. 3.2 and may be described as follows. For each pair of points of the input, there is one weight associated with each of the four possible combinations that can occur at the input. These combinations are detected by association units that fire if and only if one particular pattern is present on the input pair. Such association units are called *masks*, hence this is a 'mask perceptron'. There are four masks for each pair of inputs, corresponding to the four possible combinations. It is clear that if a solution (in terms of suitable weights A0, A1, ..., C2, C3) can be found, and if any two weights within one group associated with one particular pair (say A0 and A3, which are both related to the input pair $\langle r1,r2 \rangle$, but *not* A0 and B3, which are related to different pairs; $\langle r1,r2 \rangle$ and $\langle r2,r3 \rangle$) turn out to be equal, then the two masks concerned can be replaced by a single association unit. As an example, say that weights A2 and A3 turn out to be equal, then (referring to fig. 3.2) the combined effect of these two weights on the perceptron may be described as having value A2 (or A3) if the pair $\langle r1,r2 \rangle$ has a value of $\langle 1,0 \rangle$ *or* $\langle 1,1 \rangle$: that is, whenever r1 is 1. Hence the 1,0 and 1,1 masks could be replaced by a direct connection of A2 (or A3) to r1 with the omission of A3 (or A2).

It is for this reason that a mask perceptron is seen to be more general than one with more 'tailored' association units and if the mask device is shown not to be capable of a particular task, we can be sure that a perceptron with 'tailored' A-units will not be capable of doing the same thing either.

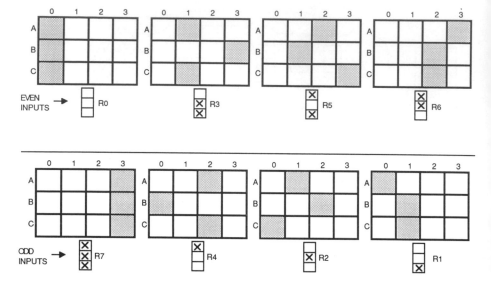

Fig. 3.3 Firing patterns for odd and even numbers of 1s and the input.

The firing patterns at the 12 inputs, the 8 possible input patterns (R0 to R7), are shown in fig. 3.3 as tables (a grey area in square A2 for example, means that mask A2 is firing).

This figure can be used to create the inequalities that are implied by the task. For example, R7 > T and R0 < T implies that R7 > R0 which may be written as:

$$A3 + B3 + C3 > A0 + B0 + C0 \tag{3.1}$$

We have 16 such inequalities that are oozing with evidence that the function cannot be achieved by the MCP. One such group is described below.

It is necessary that R4 > R5. This implies that:

$$A2 + B0 + C2 > A2 + B1 + C3$$

That is $\qquad$ B0 + C2 > B1 + C3

also, R4 > R6 implies $\qquad$ A2 + B0 > A3 + B2

R2 > R3 implies $\qquad$ B2 + C0 > B3 + C1

R2 > R6 implies $\qquad$ A1 + C0 > A3 + C2

R1 > R3 implies $\qquad$ A0 + B1 > A1 + B3

R1 > R5 implies $\qquad$ A0 + C1 > A2 + C3

Adding these six inequalities we get:

$$2A0 + A1 + A2 + 2B0 + B1 + B2 + 2C0 + C1 + C2$$
$$> A1 + A2 + 2A3 + B1 + B2 + 2B3 + C1 + C2 + 2C3.$$

Cancelling equal terms leaves:

$$2A0 + 2B0 + 2C0 > 2A3 + 2B3 + 2C3$$

Dividing both sides by 2:

$$A0 + B0 + C0 > A3 + B3 + C3$$

This is in complete contradiction of our very first inequality (3.1), and therefore the task cannot be accomplished with an order-2 perceptron.

Of course an order-3 perceptron can do the job but in a trivial way: it simply requires one association unit which detects parity at its input. Minsky and Papert used a sophisticated algebraic argument which shows that what we have found above for a 3-input perceptron is true for any (K-input) perceptron. So, the order required for parity detection is always at least K, that is, the number of inputs.

3.2.2 Connectedness

As defined at the start of this chapter, connectedness turns out to be a less severe problem than parity in the sense that it may be achieved with perceptrons of order less than the size of the input image. However, Minsky and Papert's criticism centered on the fact that a connectedness perceptron cannot be of fixed order – that is, its association units need to grow with the size of the image that needs to be assessed. Again, it is felt that this is not the place to reproduce the whole of various algebraic proofs that demonstrate this point rigorously: it is the crux of these proofs that is presented by the use of a pair of examples.

The procedure consists first in showing that to have a connectedness perceptron it is necessary to have a *one-in-a-box* perceptron and second that the order of such a perceptron is not fixed, but grows with the size of the problem. But first, what is a one-in-a-box (*oiab*) perceptron?

Imagine an image that is divided into several (say, m) different and non-overlapping areas called 'boxes' The oiab perceptron fires if and only if there is at least one black picture point in each of the m areas or boxes. Consider now the image in fig. 3.4. It is seen that for this basic disconnected pattern, in order to find a connected pattern, it is necessary to put at least one black square in each of the m white lines. This then becomes precisely the oiab problem.

To understand the basis of the argument, consider the system of three boxes each with three squares shown in fig. 3.5. It will now be shown that the oiab perceptron is of order-2.

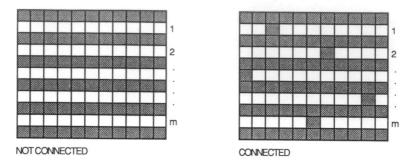

NOT CONNECTED   CONNECTED

Fig. 3.4 Examples of connected and not-connected patterns.

There are only three types of association unit with order-2 or less: first, there are those that are of order-1 (that is, with only one input). We call these 'type A': there are nine of them. Then there are those of order-2 but which have both inputs in the same box (say type B: there are nine of these too). Finally, there are those of order-2 that have their two inputs in different boxes (say type C: there are 27 of these). Taking the masks approach which was used in discussions on parity above gives rise to the perceptron with 45 mask association units in fig. 3.5.

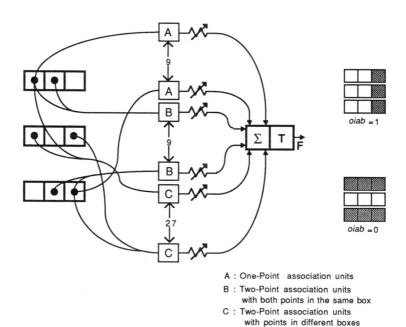

A : One-Point association units
B : Two-Point association units
     with both points in the same box
C : Two-Point association units
     with points in different boxes

Fig. 3.5 A one-in-a-box (oiab) perceptron.

It is clear that all association units of the same type (A, B or C) must have the same influence on the perceptron. Therefore they must all have the same weight (Minsky and Papert call this a result of a *group invariance* theorem). Let the weight of A-type units be A, B-type units B and C-type units C. Further, let the number of A-type units that are firing for a given pattern be **a** and so on for B and C units. The perceptron function can then be expressed:

$$\mathbf{a}A + \mathbf{b}B + \mathbf{c}C > T \qquad \text{for oiab to be true.}$$

We shall not solve this set of inequalities fully, but just consider one pair of patterns shown in fig. 3.5. The oiab = 1 pattern is one with fewest firing association units which must nevertheless be greater in terms of the perceptron equation than that oiab = 0 pattern which has the most firing association units in that group. In order to illustrate the point, we let $A = 3$, $B = -2$, $C = 0$ and $T = 8$. For the oiab = 1 pattern there are 3 of the A-type units firing, so **a** = 3; there are no B-type units firing, so **b** = 0. The value of **c** is not of interest as C has been made zero. This makes the left-hand of the inequality = 9 which is greater than 8 and hence valid. For the oiab = 0 pattern **a** = 6, **b** = 6 (and **c** = 9) making the left-hand side of the inequality become 6, which is less than 8, showing that the perceptron has properly distinguished between the two cases. It may be shown that the given choice for A, B, and C is a general solution for images divided into 3 boxes (m = 3) each with three squares.

Now, instead of three 3-element boxes, we have three 4-element boxes as shown in fig. 3.6. Again we shall test whether the oiab perceptron, and hence the connectedness perceptron, can be of order-2. The inequality is still the same one as above. For the oiab = 1 case in fig. 3.6, **a** = 6, **b** = 6 and **c** = 9. But for the oiab = 0 case, **a**, **b** and **c** are again **a** = 6, **b** = 6 and **c** = 9 and therefore, no weight values will distinguish between the two cases one of which has oiab and the other

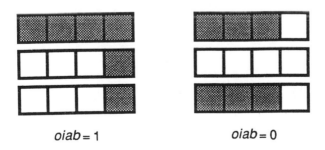

oiab = 1   oiab = 0

Fig. 3.6 A oiab perceptron with four squares in each box.

of which does not. This is evidence, therefore, that in a limited example at least, the order of an oiab perceptron and hence a connectedness perceptron is not fixed, but grows with the size of the problem. In fact, Minsky and Papert have shown that the order of a perceptron for connectedness is greater than or equal to $C(K^{0.5})$ (or, put another way, $C\sqrt{K}$) where C is some constant and K is the number of inputs to the perceptron.

3.3 DIAMETER-LIMITED PERCEPTRONS

Probably the best known of Minsky and Papert's proofs of the inadequacy of perceptrons is the one which shows that a *diameter-limited* perceptron cannot compute connectedness. But what is a diameter-limited perceptron and why is it significant?

A diameter-limited perceptron is one in which the association units are connected to points that are in the vicinity of one another in the input image. Indeed a distance D is associated with such units and is the maximum physical distance between any inputs to the association unit. The significance of such schemes is that they have physiological implications. The early stages of vision in mammals are known to be handled by fixed-logic cells that are a bit like the association units of a perceptron and which are diameter limited. The fact that we can easily see connectedness in some (but not all) patterns suggests that the computation is done in a manner more complex than suggested by perceptron models.

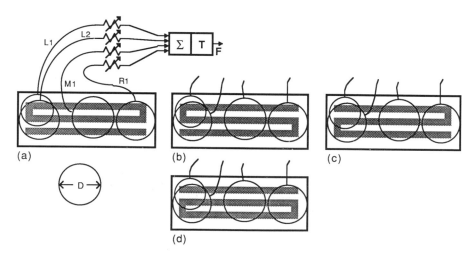

Fig. 3.7 An impossible task for diameter-limited perceptrons.

The proof is based on the four images shown in fig. 3.7 where it is assumed that many association units with a maximum diameter D exist. The figure is constructed by making the distance between its short ends several times greater than D. This is done after D becomes known, suggesting that such a figure can always be constructed for a given D. Clearly only (b) and (c) are connected and we require that the perceptron should fire for these two images and not fire for (a) and (d).

The association units may be divided into three groups: the left group L1, L2, ... the middle group M1, M2, ... and the right group: R1, R2, ... Comparing (a) and (c) it is evident that it is only the left group which is capable of sensing the difference. This requires a higher total sum of the weights connected to this group for (c) than for (a). Now comparing (a) and (b), it is the right group that has higher weights for (b) rather than (a). However, these two requirements give (d) an even higher weight score which implies that if a suitable threshold is found to classify (b) and (c) properly, that threshold will be exceeded for (d), classifying it as being connected which it is not! What has happened, of course, is that the MCP part of the perceptron is being required to detect parity which it cannot do, as we have shown earlier in this chapter.

3.4 MULTIPLE NEURON SYSTEMS

Much of what cannot be achieved with a perceptron is a result of the restriction that the MCP part of the device can only perform functions that may be represented by a cutting plane in the geometrical method of representation discussed in the last chapter (e.g. fig. 2.4). Earlier in this chapter we referred to these as 'linearly separable' functions. It is possible to show, however, that if several MCP models are connected to the same input points, then a greater variety of functions can be achieved, provided that one can find a way of combining the output of the multiplicity of these devices. For example, say, that the parity function is required through some combination of MCP units. Consider the two linearly separable 2-input functions in fig. 3.8:

$$X1 + X2 > 0.5$$

and

$$-X1 - X2 > -1.5$$

It is clear that the two truth tables F1 and F2 generated by the two inequalities are:

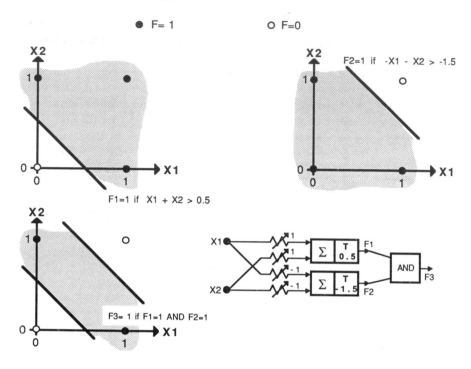

Fig. 3.8 Using two neurons to achieve parity.

X1:	0	0	1	1
X2:	0	1	0	1
F1:	0	1	1	1
F2:	1	1	1	0

The desired function is:

F3:	0	1	1	0

because it requires that the output be 1 when the number of 1s in the input is odd. This may be obtained by performing a logical AND between F1 and F2. This means that the combined circuit shown in fig. 3.8 could perform the parity desired function. It now looks as if the diameter-limited connectedness problem of fig. 3.7 has been solved. Alas, this is not true. Without going into details, the principle of adding AND gates to pairs of neurons becomes difficult when applied to the vast numbers of association units which would have to be deployed for the infinity of elongated connected and not-connected figures that can be drawn in a manner similar to that of fig. 3.7. Therefore, more general approaches are required and these are discussed in the next section.

3.5 UNIVERSAL TWO-LAYER PERCEPTRONS

The discovery of the solution to the parity problem in fig. 3.8 both creates a problem and opens up a new line of thought. The problem is that placing the AND gate where we have done and knowing that it must be an AND gate (as opposed to, say, an OR gate or a NAND gate), implies some knowledge of logic design. The new line of thought is the fact that the output AND gate could be an MCP element instead, as shown in fig. 3.9.

This is easily demonstrated as the AND function is linearly separable. Indeed, for a 2-input MCP it is given by the inequality:

$$X1 + X2 > 1.5$$

A general principle drawn from the theory of logic circuit design is that any logic function of k variables $(X1, X2, \ldots, Xk)$, having 2^k columns in its truth table, may be implemented as follows. Take the first column that requires a 1 at its output. Say $k = 5$ and this column has $X1 = 0$, $X2 = 1$, $X3 = 0$, $X4 = 1$ and $X5 = 1$. Then this column adds its 1 to the truth table when:

$$NOT(X1) \text{ AND } (X2) \text{ AND } NOT(X3) \text{ AND } (X4) \text{ AND } (X5)$$

This is a *column expression*. A logic designer would implement this column by using NOT gates (which turn a 0 into a 1 and *vice-versa*) for the $NOT(Xj)$ terms. He or she would use an AND gate with k inputs (which outputs a 1 only when all its inputs are 1), one for each input variable inverted (NOTted) or straight according to the column expression, to add the 1 to the truth table. He or she would do this for any column that requires a 1. The overall output is based on the logic:

the circuit outputs a 1 if
            column a is 1,
        OR column b is 1,
    . . . and so on for all columns that are 1.

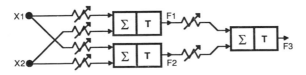

Fig. 3.9 A two-layer system.

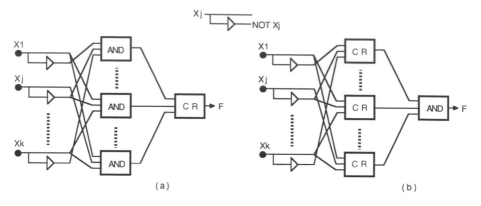

Fig. 3.10 Canonical forms of logic circuits.

This means that the output of all the AND gates is connected to an overall output OR gate (which outputs a 1 if one or more of its inputs are 1). This so called *first canonical form* circuit is shown in fig. 3.10(a). It may also be shown that an alternative form (the *second canonical form*) can also be used to implement any logic function. This is shown in fig. 3.10(b). Here every column with a zero in the truth table merits an input OR gate with inversions for inputs that are 1 in the column. The output gate is an AND gate in this case. It is left to the reader to convince herself that this second method works as well as the first. In fact, the multiple neuron solutions to the parity problem shown in fig. 3.8 are based on the second canonical form. (Those who would like a more leisurely explanation of these logic design principles are recommended to read a fundamental book such as Stonham (1987).

From this it is possible to define an 'architecture' consisting of two MCP layers which is capable of performing *any* logic function. This is based on the fact that the MCP node can perform both the AND function and the OR function on its inputs with any of these inverted. (In geometrical terms this is equivalent to the use of the hyperplane to isolate just one corner of the hypercube.)

So if the function has a majority of 1s, then a system containing a first-layer MCP for each 0 and an output AND function can achieve any such function. Similarly, if there are fewer 1s in the truth table, there is a need for an MCP element for each of these 1s and an output OR function. The obvious conclusion is that if there are k input variables, a system containing $2^{(k-1)}$ (i.e. half of the number of lines in a truth table) MCP elements in the first layer and one MCP with $2^{(k-1)}$ inputs in the second. An example for $k = 3$ is shown in fig. 3.11.

The feasibility of this architecture is based on the principle that if

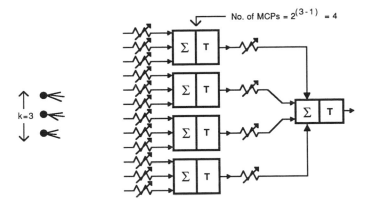

Fig. 3.11 A universal two-layer net.

there are more 1s in the truth table, the first layer will learn to be OR gates and the second will become an AND gate (also through learning). The fact that this is difficult will be discussed later, but the fact that this architecture may be expensive can be seen now.

3.6 COST OF THE UNIVERSAL ARCHITECTURE

The hopes for neural computing lie in situations where k is very large. For example, if the universal architecture were to be used for image processing, the smallest image 'patch' that may need to be recognized may be of the order of 10×10 binary picture elements. The universal perceptron would require 2^{99} MCPs (i.e. more than 10^{30}) in the first layer and a second layer device with the same number of inputs, for work on a trivially small image. This is highly impractical on several counts.

Technologically, the amount of 'weight' memory required by this single device is greater than the combined memory of all of the world's computers by a factor greater than 10^{10}. It also exceeds the size of an average brain by a factor of about 10^{20}. Furthermore, there is no generalization in this system at all. So why have we introduced the concept at all?

The concept is important because it provides an antithesis to the Minsky and Papert objection to non-universal MCPs. There are two extreme views involved. The universal view says that everything is possible at, perhaps, great cost. The other holds that single layer schemes, although looking inexpensive, are not capable of achieving some tasks. This suggests that the art of designing neural nets is one of finding cost-limited solutions of a non-universal kind which include multi-layer nets. The universal argument is there as a theoretical backstop to show that the Minsky and Papert objections need not be as damning as they first seem.

3.7 HARD LEARNING

We finally come to the topic which, because of its importance, has given a title to this chapter. This arises from the realization that single layer perceptrons are not all that useful, and that several layers may have to be used to create a general computing medium.

In Chapter 2, we saw that MCP nodes can be trained by 'delta' rules which require that weights be adjusted incrementally so as to remove a measured error at the output of the MCP node. However, looking back at the neural net in fig. 3.9, it is clear that the only way in which a delta learning rule could be applied is by knowing exactly what functions the first-layer units are to perform. This goes against the grain of the neural computing paradigm which is based on the principle that nets can be trained by outward examples. In other words, any training algorithm which is used with multi-layer networks can only rely on error measurements taken at the output layer.

This is called *hard learning* and is at the centre of current debate in neural computing. In Chapters 7 to 10 of this book we shall look at some ways in which the problem of hard learning is overcome. These are based on hill-climbing techniques that rely on the principle that local weight adjustments, based on appropriate local measurements, may be made to reduce the errors at the output of the net.

Here, we have merely acknowledged that the focus of contemporary neural computing is on systems that overcome the limitations exposed by Minsky and Papert. This means that two other problems need to be solved. One is the hard learning question and the other, as yet unmentioned, is the selection of appropriate network topologies which, as they cannot be universal, include the desired solution in the range of functions they offer.

On the latter point, it is important to realize that any computing methodology has a need for human intervention. For example, special-purpose hardware has to be designed by a human designer. No conventional computer can operate without human-designed algorithms. In the same way the human user of neural nets will have to be concerned with the design of nets. In general purpose computers of the future that have a neural component, there will be a need for someone, equivalent to a systems programmer in conventional computing, to organize network topology to meet the demands anticipated from the machine's end user.

EXERCISES FOR THE READER

1. A 'symmetry' function is one which outputs a 1 when the input pattern is symmetrical about some axis. Consider the 4-input function below:

   X1: 0 0 0 0 0 0 0 0 1 1 1 1 1 1 1 1
   X2: 0 0 0 0 1 1 1 1 0 0 0 0 1 1 1 1
   X3: 0 0 1 1 0 0 1 1 0 0 1 1 0 0 1 1
   X4: 0 1 0 1 0 1 0 1 0 1 0 1 0 1 0 1

   F1: 1 0 0 0 0 0 1 0 0 1 0 0 0 0 0 1

   The 'axis of symmetry' is drawn horizontally between X2 and X3 (as defined in the early parts of this chapter). $F1 = 1$ when X1, X2 = X4, X3. Show that an order-1 perceptron cannot achieve this function.
2. Show that an order-2 perceptron can perform the symmetry function provided that the association units are capable of performing the parity function.
3. Find a 2-layer solution to the symmetry problem which uses a minimal number of MCP nodes in the first layer, but which is constrained by being given only one OR gate as its second layer.
4. For the circuit in fig. 3.9 it is possible to invent a training algorithm which searches through all significant values of the six weights. By first calculating how many significant weight values would be needed for each node, calculate the total number of combinations that would have to be considered. How feasible is this method for larger problems?
5. As additional reading it is worthwhile to carry out a literature review of what is known of the way that the brain controls learning in neurons. Crick and Asanuma (1986), is a good starting point.

4

Making neurons

The future success of neural computing will depend on the availability of novel hardware, capable of supporting a high degree of parallelism and a great deal of memory. This is a new challenge for the computer designer as it requires rethinking ways in which memory can be achieved in silicon, and the way in which parallelism can be achieved without incurring prohibitive wiring costs. In this chapter we first review methods of designing analog memories as these are 'natural' to neural models. However, we then go on to show that digital methods may, nevertheless, have greater promise. Semi-parallel emulations are discussed as well as the potential for optical implementations*.

4.1 THE NEED TO MAKE NEURAL NETS

In the introductory chapter it was suggested that neural nets not only offered ways of solving problems in artificial intelligence that cannot be solved in other ways, but also promised high speed in the execution of such tasks. There is a hurdle however: the promise depends on the inherent parallelism of neural nets, which means that if they are seen merely as interesting algorithms for conventional serial computers this promise cannot be realized. Thus, as researchers began to study neural nets seriously, they were obliged to address the issues involved in making special-purpose parallel equipment.

There are a number of options open to contemporary scientists. These range from dedicating a processor, such as a transputer, to the emulation of each part of a net and then letting several of these work in parallel, to the development of special silicon chips which carry out the function of one or more nodes. In this chapter we shall concentrate on the solution of some fundamental problems that bedevil most of these

---

*It is felt that a consideration of practical issues associated with the making of neural nets provides insight into the practicality of using such systems in serious computations. Hence some technical detail is necessary. This chapter will be more easily understood by those with a little knowledge of electronic circuitry and physics. Those without such knowledge can skim through the material, or bypass it altogether, without affecting their understanding of the broader principles contained in this book.

approaches. One such problem is that of manufacturing the weights of a MCP-type node.

4.2 ANALOG WEIGHTS

As already stated, the MCP node requires a continuously variable quantity to represent an input weight which acts as a multiplier of the input value. In practice this means that it is necessary to find some electronic component which can be set by an electronic signal (generated by some machinery which implements the learning rule) and remains set even when the incrementation signal has been removed. In other words the weight must be an analog memory. The obvious way for an electrical engineer to achieve this is to use a variable resistance: the type of component that is used as a volume control in audio equipment. The only snag is that the input quantity which alters the resistance is usually a physical force, such as the torque exerted by the fingers that turn the volume control.

To replace these human fingers by something that is sensitive to an electronic signal it is necessary to use some kind of a motor which rotates in response to the incrementing signal, thus adjusting the resistance. Once the energizing power from the motor is removed the weight remains set. Such an arrangement is shown in fig. 4.1 and was used in a machine built by Wilf Taylor at University College, London in 1959 (Taylor, 1959). The amount by which a weight is adjusted in this system depends on the length of the pulse applied to the motor.

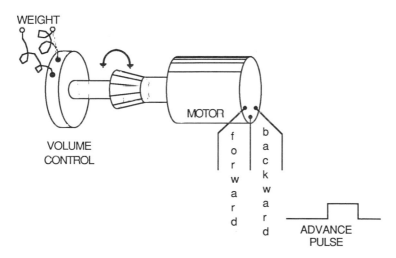

Fig. 4.1 Motor-driven weight adjustment.

With a suitable arrangement, the motor may be made to go backwards or forwards, so making it possible to implement the delta learning rule. Although this idea was interesting, the implementation of a system containing 100 MCP units required an entire room filled with motor-driven volume controls, hardly auguring well for the extension of the technique to systems that may require millions of such components.

Several other attempts have been made to design analog weights. For example, in the 1960s Widrow built a device called the Memistor which consisted of a thin wire set in an electrolyte that contained another metal. Pulses of current were used to deposit layers of metal on to the wire or to remove them, thus changing its resistance. This idea, too, was ingenious, but had little future.

Although it will be seen that digital techniques offer sensible ways of designing weights, analog systems are continuing to receive attention. Designers of very large scale integrated (VLSI) silicon chips, are still considering ways of making analog weights. For example, one such attempt is reported by Stuart Mackie of AT&T, Bell Laboratories (Mackie, Graf and Schwartz, 1988). The scheme is shown in fig. 4.2.

To start with, the two capacitors Q_1 and Q_2 are charged up to the same level. Their voltages are sensed in the opposing inputs of a differential amplifier the output of which is proportional to $Q_1 - Q_2$. So, initially the output w (the weight) of the amplifier is zero. The weight is incremented by shifting charge from one capacitor to another by the triggering of the MOSFETs (this is a mnemonic for the mouthful:

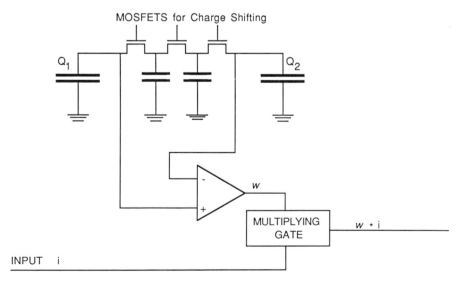

Fig. 4.2 The Bell Labs capacitative weight.

Metal Oxide Silicon Field Effect Transistor – in other words, a transistor which can be made to conduct a current or not) in order to control the direction in which the charge increment is to be effected. The intermediate capacitors are there to hold the charge increments that are being transferred. Being differential, the functioning of this system is not heavily reliant on the retention of charge and, it is claimed, only about 1% of charge is lost every 5 minutes at room temperature, and the loss can be reduced to zero if the system is cooled to $-100\,^\circ$C. It is further claimed that accuracy in the order of one part in 250 can be obtained in the creation of these weights. All in all, this seems rather complex considering that the storage is equivalent to just three bits. In fact, the comparison between analog and digital implementations of weights leads us to describe a seemingly fundamental law which favours digital memory. This was identified by Norbert Wiener in 1947 and will be discussed next.

4.3 LEAST COST STORAGE: ANALOG VERSUS DIGITAL

Wiener (1947, Chapter V) was concerned with methods of 'recording numbers clearly and accurately' at least cost. This, evidently, is a matter of concern to every designer of neural chips, since it applies to the technology of the weights. Say that a device can record information with an accuracy of one part in n. Normally we would expect a more accurate device to cost more than a less accurate one and we assume, for the purpose of this argument, that the cost, C, is proportional to accuracy (although the same argument applies if one merely assumes that cost increases only roughly with accuracy). In fact, if one thinks of the device as a meter with a pointer that must finish in one of n well-defined regions in order to indicate a number, it is clear that having just one region would not convey any information and should not contribute to the cost. Therefore the cost of the device should be counted only for regions in excess of 1 and may be written as:

$$C - (n - 1)A$$

where A is some arbitrary constant which depends on the method of manufacture.

The amount of information, I, contained in n messages is $I = \log_2 n$ bits, hence the cost equation may be written as:

$$C = (2^I - 1)A$$

The key question here is: 'Is it better to distribute the information over several less accurate devices or keep it all in one highly accurate device?'. If we divide information I between, say, two devices the total cost will be:

$$C = 2(2^{1/2} - 1)A$$

Similarly dividing I over N devices the cost becomes

$$C = N(2^{1/N} - 1)A$$

It may be shown that this function decreases as N increases. For example, A = 1, I = 16, we have:

N	C
1	65 535
2	510
4	30
8	24
16	16

Now we note that $2^{1/N}$ must be an integer and that the least value for this that can be achieved is 2 (when N = I) and when each device has only two states. This simply says that if information is to be stored at all, it can be done most cheaply in binary code with on/off switches.

The years have shown Wiener to be right. Although the history of computer engineering is not devoid of attempts at making non-binary stores, they have not survived. The neural device engineer should take heed of this and concentrate his or her VLSI efforts on digital weights. But how is a digital scheme turned into a neuron? This is the topic for the next section.

4.4 BINARY NEURAL CHIPS

VLSI manufacturers have been much influenced by the models of neural nets which contain M nodes, each with M inputs which enable their users to make autoassociative nets with M neurons (see Chapter 1) in which every neuron may be connected to the output of every other neuron. Here we concentrate on the chip itself. The way that the connections are made in a system that contains such chips is considered to be a problem for the computer designer which is so dependent on the electronic detail of the chip that it is beyond the scope of this book. A typical block diagram for a chip is shown in fig. 4.3.

The chip that represents the weights of the system is an array of M × M registers, each register containing the value of a weight. This

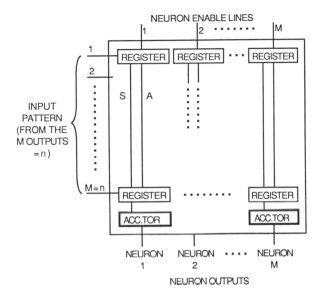

Fig. 4.3 Block diagram for a binary neural chip.

yields M neurons each with M weighted inputs (in general, the number of inputs to a neuron is designated n, but here n – M). Typically, devices with M as large as 64 can be made with relative ease, resulting in chips that contain $64 \times 64 = 4096$ weights. Clearly this type of chip needs to work in conjunction with another controlling processor, which is not shown in the diagram. It is this processor which receives the patterns from the outputs of the neurons, generates patterns for their inputs and updating information for the weights. The operation goes as follows:

Use:

1. To process an input pattern (assumed to be binary, as before), those input lines which correspond to 1s in the pattern are activated one by one, addressing all the registers in the activated row (those input lines that receive 0s are, naturally, not activated).
2. The registers contain weight values and (if activated) these are added into the accumulators, column by column (that is, neuron by neuron) using the S (standing for 'sum') lines. At the end of this process the accumulators contain the sum of the activated weights as required by the neuron function.
3. Each accumulator can contain a threshold which, if exceeded, puts a 1 on the neuron output.

4. The output vector can therefore be generated in, at most, M operation steps.

Training:

1. The input pattern and the desired output pattern are known.
2. The erroneous outputs can be identified and the delta rule, assumed to be resident in the control processor, can be applied.
3. This is done by a combination of energizing an A line which addresses all the weights of a neuron selected for treatment and then selecting the weights energized by the input pattern, one by one to apply the weight incrementation rule.

Of course, in practice, it may be necessary to build nets that are larger than the limits imposed by fabrication techniques. Therefore there must be provision for the sort of chip we have just described to be connected to several other chips so as to make a larger net. This means that it must be possible to add the contents of several accumulators to one another, if larger neurons are required, and to extend the weight address lines to neurons in other chips. A complete system might also provide easy means of loading learnt weight values from the registers into some backing store so that they may be used again at a later time without having to go through the training process again. This makes such systems into 'general purpose' devices. Every time they are taught something the value of the weights appropriate to one particular task is stored. The system can then be cleared and taught another task and the new weights can again be stored away. Thus a library of tasks (represented by sets of weight values) can be created to run on the same hardware as and when required.

4.5 EMULATORS

Bearing in mind that the function of neuron j is given by

$$F_j = 1 \text{ if and only if } \sum_k w_k \cdot i_k \text{ exceeds some threshold T}$$

it is clear that a special microprocessor chip could be built that simply implements this function and that one such chip could be used for each neuron in the system. Such a chip would then be said to emulate (or simulate) a neuron. A typical arrangement for such a device is shown in fig. 4.4. This system has been developed by Simon Garth of the Texas Instruments Company (Garth, 1988). Here the 'neural chip' performs the 'sum-of-products' equation set out above on neural inputs stored in the local memory, storing the result in local memory under the control

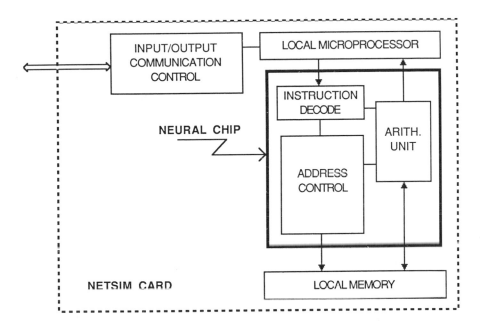

Fig. 4.4 A neural emulator.

of a local microprocessor. Clearly it would be wasteful to use such a chip to represent just one neuron. Since a neuron is characterized merely by values of its weights and a threshold, the local memory in fig. 4.4 could be used to store the weights and thresholds of several neurons, together with their current input patterns, and the neurons could be 'interrogated' one after the other.

The chip is sited on a card (in this case called NETSIM) which contains not only the necessary control processor and local memory, but also a special communications chip which keeps track of where input information comes from and where output information goes to. This allows several NETSIM cards to be grouped together, under the control of yet another host computer (such as a conventional personal computer), to form what can be called a *neurocomputer*.

This type of system is called an *emulator* (a technical term for a simulation done in hardware) because, in contrast to the direct implementation of fig. 4.3, it performs the neural node calculation serially, synapse by synapse, neuron by neuron. It also performs and executes the weight updates during training. Thus for any array of M neurons with M inputs, the emulator takes M^2 steps, in contrast with the M steps taken by the parallel scheme described earlier. Despite this, a single NETSIM card can generate the response of a 256-input, 256-neuron system in about 1/20 s.

Perhaps the more telling performance figure is the speed with which weights can be incremented. For example, Garth quotes four million synapse updates per second. This sounds better than it is, bearing in mind that there are 65 536 synapses in a 256 × 256 system, and therefore one round of incrementations for all the weights would take about 1/60 s. As most applications of a system of this size may require tens of thousands of updates for each weight, the fact that this is done serially in the emulation means that training could take many minutes, or even an hour or so in difficult situations. Clearly the direct implementation (fig. 4.3) operates M times faster than the emulation (fig. 4.4). However, *both* of these systems are much faster than simulations on conventional computers that do not use specially designed neural chips.

There are many schemes being developed involving emulators which are slightly different from the one discussed above. For example, the Hecht-Nielsen Neurocomputer Corporation has been marketing PC-based systems similar to NETSIM but endowed with a broader range of neural training and running algorithms, some of which are discussed in the latter parts of this book.

Neural computing has captured the imagination of many researchers in computer architectures. This means that a wide variety of known techniques are being investigated with the aim of developing efficient emulations. Typical is the work of Philip Treleavan at University College, London, who has developed a neural emulation chip based on a conventional idea in communications: the packet-switched network (Reece and Treleavan, 1988). The possibility of using a transputer for the emulation of neural functions is also being explored. A transputer is a microprocessor chip designed to work in concert with other such chips in parallel systems. It therefore already contains the communications circuits that were seen to be needed in the NETSIM card. However, being an 'off-the-shelf' general-purpose device, the transputer is better known and in more widespread use than NETSIM, and benefits from large-scale production cost advantages. David May and Roger Shepherd (1988) give a good description of the device in the context of neural computing.

4.6 NOTE ON TRAINING TIME

Clearly, as suggested above, it could take quite a long time to train a neural net of a substantial size. There is a school of thought that argues that this does not matter a great deal, as it has to be done only once, but that the running time is of prime importance. This may be true in some situations, but not in all. For example, medical computing devices which classify back complaints on the basis of measurements, or systems which have learnt to translate text to speech, may have a fixed training set and need to be trained only once. However, other applications such as a neural vision system that checks the quality of pieceparts in a factory, may need frequent retraining to accommodate design changes. A second school of thought would, therefore, support the notion that training time may well need to be kept low in order to make a system usable.

The first way of thinking also leads to the notion that learning can be done 'off-line', perhaps in a conventional simulation, as long as speed can be achieved through special hardware at run time. It is this argument that is often used to support optical implementations of neural computers. These are discussed next.

4.7 OPTICAL NEURAL NETS: THE PSALTIS AND FARHAT MODEL

In recent years, the possibility of designing computers using optical components has been getting closer to reality. The increasing desirability of making parallel machines has disadvantaged electronic systems due to the increased cost of wiring. In optics, it is possible to use light beams to carry information and to exploit the fact that they can be directed by lenses. Indeed, light beams can cross without any danger of the information they carry becoming confused. It was with these advantages in mind that Demitri Psaltis and N. H. Farhat proposed the simple arrangement of light-emitting diodes, light receptors and lenses shown in fig. 4.5.

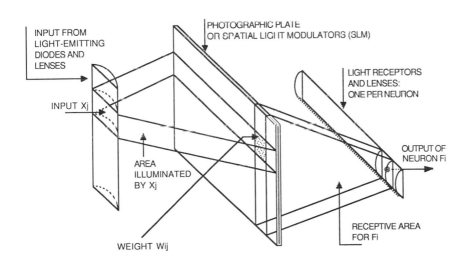

Fig. 4.5 A neural system based on diode arrays.

It is assumed that the input is brought to the system through electric wires that energize an array of light-emitting diodes. These devices are commonplace, for example, conventional infra-red remote control systems for home television sets contain light-emitting diodes in the handset and the light-sensitive device situated in the television set is also a diode. The lens of the input array is arranged so as to create a horizontal illumination area as shown, while the lens for the receptive diodes is arranged so as to have a vertical field. Clearly the amount of light transmitted between the input diode (Xj) and the receptive diode (Fi) then depends on the intensity of the photographic film at the intersection of these two fields. Say that this intensity is Wij. The total intensity of light reaching a particular receptor (Fi) is therefore:

$$\sum_j Wij \cdot Xj$$

This is precisely the 'sum' part of an MCP node equation. Psaltis suggested that the rest of the neural node task (the threshold) could be done by electronic circuitry following the receptor diode array. Thus optics would be used at the level where it is most effective: where the greatest parallelism is required.

The question that remains unanswered is how should the photographic plate be 'trained' in order to store the appropriate information. The simple, but of course slow, answer is that the weights can be developed by training a simulation of the system running on a conventional computer. The weights can then be projected from the computer onto the photographic plate. Here the argument used earlier comes into play: for applications which do not need continuous retraining, the above method would suffice. However more sophisticated techniques are in the offing: these are based on a device called the spatial light modulator (SLM) which bears a resemblance to the familiar liquid crystal display found in digital watches. The crystal may be divided into an array of dots, each of which can be addressed in order to control its light transmission. Clearly this implies that the information which determines the intensity of each point is stored elsewhere (e.g. in a conventional computer memory). Despite this requirement for mixed electronic/optical technology, such systems offer a promising means of exploiting the potential of optics to make a large number of parallel connections at low cost.

4.8 HOLOGRAPHIC NEURAL NETS

Holography offers additional opportunities for exploiting the optical domain. The essential feature of a hologram is that it can direct a light beam in a direction determined by the information stored as an interference pattern on a tiny area of film. Indeed, the familiar notion of a holographic picture which is seen in three dimensions is based on the property of being able to reconstruct the intensity of a light ray as well as the direction in which it was transmitted.

Several methods have been proposed for using holograms in the creation of neural nets. In principle, the scheme shown in fig. 4.6 is the basis for many of them. In this arrangement the input to the neuron is obtained by means of a spatial light modulator whose operation has briefly been described. The weight of each input is determined by the intensity with which each element of the SLM is illuminated. This intensity is controlled by the hologram which, on being illuminated by a reference beam, produces an accurate pattern of light intensities in the plane of the SLM. The light shining through each element is then given by.

Wa·Xa,

where Wa is the amount of illumination coming from the hologram, and Xa the transmission value of the SLM element. The full lens arrangement for focusing the total light coming through the SLM is not shown, but it is all directed towards a detector whose output is the desired form of the summing part of the neuron equation. Again it is assumed here that the thresholding can be done electronically, in systems connected to the detector output.

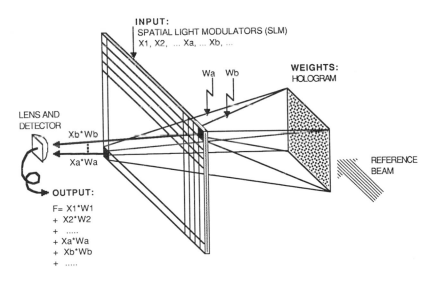

Fig. 4.6 A holographic neuron.

There are other reasons for the interest in making neural elements by means of optics. First, in the arrangement of fig. 4.6 it is quite possible to use a higher degree of parallelism. The hologram could be just one area of a larger M × M (say) sheet of such holograms. Each could hold the weight information for a different neuron and be individually focused towards one of an M × M array of detectors after passing through the SLM. This means that the SLM input pattern would be processed individually and in parallel on M × M neurons simultaneously.

A second reason for a high level of interest in holographic methods comes from the possibility that the entire processing procedure in a neural net could be done optically. This is facilitated by the existence of materials such as gallium arsenide which have non-linear transmission characteristics that make possible the fabrication of optical thresholding devices. Such a material maintains a low level of transmitted light as the incident light level is increased. At some critical incident light intensity the material abruptly alters its molecular structure and allows a high degree of light transmission (*transmittance*), giving the desired threshold function. Abu-Mostafa has designed an autoassociative system (as defined in Chapter 1) made exclusively of optical computing components (Abu-Mostafa and Psaltis, 1987). It will be seen in Chapters 6–15 that autoassociative systems have a central role to play in neural computing in general.

4.9 SUMMARY

In this chapter we have surveyed the principles of some of the methods that are currently under investigation for the eventual implementation of large neural nets with which some real computation can be done. It will be seen in the rest of this book that neural nets require very large amounts of memory in order to start performing such realistic computations. The technological concern, therefore, boils down to finding ways of exploiting the falling cost of memory and minimizing the cost of making parallel systems. Many hopes are placed on VLSI techniques, with optics waiting in the wings. Optical techniques are still in their infancy and need to become better established before they can lead to practical systems.

EXERCISES FOR THE READER

1. It is not easy to determine the required accuracy of a weight. Can you think of ways that one might go about it? (Hint: start with a 3-input MCP model and calculate the number of significant hyperplane positions).
2. What happens if the chosen accuracy of weights is too low? (Hint:

consider a 2-input MCP model in which the weights are just two-valued).
3. Discuss the advantages and disadvantages of optical neural implementations in contrast to electronic ones
4. Write a program in an assembly-like language to simulate an MCP node and calculate how many machine cycles are required to process its input data.
5. Write an essay on the Abu-Mostafa/Psaltis (1987) method of achieving autoassociation.

5

The secrets of the WISARD

The main secret of the work described in this chapter is *weightlessness*: the use of memory nodes whose function is altered not by the changing of weights but by altering the contents of a memory device. In the world of neural computing, this approach is seen as being somewhat unorthodox. It starts by using a conventional random access memory as a neural node. It is shown that a single-layer group of such nodes (called a *discriminator*) acts very much like a single-layer perceptron. The advantages of the discriminator approach are that its behaviour is amenable to simple analysis and that it is easily implemented with conventional computer hardware. This chapter looks at a multi-discriminator system used in industrial settings: the WISARD. A way of calculating and optimizing the behaviour of this system is given. On the whole, it turns out that usable neural systems with a clear, predictable performance may be obtained through the multi-discriminator approach.

5.1 WHAT IS THE WISARD?

WISARD stands for **WI**lkie, **S**tonham and **A**leksander's **R**ecognition **D**evice. It is an adaptive pattern recognition machine which is based on neural principles. The prototype was completed in 1981 at Brunel University in London by a team under the direction of one of the authors (Igor Aleksander). Bruce Wilkie was the design engineer and John Stonham his faculty supervisor. The machine was subsequently patented and produced commercially in 1984. The object of this chapter is not to sing the praises of these machines or describe their operation in great detail, but rather to examine the principles on which these are based. The history of these principles goes back to 1965, when IA suggested that a simple memory device (which, nowadays would be called a ROM: read-only memory) has neural-like properties (Aleksander, 1965). The ROM is a once-only learning device. Over the years, it has been shown that the same neural-like properties are held by RAM (random access memory). RAM devices can learn and relearn. We examine these learning properties of RAM systems in this chapter and develop simple ways of analysing networks of such devices.

Broadly, the difference between an MCP node and a RAM node is that the RAM can achieve any of the functions of its inputs but cannot generalize. This makes it appear to be a less interesting device than the MCP. However we shall show that networks of RAM nodes do generalize and that this makes them as interesting as networks of MCP nodes (if not more so). The main advantage of the RAM node is that systems may be built using conventional digital circuitry, without the need to develop special VLSI devices. It will also be shown that learning in RAM nets is much faster than in MCP nets.

5.2 THE RAM NODE

The random access memory device is the silicon building brick of the local memory of any modern computer. It is the component which, in conjuction with the silicon processing chip, has been responsible for the microprocessor revolution. Prior to the early 1970s the usual way of achieving local memory in a computer was by means of intricately threaded ferrite rings. Such systems were bulky, expensive and limited in capacity. The advent of the silicon RAM transformed the computer industry. The capacity of such chips has continued to improve spectacularly, so that whereas the price of, say, an armchair would cover the cost of one chip containing about 100 bits of memory in 1970, the price of the same chair in 1989 buys about 10 000 000 bits of memory distributed over a handful of chips. Designing neurocomputers which exploit silicon RAM leads more directly to usable machines of significant capacity than relying on node designs which still require VLSI development.

Figure 5.1 is a simplified diagram of the way in which a RAM operates. This is not the description of any particular circuit, it is intended merely to clarify an explanation of what a RAM does.

The principal components of this device are an address decoder, a group of memory registers, a data-in register and data out register. To store information, an N-input binary *address* is supplied to the input of the decoder. The output of this decoder has 2^N lines, one for each possible address, i.e. a combination of 0s and 1s on the N input terminals. The presence of one such pattern at the input of the decoder, energizes the corresponding line and makes the memory register connected to the line active. The active memory register absorbs the data held in the data-in register and stores it.

In fig. 5.1, it is assumed that the pattern 00 . . . 01 is present at the input of the decoder, energizing the second line from the top. This causes the data present in the data-in register (101 . . . 0) to replace the current content of the second memory register. If data is to be retrieved from the RAM, again the address is chosen and given as input to the

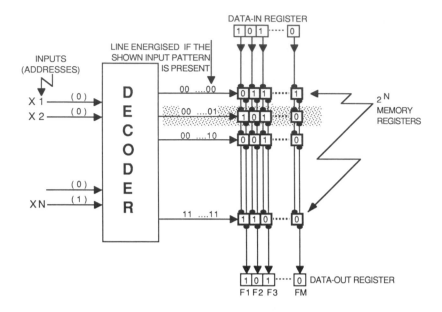

Fig. 5.1 The random-access memory (RAM).

decoder, but this time the content of the selected memory register is copied to the data-out register. Clearly much detailed control circuitry has not been shown in fig. 5.1. In particular, circuitry and an additional input line are required to indicate to the RAM whether it is in the retrieval or the recording state (more conventionally these are called the 'read' and 'write' states).

For a typical, commercially available RAM chip, M (the number of bits of information that can be stored in each memory register) is 8. This type of chip is said to be 'byte-oriented': a byte being eight bits. Typically, N could be 18 and this would be called a 256 kilobyte RAM (2^{18} is 262 144, but it is conventional to name these devices with the first three digits of the nearest power of 2 which, in this case, is 256).

In order to relate the RAM to the neuron, two further points need to be understood. First, it is noted that, taking one column of the memory registers at a time, the values of this colum can be set independently, and represent precisely the truth table of a logic device with one output. As whole words are always written into the memory, one row at a time, this independent setting of a particular bit in a column is done by selecting the selected bit in the word, leaving the other bits unaltered. Therefore a RAM with M bits in the memory register, can be thought of as M RAMs each with one bit per memory register, and each connected to the same N input variables. This notion is shown in

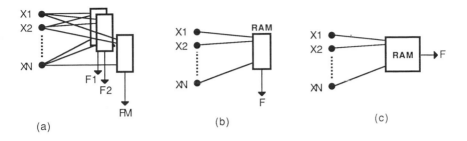

Fig. 5.2 (a) The RAM shown as M RAMs each storing 2^N bits (one per address pattern); (b) RAM storing one-bit words; (c) conventional way of drawing (b). Note: all RAMs contain their individual decoders, which are not shown in the figure.

fig. 5.2(a). Were the same input address used in fig. 5.2(a) as in fig. 5.1, the second bit in each RAM would be activated. Note that the decoders are not shown in fig. 5.2(a), but it is implied that there is one in each of the M RAMs.

The second step is to concentrate only on one of these one-bit-per-word RAMs as shown in fig. 5.2(b). Here, the data-in memory has not been shown, and the data-out memory of one bit and the decoders can be assumed to be resident inside the boundary of the RAM.

So, the sense in which fig. 5.2(b) is *like a neuron*, is that, given an input at X1 to XN, and a desired output to be held at the data-in terminal, setting the RAM into the reading mode will cause it to 'learn' this desired response, and this can be overwritten by a subsequent training step.

The sense in which fig. 5.2(b) is *not like a neuron*, is that there is no need for a sophisticated training algorithm – the setting for one input does not affect another and, therefore, the description in the last paragraph *is* the training algorithm. Admittedly, there is no generalization in the RAM itself. While this could be seen as a disadvantage, it is shown in the subsequent sections that *networks* of RAMs generalize in a way which is similar to networks of neurons. In other words, the RAM is like the TAN (in Chapter 1) without a firing rule.

5.3 THE RAM DISCRIMINATOR

The simplest RAM network with properties of generalization is called a *discriminator* and is shown in fig. 5.3. This consists of a layer of K RAMs with N inputs and thus each RAM stores 2^N one-bit words, and the single layer receives a binary pattern of KN bits. It is assumed that,

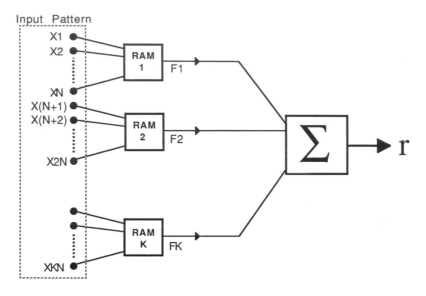

Fig. 5.3 A RAM discriminator.

before any training takes place, all the memory cells in the RAMs are set to 0. Training consists of applying an 'input pattern' of 0s and 1s at the input terminals shown in fig. 5.3. This is called a *training pattern* and is an example of the class of patterns to be learnt by the discriminator. To record this pattern, a 1 is stored in that memory location of each RAM which is addressed by this input pattern. Effectively, this causes each RAM to record the occurrence of part of the input pattern – the part 'sampled' by that RAM. This is done for other input patterns, leading to further 1s being stored in the RAMs.

The RAMs can be switched from a 'write' mode for training as described above, to a 'read' mode during which time what has been learnt can be used. In this latter phase, when another, previously unseen, pattern is later presented at the input, the summing device (designated Σ) produces a number which is equal to the number of RAMs that output a 1.

This number is said to be the *response* of the discriminator and is given the symbol r. Clearly, if one of the patterns used in the training set were to be entered later at the input of the net, it would find storage locations that contain a 1 in each of the RAMs and therefore r would have its maximum value of K, whereas, if the unknown input pattern were to be totally different from any of the training patterns (in the sense so that no RAM would receive an individual input on which it had been trained), then the value of r would be 0. Therefore, r is, in some way, a measure of the similarity of an unknown pattern to each of the patterns in the training set. It is worth looking at this idea in greater depth, illustrating generalization with a specific example, and then providing a general analysis.

5.4 ANALYSIS OF THE RAM DISCRIMINATOR

Rather than providing an overall analysis at this stage, we shall consider a simple example which begins to show how predictions of the behaviour of a discriminator may be calculated.

For the system shown in fig. 5.3, imagine that the net is trained on an input of all 1s and, in addition, on a set of KN different patterns, each of which consists of a string of 1s containing precisely one 0. Consider now the input of a pattern of 1s containing two 0s. If the two 0s occur at the input of two different RAMs each of these RAMs will receive an input address with only one 0 in it. As these two RAMs have been trained on just this input, they will both respond with a 1 and the result will be that $\mathbf{r} = K$. The probability of this occurrence may be calculated as follows. Given the first 0 in a particular RAM input, there are $N - 1$ sites for that RAM to receive the other 0. Alternatively, there are $(K - 1)N$ sites outside this RAM in which the second 0 could occur. The sum of these two events is $KN - 1$, so the probability of $\mathbf{r} = K$ is:

$$P(\mathbf{r} = K) = (K - 1)N/(KN - 1)$$

If both 0s occur at the input of the same RAM, $\mathbf{r}$ will be $K - 1$.
So, the probability of $\mathbf{r} = K - 1$ is:

$$P(\mathbf{r} = K - 1) = (N - 1)/(KN - 1).$$

Putting some figures to this, consider $N = 4$ and $K = 4$. Then

$$P(\mathbf{r} = 4) = 12/15 = 0.8$$

$$P(\mathbf{r} = 3) = 3/15 = 0.2$$

So, the most likely response to such patterns is $\mathbf{r} = 4$, which proves the point about generalization: patterns similar but not identical to those in the training set generate the same response as those in the training set. It is worth noting that the $N = 4$, $K = 4$ system requires training on only 16 single-0 patterns, while there are 120 patterns with two 0s of which 80% will evoke a response of 4, and 20% a response of 3.

The most likely response to any pattern may be calculated in a similar way, provided that the number of 0s and 1s in such a pattern is known.

5.4.1 Analysis

We use fig. 5.4 as an aid in visualizing the nature of this analysis.

We assume that a RAM with N inputs is connected quite arbitrarily somewhere within an image area whose dimensions are chosen to be one unit by one unit as shown in (a). Also in (a) is the first training pattern for this net, T1. Before going further, we shall show how the net responds to an unknown test pattern U shown in (b). For a RAM to output a 1 for U, all its N inputs must receive exactly the same pattern for T1 and for U. In (c) the overlap area that is the same for T1 and U is shown in black. Let us say that it measures A1 area units. (As the total area of the image is unity, A1 must be less than 1.) If any point within the image can be selected with equal probability, the probability of such a point being in A1 is A1/1, that is, precisely A1. As this is the probability for receiving the same input in T1 and U for any of the inputs of the RAM in question, the probability for all N RAMs being so connected is $A1 \times A1 \ldots \times A1$ (N times), i.e. $(A1)^N$. That is, the probability of an arbitrarily connected RAM outputting a 1 is $(A1)^N$.

Assume now that there is a large number of such arbitrarily connected RAMs. By the law of large numbers, a proportion $(A1)^N$ of this number would fire with a 1 and the rest with a 0. This is called the *relative*

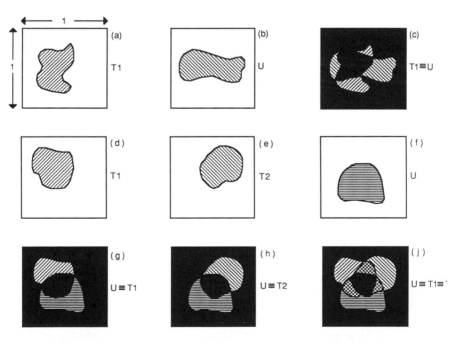

Fig. 5.4 Discriminator analysis based on overlapping areas.

response of the net, **R**. So the absolute response **r** for a net with K RAMs is

$$\mathbf{r} = K\mathbf{R} = K(A1)^N$$

The same form of reasoning can now be extended to a system trained on two patterns T1 and T2 as shown in fig. 5.4(d) and (e) respectively. The unknown pattern, U, is shown in (f). This time, the arbitrarily connected RAM will output a 1 if all its inputs are in the overlap area between T1 and U (shown in (g) as a black area and dubbed A1) or in the overlap area between T2 and U (shown in (h) as a black area and dubbed A2). Again the probability of connecting a RAM to the first of these areas is $(A1)^N$ and the second is $(A2)^N$. To get the total probability of the RAM firing with a 1, the probability of these two events can be added, provided that one subtracts the event of connecting to an area *common to the two events* which would otherwise be counted twice. This area is shown in black in (j) and is the overlap of U, T1 and T2. We call this area A12 and note that the probability of connecting to it is $(A12)^N$. So, the relative response for the system trained on two patterns is:

$$\mathbf{R} = (A1)^N + (A2)^N - (A12)^N. \tag{5.1}$$

The final step of this analysis is to extend equation (5.1) to any number (say E) of training patterns T1, T2, T3, ..., TE. The form of such an expression is the same as (5.1). That is, first U is overlapped with all the training patterns to calculate the contribution to the response, then overlap with pairs has to be removed to correct for double counting: but this takes away too much as it also removes the overlap of three training patterns once too often and this has to be put back, and so on. Formally, this is written as:

$$\mathbf{R} = (A1)^N + (A2)^N \ldots + (AE)^N - (A12)^N - (A13)^N$$

$$- \ldots - (A1E)^N \ldots - (A[E-1]E)^N + (A123)^N$$

$$+ (A124)^N \ldots \quad \ldots \quad \ldots - (A1234 \ldots E)^N \tag{5.2}$$

(The last term in an equation such as this is negative if E is even and positive if E is odd).

This formidable looking formula is really no different from (5.1), there is just more of it. The main characteristic of the system (and equation (5.2)) is that **R** is 1 if U is one of the training patterns. This can be understood either from the description of the system in the earlier parts of this chapter or from realizing that if, in equation (5.2), U = T1, say, then A1 = 1 and the rest of the equation adds up to 0. Also if U is close to any one of the training patterns, this makes **R** close to 1 by an amount which we shall find depends on N.

A legitimate question that can be asked at this point is why is it worth going to all the trouble of inventing discriminators, since the value of **R** as given by (5.2) could clearly be calculated on any computer. In other words, U could be compared to all the stored training patterns and their combinations, thereby generating all the overlap counts needed by equation (5.2). The value of **R** could then be computed as a result of this exhaustive search. On the other hand, a specially built hardware discriminator delivers **R** in just one computation (one pass through the net) thus avoiding long searches and overlap calculations as would be carried out in a simulation on a conventional serial machine.

The usefulness of equation (5.2) is that it allows the design engineer to gain an understanding of the effect of altering the value of N. We shall illustrate this by means of a few examples.

5.5 EXPECTED DISCRIMINATOR PERFORMANCE: SPECIFIC CASES

5.5.1 Position detection

A discriminator is required to detect the vertical position of a vertical bar and report on the distance of the bar from the central position.

This could be the sort of task that is required in order to keep a robot, which is guided by a visual system, moving along a line painted on a surface. The task is shown in fig. 5.5. T1, the only training pattern, is seen to be a bar of width $1/3$ units where the width and the height of the entire window are one unit. The test pattern U could have a vertical bar of the same width as T1 but anywhere that is wholly within the window. The distance of the bar from the left-hand edge is D, and the maximum value of D is $2/3$.

As D is increased from 0 to $2/3$, the overlap A1 between T1 and U increases linearly with D from $1/3$ (due to the overlap in the white area at the right of the two images) to 1 when the two images overlap totally at $D = 1/3$. As D is increased further, A1 falls linearly to $1/3$. The overlap area in A1 is shown in black in fig. 5.5 for a value of D between 0 and $1/3$. Remember that the response of the discriminator is given by:

$$\mathbf{R} = (A1)^N$$

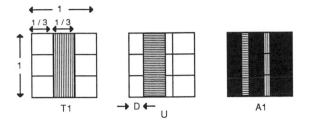

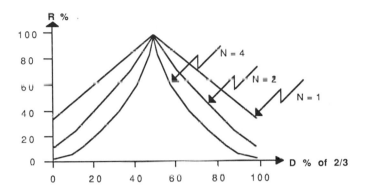

Fig. 5.5 A discriminator for centering on a bar.

It is seen that for $N = 1$, the response is merely a linear indication of the position of the bar from the central, trained, position. The effect of higher values of N is to 'sharpen-up' this detection, that is, indicate a displacement from the central position by a greater drop in **R**. This is a general rule in systems of this kind: the higher the N, the greater is the degree of discrimination (or acuity) of the discriminator. Or, putting it yet another way, if the discriminator has to detect the difference between patterns that are very similar, it will require a greater value of N than if the patterns are more distinct.

On a casual reading of the above example, one might come to the (wrong) conclusion that values of N other than 1 are merely an embellishment, an added bonus. However, it can happen that the discriminator is required to respond strongly (positively) to several patterns that are quite diverse from one another, and yet to distinguish these from others. This is illustrated in the next example where it is shown that higher values of N are not only optional, but essential. In fact, it is only in the use of values of N greater than 1 that the practical value of this type of system lies.

5.5.2 Detection of verticality

Imagine that the discriminator is now required to respond strongly for any vertical bar of a width $1/3$ units (assumed to be totally within the field of view) and a horizontal bar of the same width. Also assume that the discriminator is trained only on T1 as shown in fig. 5.5. Then the response to any horizontal bar of width $1/3$ is dictated by a value of overlap, say, $A1'$ (referring to the horizontal bar, say U'), of $5/9$.

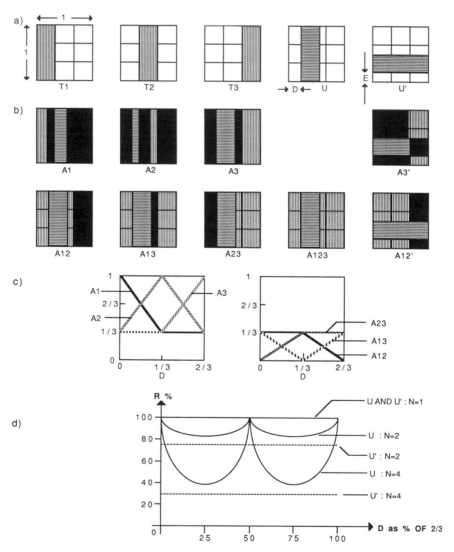

Fig. 5.6 Detection of verticality.

(Note: this includes the overlap of 'non-bar' parts of the pattern.) But if the bar is vertical the overlap can be as low as 1/3. This implies that there are vertical bars that, for any value of N, will give a lower response than the horizontal bar, which is contrary to that which is required. The obvious answer to this problem is to ensure that the discriminator is trained on vertical bars in more than one position. A possible training set is shown in fig. 5.6(a) as T1, T2 and T3. U is a vertical bar of width 1/3 at a distance D from the left-hand edge. The overlap areas with the training set and the combinations of the training set as required by equation (5.2) are shown in black in part (b) of the figure and are set out as simple expressions in Table 5.1.

The last of these is due to the fact that there is no overlap area common to the three training patterns. The other relationships are plotted as a function of D in fig. 5.6(c). For example it is shown that A1 starts at 1 for $D = 0$ and falls to 1/3 for $D = 1/3$ and remains at this value as D increases to 2/3.

It can also be seen that the corresponding overlap areas of U' are independent of E, and the same for the three training patterns. A3' and A12' are shown in fig. 5.6(b). These areas can be expressed as:

$$A1' = A2' = A3' = 5/9$$

$$A12' = A13' = A23' = 2/9$$

$$A123' = 0$$

In this case equation (5.2) becomes:

$$R = (A1)^N + (A2)^N + (A3)^N - (A12)^N$$

$$- (A13)^N - (A23)^N + (A123)^N$$

Table 5.1 Terms contributing to the response in fig. 5.6

Overlap	D = 0 to 1/3	D = 1/3 to 2/3 (not shown in fig. 5.6)
A1	$1 - 2D$	$1/3$
A2	$1/3 + 2D$	$1 - 2(D - 1/3)$ (or, $1/3 + 2(2/3 - D)$)
A3	$1/3$	$1/3 + 2(D - 1/3)$
A12	$1/3$	$1/3 - (D - 1/3)$
A13	$1/3 - D$	$D - 1/3$
A23	D	$1/3$
A123	0	0

This expression is sketched out in fig. 5.6(d) for U and U' as well as for $N = 1$, 2 and 4.

It is clear that for $N = 1$, $\mathbf{R} = 1$ both for U and U' and therefore the discriminator fails to provide the desired discrimination. Higher values of N are required and it is seen in the sketch of the values of $\mathbf{R}$ against values of D that, when N is greater than 1, U leads to a higher response than U' for all D. A worst case occurs (in the sense that $\mathbf{R}$ for U is very close to the $\mathbf{R}$ for U') when $D = 1/6$ (U is half way between T1 and T2) for which $\mathbf{R}$ evaluates as:

$$\mathbf{R}(\text{for U}) = (2/3)^N + (2/3)^N + (1/3)^N - (1.3)^N$$

$$- (1/6)^N - (1/6)^N + (0)^N$$

$$= 0.833 \ldots \text{ for } N = 2$$

and $\qquad = 0.391 \ldots \text{ for } N = 4.$

A similar value of $\mathbf{R}$ (for U) occurs for $D = 1/2$, that is, U is half way between T2 and T3. Now, $\mathbf{R}$ (for U') can be calculated (remembering that it is not dependent on D) in a similar way. We obtain:

$$\mathbf{R} \text{ (for U')} \quad = 0.777 \ldots \text{ for } N = 2$$

$$= 0.283 \ldots \text{ for } N = 4$$

It becomes clear that the discriminator achieves its desired task for values of N of 2 or higher. In fact, the higher the N the better; for the worst case calculated above, the ratio between the responses to the vertical and horizontal bar is 1.07 for $N = 2$ and 1.38 for $N = 4$. Therefore the advice for the designer is that high values of N lead to better discrimination in the discriminator. However, the designer will also soon realize that high values of N are expensive. The amount of memory contained in a RAM is 2^N, and hence every time that N is increased by 1, the cost of the discriminator doubles. This can be partly compensated for by using fewer RAMs in each discriminator but it is the 2^N trend that is dominant.

The use of systems of this kind for the detection of image features as discussed above is described in full in Aleksander and Wilson (1985).

5.6 MULTI-DISCRIMINATOR SYSTEMS: THE WISARD

A multi-discriminator system has each of its discriminators trained to a different class of object. If the task is one of recognizing the hand-

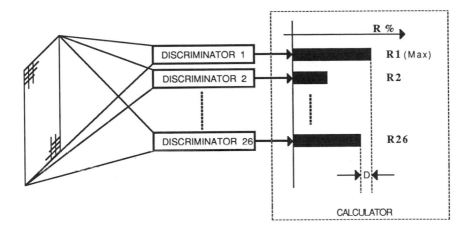

Fig. 5.7 A multi-discriminator system (the WISARD).

printed letters of the alphabet, say, then the scheme would contain 26 discriminators, one for each letter. The notion of a multi-discriminator system is quite general and takes the form shown in fig. 5.7.

The WISARD is a hardware implementation of this scheme directed towards the recognition of images. The hardware will be discussed later – here we concentrate on the principles of the arrangement.

We assume that there are 26 discriminators, each of which covers a binary 'image' with K RAMs of N address inputs each. In theory (such as led to the calculations and predictions in the examples of the last section), it is assumed that the K RAMs are randomly connected to the image with no constraints; in practice, a constraint is added – each image input is connected to precisely one RAM input. In other words the size of the image is KN binary picture points. This is done to ensure that the image is evenly covered with a minimum number of RAMs. Several points should be noted here

1. Although one talks of 'images', these ideas can be applied to any binary data (e.g. sampled speech signals).
2. Although one refers to binary picture points, an image could use more than one binary input per picture point. For example, if 16 grey levels are used there are at least four binary inputs for each such point. In this case it is assumed that all these binary points are input randomly to the learning net.
3. Whether the discriminators have identical input connections or not hardly matters. Each discriminator is trained to its own class of pattern, and therefore whether it is wired similarly to or differently from other discriminators is not of much consequence.

It is assumed that at the start of any training regime, all the RAMs of all the discriminators are set to 0. The training consists of setting to 1 the outputs of all the RAMs in the discriminator which are required to recognize the desired class. Say that a 26-discriminator system is being trained to recognize hand-printed characters, that the system is currently being trained to recognize a hand-printed letter A, and that discriminator 1 is designated to recognize As. Then discriminator 1 is trained to respond to a version of A with a 1 at all the RAMs it possesses. This is repeated for many other slightly different versions of As. The entire process is repeated for many examples of each of the other letters, taking care that only the appropriate discriminator for each letter is trained.

After training is complete, a response $\mathbf{R}j$ (% of K RAMs that output a 1) will occur at the jth discriminator (indeed, this is true for all values of j from 1 to 26) for the presentation of an unknown pattern to the entire system. The system recognizes the unknown pattern as belonging to the class for which $\mathbf{R}j$ is highest. This comparison and selection is performed by the calculator section of the system shown in fig. 5.7. The key mechanism at work in determining the response of each discriminator is that described by equation (5.2). Some examples will be used to illustrate this, but first, two more tasks performed by the calculator need to be described. The first is a measure of absolute confidence. This is merely the actual value of the highest $\mathbf{R}j$. Should this be close to 100%, the system is saying: 'Not only is this a member of class j, but also it is very much like one of the training patterns in that class.' Should the highest $\mathbf{R}j$ be low, however, this can be interpreted as the system saying: 'This pattern is not much like any that have been used in training, but, if pushed, I will say that it is a member of class j.'

The second additional task done by the calculator is to provide a measure of relative confidence $\mathbf{C}$. This is calculated by looking at the difference D between the highest $\mathbf{R}j$ and the second highest. $\mathbf{C}$ is then given by the simple formula:

$$\mathbf{C} = D/\mathbf{R}j \tag{5.3}$$

To illustrate the operation of this system we look at an example which involves the prediction of its performance when faced with having to recognize patterns in the presence of noise.

5.6.1 Example: detection of images in noise

One of the very important areas of application of neural nets is in the monitoring of premises for the presence of intruders. Figure 5.8 shows a highly stylized version of what this entails.

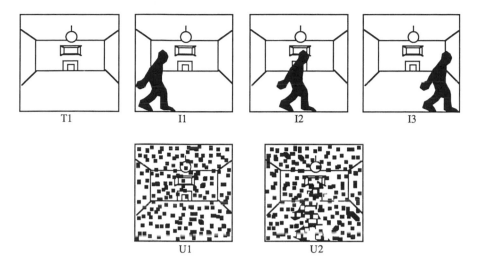

Fig. 5.8 Intruder detection in a noisy image of a room.

The task centres on training one discriminator on a particular scene (a room or an airfield, say) under normal conditions, that is, with no intruders present. A second discriminator is trained with intruders in many possible positions. This has sometimes to be done under very poor lighting conditions, and so the machine is required to operate correctly even with very poor images. Noise (which looks like 'snow' on a television set) occurs when TV cameras are made to operate in very poor lighting conditions. On a binary image we represent this as the alteration of some picture points from black to white and from white to black. Noise is measured in percentage terms, as a percentage probability of a picture point being affected by it.

Figure 5.8 shows the normal image (T1) of a room on which discriminator 1 is trained. I1, I2 and I3 are images containing an intruder on which discriminator 2 is trained. U1 is a test pattern which is intruder-free, but contains roughly 40% noise, while U2 is a test image containing an intruder and 40% noise. Using the theory developed earlier, the responses of the two discriminators to the two test patterns may be calculated once the effect of noise has been formulated. This is done as follows. Taking the overlap between any training pattern X and some unknown test pattern V as being A, then, given s% noise, the A area will lose s% (i.e. it will be $A(1 - s/100)$), while the $1 - A$ area will gain an overlap of $(1 - A)s/100$. Hence we have an expression for the noisy overlap A' as a function of the non-noisy one:

$$A' = A - As/100 + (1 - A)s/100.$$

This may be simplified a little to:

$$A' = A(1 - 2s/100) + s/100$$

So, using equation (5.2), assuming that the intruder shadow covers 1/6th of the image and that the shadows in I1, I2 and I3 do not overlap, then using the overlap values modified by noise as shown above, the *relative confidence* of the 2-discriminator system may be calculated from (5.3) and tabulated as shown in Table 5.2 (rounded) for $N = 8$:

Were only one discriminator used (say discriminator 1), putting a threshold on the response that discerns the presence of an intruder could be done only if the exact amount of noise were known beforehand. That is, were it known that the noise was precisely 20%, the presence of an intruder of the size assumed would cause the response of the discriminator to fall from 17% to 5.7%, which would be easily discernible with a threshold of say 10%. But were the noise to change from 20% to 30% this would be interpreted as the presence of an intruder and would raise a false alarm.

However, in these calculations it is the relative values of the two discriminators that are indicative of the presence of the intruder, **R1** being greater than **R2** without the intruder and the reverse when the intruder is there. This is true of any noise value up to 50%. Of course, 50% noise obliterates any meaningful pattern, as it is no longer possible to know whether any bit has its true value or a value due to noise. The confidence, too, is an indication of the level of noise. Perhaps it is worth noting that the confidence is greater in the presence of the intruder: this is due to the fact that the 'intruder-detecting' discriminators have had more training and generally give a stronger response to anything. In

Table 5.2 Responses of the system trained as in fig. 5.8

Noise	Intruder absent			Intruder present		
s%	R1%	R2%	C%	R1%	R2%	C%
0	100	58	42	23	100	77
10	43	28	34	12	43	72
20	17	13	25	5.7	16	65
30	5.7	4.9	14	2.5	5.7	55
40	1.7	1.6	3.7	1.1	1.7	37
50	0.39	0.39	0	0.39	0.39	0

(In these calculations it is assumed that the intruder has overlapped with one of the intruder training patterns.)

practice, this imbalance could be corrected by training the non-intruder discriminator on noisy images.

In a more general sense, it is the fact that there is no need to select a threshold that gives strength to the multi-discriminator method. Put simply, it allows the system to say, 'The image before me is nothing like the images that I have been trained on, but if pressed, I will say that it is more like X than any other training pattern.'

The WISARD is currently being used in security applications such as described above and in quality control tasks where it is used to identify and classify faults in products and to measure the alignment of piece-parts on production lines.

5.7 THE WISARD ARCHITECTURE

This section gives details of the hardware that has been engineered by Computer Recognition Systems in the UK to produce a commercial version of the WISARD idea. Those not interested in digital structures can skip this section, with the realization that what is being described represents a clever use of conventional digital hardware techniques. There is no need to develop special chips, the scheme relies on the use of conventional random access memory devices. Figure 5.9 shows a block diagram of the system.

Most of this equipment is a general-purpose image processing system.

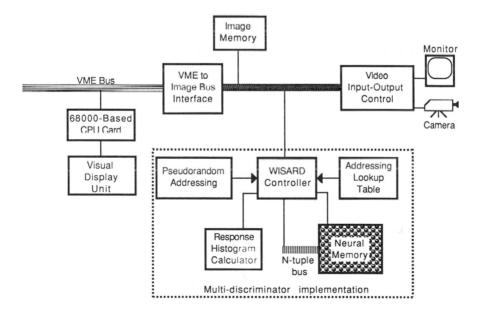

Fig. 5.9 Details of the WISARD architecture.

A video input/output controller digitizes the image picked up by the camera and transfers the resulting bits to an image memory or 'framestore'. Typically this picks up an image of 512×512 picture points (or pixels), which in the case of WISARD are only on or off. The digitized image may be output, again *via* the image bus and input/output controller, and displayed on a monitor over the original image. The controller can also allow the user to select the size and position of the digitized image.

The part of the system described so far is interfaced to a standard microprocessor system which carries the control software for the entire system and allows the user to select parameters displayed in 'menu' fashion on the visual display unit. The not-so-conventional part of the system is shown within the dotted frame and mainly consists of a large memory which can be partitioned to act as the notional system shown in fig. 5.8. The way in which this partitioning may be achieved is shown in fig. 5.9.

Under control of the 68000 microprocessor chip, the user can select a value of N and the size of the window which he wishes to use (say $X \times Y$). This determines the number of notional RAMs per discriminator (XY/N). The number of discriminators available is M, that is, each bit of a stored word contributes to the output of a different discriminator. If the total amount of memory available is 2^A words of M bits it requires A address terminals. N of these are used as RAM inputs while the other $A - N$ are used to index the individual RAMs. Therefore the number of RAMs per discriminator cannot exceed 2^{A-N}.

The random connection to the input image is arranged by a pseudo-random generator, or a predefined lookup table which build up the N

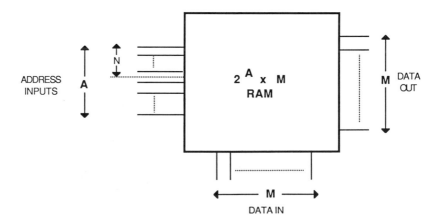

Fig. 5.10 Partitioning a large memory to make the neural memory.

address values for the memory after 'picking off' specific picture points from the image memory. The other $(A - N)$ address terminals of the memory are addressed in a systematic manner each time a complete group of N (N-tuple) has been brought together. During training only one of the M terminals (corresponding to the discriminator being trained) is energized at any one time and set to 1. The rest of the M terminals are left in the 'non-writing' state. During the 'use' phase, counters carry out a tally of the number of 1s that are generated by each of the M data-out lines, providing the histogram of **R***j* responses on which the output of the system can rapidly be calculated. The user can set values of confidence and response that are required to drive overall output lines (e.g. robot controls or relays that operate gates on a conveyor belt).

Clearly the operation of this system is serial, but the access time of the image memory can be made high enough for all the RAMs in the neural memory to be addressed within a short time. Some typical figures are given below.

Size of neural memory: 2 Megabytes
Value of M: 8
Value of A: 20
Value of N: 4
Number of RAMs per discriminator: $2^{20-4} = 64\,536$
Number of input image points that can be covered by a
  discriminator: $4 \times 64\,536 = 2^{18}$
This means that a 512×512 image (2^{18}) can be completely covered.
Time for a training or testing operation of the entire net
  (independent of N and window size): 0.08 seconds.

Provision is made in the WISARD for partial coverage if large windows are being used with large values of N. The parameters (N, M, window size and position, coverage) are selected by the user from the menu on the VDU. A warning is issued if the memory requirement is exceeded.

Further details on the architecture of the commercial version of the WISARD are in Aleksander, Thomas and Bowden (1984).

5.8 SUMMARY

In this chapter we have introduced several concepts: first, that the random access memory shares with most neural node models the property of being a trainable, variable function element. It has the distinction of being universal, in the sense that it can be trained to perform any binary function of its input terminals, while it also has the disadvantage of having no generalization. This is quickly corrected by the introduction of the second concept: the RAM discriminator. This has been shown to have properties similar to a perceptron: generalization based on a random sampling of an input 'image'. The third concept is that of a multi-discriminator system of which the WISARD machines are a particular family of physical implementations which can be used in real pattern recognition tasks.

There are also two major ideas that distinguish this type of work from neural computing based on variable weights. First, the behaviour of discriminators can be expressed as a probabilistic measure of the overlaps of training images and the unknown image. This provides a direct analytic tool, both for the assessment of given physical structures with respect to patterns with known overlap properties, and for the design of systems that will achieve a desired performance. But the underlying theme is this: here is a method of neural computing which, in the broad, does all that can be done with systems based on the McCulloch and Pitts model, but can be implemented with conventional computer component – RAMs.

EXERCISES FOR THE READER

1. For the $N = 4$, $K = 4$ discriminator (similar to the example related to fig. 5.3) calculate the most likely response to a pattern with Z zeros, given that the system is trained on the all-1 pattern and the 16 single-0 patterns. Provide numerical answers for $Z = 3$ and $Z = 4$ having first derived a general formula for Z.
2. What response would be predicted were expression (5.2) used. Discuss the difference between this and what was obtained in exercise 1 above. How does this discrepancy affect larger systems?
3. Discuss the similarities and differences between the WISARD type of arrangement and a single-layer, multi-neuron perceptron.
4. A 2-discriminator WISARD arrangement, operating on a square window, has one discriminator trained on an image for which all points to the left of a central vertical line are black and the rest white. The other discriminator is trained on the above image rotated clockwise through 90°. How could the measure of relative confidence be used to indicate when the rotation is 45°? What value of N is required to ensure that a 1% reading of relative confidence should correspond to no more than a ±3° error on the value of 45°.
5. For the example of intruder detection in fig. 5.8, select a minimum value of N which ensures that a confidence of at least 6% can be obtained in the absence of the intruder. What confidence does this imply in the presence of the intruder in one of the trained positions? What happens when the intruder is half way between the left of the image and the middle? (For all these calculations, assume that the

intruder is a rectangle 1/6th of the area of the entire image and half the image in height.)

6

The Hopfield breakthrough

In 1982 John Hopfield published a most influential paper which drew attention to the associative properties of a class of neural nets. Although he saw this as a practical advance, it is now seen as containing a fundamental statement of a method for analysing such schemes. The analysis is based on a definition of 'energy' in the net and a proof that the net operates by minimizing this energy when settling into stable patterns of operation. We first discuss how the values of the connection strengths of the net may be calculated to produce desired stable patterns of activity and then contrast this with achieving the same behaviour by a method of training.

6.1 HOPFIELD'S APPEAL: AUTOASSOCIATION

John Hopfield, a professor of biology and chemistry at the California Institute of Technology and a consultant to Bell Laboratories at Murray Hill in New Jersey (the research laboratories of the AT&T company), was responsible for rekindling the interest of scientists in neural network analysis (Hopfield, 1982). He drew attention to two properties of interconnected (autoassociative: see Chapter 1) cells of simple non-linear devices: first, that such a system has stable states which will always be entered if the net is started in similar states and, second, the fact that such states can be created by changing the strength of the interconnections between the cells. Much of the fascination of his paper came from the realization that the properties he identified – what computer engineers call *associative memory* – are emergent in these nets. These concepts need a little explanation.

6.2 EMERGENT ASSOCIATIVE PROPERTIES: AN INTRODUCTION

Associative memory is part of the computer engineer's armoury of information storage systems. Sometimes called content-addressable memory, it differs from conventional systems as follows. The memory of a conventional computer is organized like a filing cabinet with numbered files. The numbers on the files are called addresses. The whole business of programming relies on the computer being told the addresses at which data is stored. Even simple statements in BASIC such as LET A = 4, merely assign an arbitrary filing slot in memory at which the value 4 is stored. The address is not normally revealed to the programmer, who simply refers to it as 'A' in subsequent operations. In contrast, we quote from Hopfield (1982) to illustrate the operation of a content-addressable memory.

> Suppose that an item stored in memory is 'H. A. Kramers and G. H. Wannier *Phys. Rev.*, **60**, 252 (1941).' A general content-addressable memory would be capable of retrieving this entire memory item on the basis of sufficient partial information. The input 'and Wannier (1941)' might suffice. An ideal memory could deal with errors and retrieve this reference even from the input 'Vannier, (1941)'.

So the prime task for a content-addressable memory is the completion of information in a stored record in response to the presentation of part of that full record. Engineers have proposed hardware design for such memories, and some are actually in use, see Lea (1984). The advantage of neural net approaches to this type of retrieval from memory is that they are naturally tolerant of slight distortions of the presented part of the record. In his 1982 paper, Hopfield makes the point that purpose-designed associative memories are somewhat unsophisticated in that error correction has to be done deliberately by complex design, whereas with neural net approaches the error correction is done automatically.

This is where the notion of an emergent property comes in. The Hopfield net will be seen to have naturally occurring, spontaneous properties both of retrieval by content addressing and of being able to cope with errors. Some engineers tend to be suspicious of systems that have properties which they themselves have not designed. Hopfield urged such engineers to become interested in and understand these emergent properties, as they could lead to the design of novel integrated circuits and novel computing devices. Now we shall look at the assumptions that Hopfield made in defining what is now known as a *Hopfield Model*, and the way that his analysis takes some of the mystery out of the emergent properties.

6.3 THE HOPFIELD MODEL: DEFINITIONS AND AN EXAMPLE

In Hopfield's theory a 'neuron' i has two states just like the McCulloch and Pitts model discussed in Chapter 2. The output of the neuron is

$V_i = 0$ if it is not firing and $V_i = 1$ if it is firing. Neuron i receives an input from neuron j with a strength defined by T_{ij}. If $T_{ij} = 0$ it means that i is disconnected from j. (This strength T_{ij} is exactly the same concept as the *weight* in the McCulloch and Pitts model.) The most

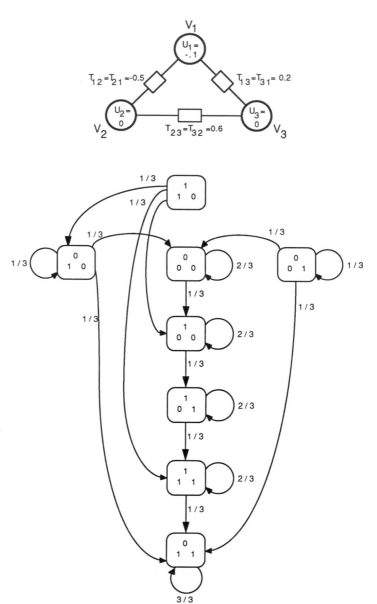

Fig. 6.1 A simplified Hopfield net and its state transitions.

important assumption made in the analysis is that there is bidirectionality in these connections, that is, $T_{ij} = T_{ji}$.

In the example in fig. 6.1, there are three neurons with respective firing states V_1, V_2 and V_3 and connection strengths as shown. The neuron in Hopfield's model has exactly the same firing rule as the McCulloch and Pitts (MCP) model:

$$V_i \text{ becomes 1 if } \sum_{j \neq i} T_{ij} V_j > U_i$$

$$V_i \text{ becomes 0 if } \sum_{j \neq i} T_{ij} V_j < U_i \qquad (6.1)$$

As in the MCP model, this firing rule assumes that each neuron has a threshold U_i which, as equation (6.1) shows, has to be overcome by the sum of all inputs to that node multiplied by their connection strengths. Armed with information giving all the weights and thresholds, it is possible to work out the sequence of firing states in the net from any given firing pattern. However, before doing this it is necessary to introduce a restriction that is characteristic of the Hopfield net: *asynchronous operation*. Each neuron fires in its own time with only a mean 'attempt rate', W attempts per second, being specified. This means that at any point in time any one of the neurons has a roughly equal probability of firing, and over a length of time of S seconds (say) every neuron will have fired, on average, WS times.

So, given a particular state, say V_1, V_2, $V_3 = 000$, we can calculate what might happen were each of the neurons in turn to be making an attempt to fire. If neuron 1 is the first to attempt to fire, the sum of the weighted inputs is:

$$0 \times (-0.5) + 0 \times (0.2) = 0.$$

Since the threshold U_1 is -0.1 the input sum exceeds it and this particular neuron will change from $V_1 = 0$ to $V_1 = 1$. This leads to the new overall state, V_1, V_2, $V_3 = 100$.

However, either of the other two neurons could fire with equal probability. The sum of the weighted inputs is as follows:

For neuron 2, $0 \times (-0.5) + 0 \times (0.6) = 0$,

which does not exceed the threshold $U_2 = 0$.
Therefore V_2 remains at 0.

For neuron 3, $0 \times (0.2) + 0 \times (0.6) = 0$,

which does not exceed the threshold $U_3 = 0$.
Therefore, V_3 remains at 0.

As we have said, these events are equally likely, therefore the transition back to the 000 state has a probability of two-thirds while the transition to the 100 state has a probability of one-third. In this way, the probability of the three possible outward transitions from each of the states may be calculated. The result is shown in full in fig. 6.1. The most noticeable feature of this is that the net will, after some time, settle in state 011. Although, at this point in the explanation, this seems not to have much to do with content addressable memory (this will be tackled later), it does call for a method of analysis which makes some predictions about this form of behaviour: the settling in some state rather than wandering around from state to state.

6.4 THE HOPFIELD MODEL: THEORETICAL ANALYSIS

(Those interested in the result of this theoretical analysis and not in its details may wish to jump to the next section where a non-mathematical summary of such results is provided.)

The way that the states in fig. 6.1 have been arranged is not incidental: they are arranged so that a transition either stays at the same height, or moves downwards. A central feature of Hopfield's analysis is that he associated each state with a quantity he called E (for energy) which diminishes every time a neuron changes its state. Let the change in energy due to neuron i changing its state be ΔE. (The symbol Δx is used in a conventional mathematical way: it means 'a change in x'.) Every time the firing rule is applied and there is a change in V_i (denoted ΔV_i), E must be reduced, that is, ΔE must be negative. Changes in V_i can occur only if V_i is 0 and the so-called *activation* ($\Sigma T_{ij}V_j - U_i$) is positive and ΔV_i is also positive, *or* if V_i is 1, in which case the activation must be negative, as is ΔV_i. Thus the product $\Delta V_i(\Sigma T_{ij}V_j - U_i)$ is always positive. So Hopfield defined:

$$\Delta E = -\Delta V_i \left(\sum T_{ij}V_j - U_i \right) \tag{6.2}$$

which ensures that ΔE is always negative when a neuron changes state according to its firing rule.

So the energy of node i which leads to the above change could be defined as:

$$E_i = -V_i \left(\sum T_{ij}V_j - U_i \right) = - \sum T_{ij}V_jV_i + V_iU_i$$

It is this form of expression that led Hopfield to define the total energy of the system at any point in time as related to the sum of E_i for all i. Remembering that $T_{ij} = T_{ji}$, he asserted the following expression for this total energy E:

$$E = -1/2 \sum \sum T_{ij} V_j V_i + \sum V_i U_i \qquad (6.3)$$

The half term is a nicety which compensates for the fact that in taking overall summations some of the terms are met twice. To explain this process we work through the calculation of energy for our 3-neuron example in fig. 6.1.

$$E_1 = -V_1(T_{12}V_2 + T_{13}V_3 - U_1)$$

$$E_2 = -V_2(T_{12}V_1 + T_{23}V_3 - U_2)$$

$$E_3 = -V_3(T_{23}V_2 + T_{13}V_1 - U_3)$$

$$E_1 + E_2 + E_3 = -2T_{12}V_1V_2 - 2T_{13}V_1V_3$$

$$- 2T_{23}V_2V_3 + U_1V_1 + U_2V_2 + U_3V_3$$

E is related to $E_1 + E_2 + E_3$ as:

$$E = -T_{12}V_1V_2 - T_{13}V_1V_3 - T_{23}V_2V_3 + U_1V_1 + U_2V_2 + U_3V_3$$

which is a specific case of equation (6.3) which applies to fig. 6.1.

Taking the example further and calculating some energy values for its states we find for state $V_1V_2V_3 = 111$ that

$$E = -(-0.5)\cdot 1\cdot 1 - (0.2)\cdot 1\cdot 1 - (0.6)\cdot 1\cdot 1$$

$$+ (-0.1)\cdot 1 + 0\cdot 1 + 0\cdot 1$$

$$= -0.4$$

If neuron 1 stops firing, the net transits to state

$$V_1V_2V_3 = 011$$

for which the energy may be calculated as being

$$E = -(-0.5)\cdot 0\cdot 1 - (0.2)\cdot 0\cdot 1 - (0.6)\cdot 1\cdot 1 + (-0.1)\cdot 0 + 0 + 0$$

$$= -0.6$$

This turns out to be the lowest value of energy among all the states, and is that state that the net will revert to in the long run. It will be shown later that it is not always the case that a net will revert to the state with the lowest energy – there could be several states in which a net can remain stable (known as 'energy wells'). The state transition diagram of fig. 6.1 is reproduced in fig. 6.2 with the energy of all the states explicitly shown. This shows that the definition of energy is such that any state transition either leaves the system at the same energy level or causes it to fall to a lower one until it can fall no more.

6.5 NON-MATHEMATICAL SUMMARY OF THE 'ENERGY' ANALYSIS

The essence of Hopfield's analysis is that he has been able to prove that

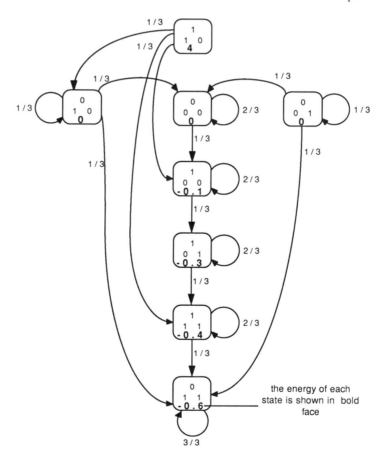

Fig. 6.2 The energy of states in the Hopfield net.

as a net, structured according to his recipe, alters state it does so in an irreversible manner: it has the tendency not to return to a previously experienced state. His proof centres on defining an 'energy' which can be calculated for each possible pattern of firing and non-firing in the neurons of the net. He has shown that every time that this state or pattern changes, the energy can only stay the same or become lower. That is, the net's state changes to one with the same or lower energy. Eventually there are no further accessible states with a lower energy, and the net remains stable in the last found state.

Unfortunately, this stability can be purely local. Being in a stable state is like being in a well surrounded by a wall (the wall being the higher energy states) without being aware of the fact that there may be deeper wells nearby.

In the next section it will be shown that these low energy states can actually be designed into a net and we shall see how two such wells can be created in a 3-neuron net of the same shape as the one in fig. 6.1.

6.6 DESIGNING ENERGY WELLS BY CALCULATION

The behaviour of a net can be of some use only if its stable states can be selected or 'created' in some way by the user. We shall distinguish between creating stable states directly by *calculating* the connection strengths that are needed and the *training* of the net where additional machinery is provided so that the net itself can make adjustments to the connection strengths to create stability for states chosen by the trainer. In this section we will look at how stable states are created by calculation.

As an example, we shall assume that *two* states are to be made stable in the net:

$$V_1 V_2 V_3 = 010 \ and \ 111$$

Recall that the energy of a neuron i is given by:

$$E_i = -V_i \left(\sum T_{ij} V_j - U_i \right).$$

This may be written as:

$$E_i = -V_i \ (\text{activation}_i).$$

For a state to be stable, none of the nodes should be activated in such a way as to change its firing condition. In other words, if the node is firing ($V_i = 1$) the activation should be positive in order not to change the firing state (i.e. stop the node from firing). Similarly if the node is not firing ($V_i = 0$) the activation should be negative so as not to cause the node to fire.

Therefore, for every stable state that needs to be included in the design, restrictions are imposed on the values of connection strengths and neuron thresholds, and values need to be found that satisfy all the restrictions implied by all the desired stable states. As an illustration we will continue using our example

We will label

$$V_1V_2V_3 = 010 \text{ as state pattern } \mathbf{A}$$

and $V_1V_2V_3 = 111$ as state pattern $\mathbf{B}$

For state pattern $\mathbf{A}$:

V_1 is 0,
therefore the activation $T_{12}V_2 + T_{13}V_3 - U_1$ must be < 0,
but V_2 is 1 and V_3 is 0,
so the above inequality becomes

$$T_{12} - U_1 < 0 \tag{6.4}$$

Similarly, for V_2,

$$U_2 < 0 \tag{6.5}$$

and, for V_3,

$$T_{23} - U_3 < 0 \tag{6.6}$$

For state pattern $\mathbf{B}$:

$$\text{for } V_1 \quad T_{12} + T_{13} - U_1 > 0 \tag{6.7}$$

$$\text{for } V_2 \quad T_{12} + T_{23} - U_2 > 0 \tag{6.8}$$

$$\text{for } V_3 \quad T_{23} + T_{13} - U_3 > 0 \tag{6.9}$$

This set of inequalities can now be 'solved' to give allowable values of the six unknowns. We shall proceed to do this informally, by choosing values arbitrarily to satisfy one inequality at a time. (We will assume that all unknowns should be in the range -1 to $+1$.)

Let T_{12} be 0.5.
Then, to satisfy (6.4), U_1 is in the range 0.5 to 1, so let it be 0.7.

From (6.7) we see that T_{13} must be in the range from $-(0.5 - 0.7)$ (that is, 0.2) to 1, so let it be 0.4.
(6.5) requires a negative value of U_2, so let it be -0.2.
(6.8) now reads $0.5 + T_{23} + 0.2 > 0$.
This means that T_{23} must be in the range -0.7 to 1, so let it be 0.1.
Finally from (6.9) $0.1 + 0.4 - U_3 > 0$.
Hence, U_3 should be in the range 0.5 to -1, so let it be 0.4.

In summary:

$T_{12} = 0.5$
$T_{13} = 0.4$
$T_{23} = 0.1$
$U_1 = 0.7$
$U_2 = -0.2$
$U_3 = 0.4$

To check the success of this allocation, the inequalities (6.4) to (6.9) can be evaluated.

$$T_{12} - U_1 = -0.2, \text{ which is less than } 0 \tag{6.4}$$

$$U_2 = -0.2, \text{ which is less than } 0 \tag{6.5}$$

$$T_{23} - U_3 = -0.3, \text{ which is less than } 0 \tag{6.6}$$

$$T_{12} + T_{13} - U_1 = 0.2, \text{ which is greater than } 0 \tag{6.7}$$

$$T_{12} + T_{23} - U_2 = 0.8, \text{ which is greater than } 0 \tag{6.8}$$

$$T_{23} + T_{13} - U_3 = 0.1, \text{ which is greater than } 0 \tag{6.9}$$

Having checked that these values satisfy the required theoretical conditions, the actual state transition diagram can be derived, as before, to check that the appropriate 'well' states have in fact been created. This is shown in fig. 6.3. It is clear from this diagram that, whatever its starting state, the net will finish, unchanging, in one of the initially determined states (A or B).

6.7 NON-MATHEMATICAL COMMENT ON THE CALCULATION METHOD

Reviewing the previous section in a non-mathematical way, we arrive at the following description. Two states were selected and values for the connection strengths (weights) and the thresholds of the neurons were calculated in such a way as to make sure that no change would take place in these firing states. It has been shown that the resulting state transition diagram contains only these two states, which means that, whatever the starting state, the net will end in one of these two states.

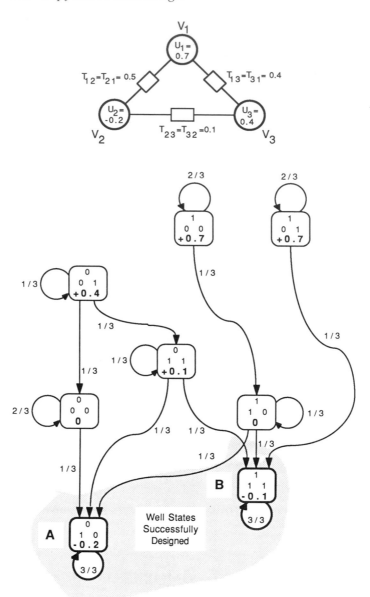

Fig. 6.3 The design of stable 'well' states.

Indeed, it is possible to make a list of starting states and end states with the associated probability of entering these end states as in Table 6.1. This is done merely by following through the paths shown in fig. 6.3. It is just possible to discern from this example that some patterns similar to one of the selected stable states (A or B) are more

Table 6.1 Probabilities of reaching the end states in fig. 6.3

Start state			End State (% Prob.)			
V_1	V_2	V_3	V_1	V_2	V_3	
0	1	0	0	1	0	100%
1	1	1	1	1	1	100%
0	0	0	0	1	0	100%
1	0	1	1	1	1	100%
0	0	1	1	1	1	25%
			0	1	0	75%

The other three starting states have 50% probability of entering either final state.

likely to lead to their similar partner among A and B, than to any other. (This is more easily seen with a larger net.) In particular, if one of the nodes is *clamped* to a value that distinguishes between the two selected states (e.g. $V_3 = 0$), the net will finish in the stable state which contains that value (state A in this example). Clamping is simply the process of preventing the chosen node(s) (like V_3 here) from changing its firing state (by means that will depend on the electronic arrangement of the net and need not be detailed here). For example, if the current state is 110 without clamping, the next state could be 110, 010 or 111 with equal probability. If V_3 is clamped to 0, the change can be back to 110 or to 010 with equal probability. That is, it will sooner or later fall into 010.

It is precisely this latter effect that led Hopfield to highlight the *content-addressable* nature of these nets. In the above, clamping V_3 to 0 causes the 01 response on V_1V_2 to be 'retrieved', 010 being the complete stored record. In the case of much larger nets, it is precisely this retrieval characteristic that could make it possible to complete the publication reference records quoted at the beginning of this chapter.

6.8 THE PROBLEM OF FALSE WELLS

It could be said that the result of the calculation in the last example was a little lucky. One of the problems with the setting up of wells in the state transition diagram of a net is that there may be other, unwanted, wells into which the net could stray. We shall illustrate this with an example. Consider an alternative set of net values as shown in fig. 6.4:

$$T_{12} = -0.5 \quad T_{13} = 0.5 \quad T_{23} = 0.4$$
$$U_1 = -0.1 \quad U_2 = -0.2 \quad U_3 = 0.7$$

Again, to check the success of this allocation (that is, that the two desired wells exist), the inequalities (6.4) to (6.9) can be evaluated:

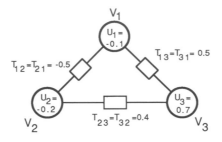

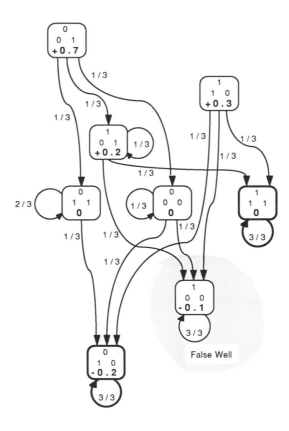

Fig. 6.4 A false well.

$$T_{12} - U_1 = -0.4 < 0 \tag{6.4}$$
$$U_2 = -0.2 < 0 \tag{6.5}$$
$$T_{23} - U_3 = -0.3 < 0 \tag{6.6}$$
$$T_{12} + T_{13} - U_1 = 0.2 > 0 \tag{6.7}$$
$$T_{12} + T_{23} - U_2 = 0.1 > 0 \tag{6.8}$$
$$T_{23} + T_{13} - U_3 = 0.2 > 0 \tag{6.9}$$

Clearly these conditions are satisfied, and this is reflected in the existence of the desired wells in fig. 6.4. However, the figure shows quite clearly the state 100 is also a well which results from the chosen values. The thought may occur that additional inequalities could have been included to avoid this occurrence, one for each non-well state. Although this is true, it would be quite impractical in a net of any size as the number of such inequalities is massive. For a 100-neuron net (which is not very large) there would be a total of 100×2^{100} (approx 10^{32}) inequalities, each of which would have to be stated.

As things stand, attempts to clamp V_3 to 0 will retrieve 100 and 010 with equal probability if the starting states are either 000 or 110. If, before the system can fire, the starting state 101 is clamped with V_3 set to 0, the net will enter the false state 100 with 100% certainty. Ways of overcoming this problem were not discussed by Hopfield in his original paper, but were tackled later by Hinton, whose work will be explained in the next chapter. See Hinton and Sejnowski (1986).

6.9 LEARNING FROM EXAMPLES, OR TRAINING

In his original paper, Hopfield made very little of the fact that a neural net can learn its stable states (wells) from examples. Only in reference to biological cells does he draw attention to the fact that weight and threshold adjustments in such systems can be made according to a model by Hebb (1949) in which the connection strength between two neurons is increased in proportion to the frequency with which the neurons fire together. In fact, the Widrow–Hoff rule described in Chapter 2 is a development of this idea, and we shall use it to show that it successfully creates energy wells in Hopfield nets.

Starting with a 3-node net as before, we assume that the connection strengths and thresholds are set arbitrarily as follows:

$$T_{12} = T_{13} = T_{23} = 0.5$$

$$U_1 = U_2 = U_3 = 0$$

We further assume that the two stable patterns that are to be taught to this net are the ones used before:

$V_1V_2V_3 = 010$ as state pattern **A**

and $V_1V_2V_3 = 111$ as state pattern **B**

The Widrow–Hoff rule simply requires that the actual activation of a node be calculated (or measured, in a practical system) and compared to some required value. The discrepancy between the two is seen as an error. A part, d, of the error is then removed by equal adjustments to the 'live' connection strengths ('live' is defined as that strength T_{ij} for neuron i, for which V_j is 1) and relevant thresholds.

For example, if the net is set to pattern **A**, V_1 should be 0 but its activation is:

$$T_{12} - U_1 = 0.5 - 0 = 0.5$$

For V_1 the desired value of this is to be less than 0, say -0.1, which means that the error is $0.5 - (-0.1)$, that is 0.6. In order to ensure that the process may converge on a solution, d is often selected by some means of experimentation, but here for the sake of an illustration, we give d a value of 1. So, we shall try to remove the whole of the error, splitting the responsibility for doing so between T_{12} and U_1. The former will be decreased by 0.3 and the latter increased by 0.3. So, now,

$$T_{12} - U_1 = 0.2 - 0.3 = -0.1$$

as required. We can track the changes in strengths and connections:

Step 0: $T_{12} = 0.5$ $T_{13} = 0.5$ $T_{23} = 0.5$
           $U_1 = 0$ $U_2 = 0$ $U_3 = 0$

Step 1: $T_{12} = 0.2$ $T_{13} = 0.5$ $T_{23} = 0.5$
           $U_1 = 0.3$ $U_2 = 0$ $U_3 = 0$

Because in the Hopfield model the connection strengths appear in the activation of several neurons, the adjustment must be done in rotation, neuron after neuron, and repeated until all the desired values are satisfied. So, considering pattern **A** and V_2, the activation function is merely:

$$-U_2 = 0$$

For V_2 to be 1 this activation must be positive, say $+0.1$, which makes $U_2 = -0.1$. So we have:

Step 2: $T_{12} = 0.2$ $T_{13} = 0.5$ $T_{23} = 0.5$
            $U_1 = 0.3$ $U_2 = -0.1$ $U_3 = 0$

Now, for pattern **A** and V_3, the activation function is:

$$T_{23} - U_3 = 0.5 - 0 = 0.5$$

But this too should be negative for V_3 to be 0, leaving an error of 0.6. This is overcome by letting T_{23} fall to 0.2 and U_3 rise to 0.3.

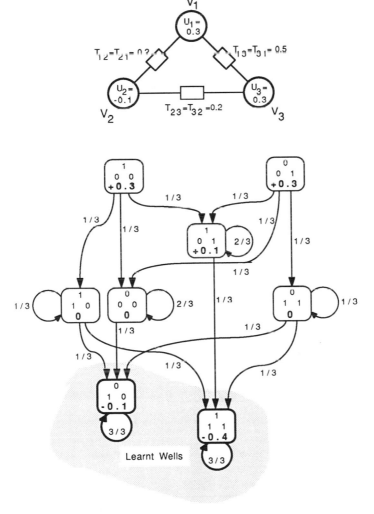

Fig. 6.5 Learnt wells.

So, we have:

Step 3: $T_{12} = 0.2$ $T_{13} = 0.5$ $T_{23} = 0.2$
               $U_1 = 0.3$ $U_2 = -0.1$ $U_3 = 0.3$

This is sufficient to make pattern **A** a stable well state.

It may also be seen that this learnt set of net parameters is also suitable, perhaps fortuitously, to keep state 111 stable (i.e. a well). At this point both patterns have been learnt. Looking at the state transition diagram as in fig. 6.5, this shows that indeed the two desired states have been learnt and that there are no false wells. (The latter, however, may also be fortuitous.)

6.10 THE IMPORTANCE OF TRAINING

In broad terms, to discover what this system is doing it is possible to make a list of starting states and end states with the associated probability of entering these end states as was done for the programmed net in fig. 6.3, see Table 6.2.

This is substantially the same as the result obtained by calculation in fig. 6.3, suggesting that training is another appropriate way of creating the desired states in a net.

From a perspective of energy analysis it becomes clear that an application of a rule such as the Widrow–Hoff learning procedure is a way of reducing the energy of a state to its minimum. In fact it is Hopfield's energy-based analysis that makes sense of such rules. Remember that the energy of the neuron i is given by:

$$E_i = -\left[V_i \left(\sum T_{ij}V_j - U_i\right)\right] = -[V_i \times activation].$$

Table 6.2 Probabilities of reaching the end states in fig. 6.5

Start state			End State (% Prob.)			
V_1	V_2	V_3	V_1	V_2	V_3	
0	1	0	0	1	0	100%
1	1	1	1	1	1	100%
0	0	0	0	1	0	100%
1	0	1	1	1	1	100%
0	0	1	0	1	0	50%
			1	1	1	50%

The three other starting states also have 50% probability of entering either final state.

From this it is noted that if the unit is required to fire but the activation is negative, the Widrow–Hoff rule requires that it be made positive. This increases the value of the term in square brackets, which decreases the energy, that is it reduces its contribution to the total energy. Similarly, if the unit is firing and it should not be, the activation function is made negative at the same time as the value of V_i is made negative. The product of the two negatives gives again a positive nudge to the term in square brackets, reducing the energy. This is beginning to sound rather involved so, let us simply track the energy of the system in the above example as the steps of the training algorithm progress:

STATE $(V_1V_2V_3)$ (Desired state highlighted)	000	001	**010**	011	100	101	110	111
Starting energy	0	0	0	−0.5	0	−0.5	0.5	1.5
After first step	0	0	0	−0.5	+0.3	−0.5	+0.1	−0.9
After second step	0	0	−0.1	−0.6	+0.3	−0.2	0	−1.0
After third step	0	+0.3	−0.1	0	+0.3	+0.1	0	−0.4

It is the last line that is reflected in fig. 6.5. It is seen from this that the effect of applying the Widrow–Hoff rule is to lower the energy of the appropriate state with respect to its 'neighbouring' states (i.e. those that differ by the firing of one node: 000, 110 and 011 in this case).

There is another important way of looking at the training of a Hopfield model. Looking at inequalities (6.4) to (6.9), they are examples of 'simultaneous equations'. These occur often in mathematics when several constraints are to be met at the same time. There are well known computational procedures for solving simultaneous equations, but they are generally time-consuming. Building a net that can be *trained* provides an automatic way of solving such equations.

6.11 FURTHER COMMENTS ON HOPFIELD'S MODEL

We have seen that, in an attempt to present neural nets as practical content-addressable memories, Hopfield made two major contributions. The first is the development of an analysis derived from physics which uses the concept of 'energy' to represent the successive firing of the net as a 'fall' down slopes determined by the connection strengths and thresholds of the neurons. The conclusion of such analysis is that the net must eventually reach the bottom of some energy well, after which it will tend not to change its pattern of firing any further. Connection strengths and thresholds can be calculated so as to create such stable 'well' states.

The second aspect of such nets is that of training. This opens the possibility that rules such as the Widrow–Hoff procedure can be used to make gradual adjustments to the net parameters until the wells are created. This is interesting because it gets around the difficulties of solving massive simultaneous equations by conventional methods, and could be used as a tool for such computations.

This work is of great fundamental significance, but there are certain practical problems relating to false minima, storage capacity and hard learning.

6.11.1 False minima

We have discussed this problem earlier in this chapter. In the next chapter we shall see how it can be overcome by the use of noise in the net.

6.11.2 Storage capacity

Given a Hopfield net of N neurons, it is appropriate to ask how many N-bit patterns the net can store as stable wells. Abu-Mustafa and St. Jaques (1985) have asked this question and come up with a simple answer: the maximum is N. In practical terms this is disappointingly low. As each stored pattern has N bits, the maximum storage capacity of bits stored by the net as stable wells is N^2.

Say that a system of N nodes requires connection strengths each of which can assume T distinct values. Recalling the ways in which neurons can be implemented digitally (as in Chapter 4) each connection therefore requires Log_2T bits, and the total number of bits in the machinery of the net is $N^2(Log_2T)$ as there are N^2 connections in the net. Therefore the Hopfield content-addressable memory requires Log_2T times as much machinery as its conventional equivalent. In practice, T is not easy to ascertain. Taking the particular case of fig. 4.3 in Chapter 4 with N = 64. In this case, 16-bit registers were used as weights.

So the total number of bits used = $N^2 \times 16$
The total capacity according to Abu-Mustafa = N^2

So there is a wastefulness factor of 16 with respect to storing 16, 16-bit records in a conventional content-addressable memory. This could be seen as the price one pays for the ability to correct errors, which is one of the emergent properties of the Hopfield model.

6.11.3 Hard learning

Without going into detail, it is clear that the Hopfield model suffers from the same hard learning probems as perceptrons (see Chapter 3).

After all, training simply requires the build-up of arbitrary functions in the nodes of the net, and these might include functions such as parity which (as we saw in Chapter 3) cannot be achieved by the node. We shall see in the next chapter that it is possible to overcome this limitation by the introduction of 'hidden neurons' into the model.

EXERCISES FOR THE READER

1. Why is the energy of the all-zero state always 0 in any net of any size? Use this fact to argue that at least one threshold must be negative for the all-zero state not to be a stable well.
2. Taking a three-node net, why cannot the following states $V_1V_2V_3 = 000, 011, 110$ and 101 be made stable wells?
3. Calculate what would happen to the system in fig. 6.3, were the Hopfield requirement of one neuron firing at a time removed. That is, assume that all three nodes are capable of changing state (if their activation so requires) at the same time, that is, at the arrival of a clock pulse.
4. Consider the network shown below

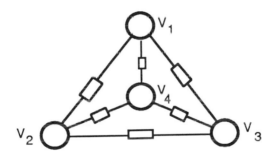

Fig. 6.6 A four-node net

Show, using the method of calculation, that weights and thresholds may be found to maintain the following stable states:

V_1	V_2	V_3	V_4
1	1	0	0
1	0	1	0
0	1	1	0
0	0	0	1

Comment on the fact that if one considers only V_1, V_2 and V_3 then these units perform the parity function using the fourth unit in an auxiliary capacity.

7

The Boltzmann solution

This chapter reports on the work of Hinton and his colleagues (1986). They added noise to the Hopfield model and called their net a Boltzmann machine, drawing an analogy between its behaviour and that of physical noisy systems. In this chapter we explain the meaning of these terms, and discuss the training techniques which lead to a better control of the energy minima defined in the previous chapter. These techniques also provide solutions to the hard learning problem.

7.1 BOLTZMANN AND NOISE

Despite the excellence of Hopfield's analysis (Hopfield, 1982), the prospect that his proposed model could be used directly in the implementation of content-addressable devices for real computers is marred by the problems listed at the end of the last chapter. We recall that two of these are the possibility of delivering wrong answers because the net gets 'stuck' in false local minima, and the inability of the net to cope with 'hard learning' problems. In this chapter we shall discuss the work done by Geoffrey Hinton and Terry Sejnowski on methods that go towards solving these two problems, see Hinton and Sejnowski (1986).

Hinton, Sejnowski and their colleague Dana Ballard were working together at the same time as Hopfield was developing his analysis, but with their attention directed towards problems of artificial vision. Their major concern was the development of computations that could interpret local intensity data of some small part of an image, so as to infer the depth and orientation of the surface represented by that data. This requires a knowledge of the intensity data in neighbouring parts of an image. They suggested that a parallel network of neural-like nodes could solve this type of *constraint satisfaction* problem (Ballard, Hinton and Sejnowski, 1983). Such a network starts with a poor interpretation of the surface properties of the image and, while it runs, improves its interpretation on the basis of learnt 'solutions'. The mechanism is very much like that of the Hopfield net, the solutions being analogous to the local minima in Hopfield's energy-like interpretation. Clearly, false minima and the inability to interpret 'hard' examples would prevent the technique from being used for vision applications and were therefore

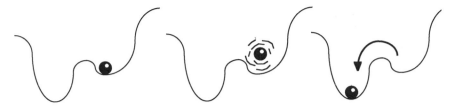

Fig. 7.1 A 'noisy' ball finds the lowest hill.

seen by Hinton and his colleagues as problems requiring solutions. In this chapter we shall not directly pursue Ballard, Hinton and Sejnowski's notion of computer vision, but we shall apply their findings directly to the Hopfield nets as described in the last chapter.

The key to ensuring that the system can escape from local minima lies in the use of 'noise': the application of a degree of uncertainty to the energy of the state. This can be illustrated by using the energy analogy and representing the state of a net as a ball on a hilly surface as in fig. 7.1.

The intuitive notion is that if the ball has an internal property that makes it 'jump about' it is more likely to spend most of its time in the lowest well within reach. The word 'noise' is used by electrical engineers and physicists to describe this uncertainty and comes from the phenomenon illustrated in fig. 7.2.

In (a) a relatively smooth current waveform is shown. If this were passed through a loudspeaker with a repetition rate of somewhere between 500 and 5000 cycles (repetitions) per second, a pure, organ-like note would be heard. However, if (b) were passed through the same loudspeaker, the same note would be accompanied by a nasty hiss. It is this hiss that the engineer calls noise. Listeners to distant radio stations will be familiar with this effect.

It was Ludwig Boltzmann, the Austrian physicist, who, towards the

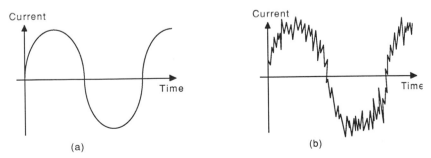

Fig. 7.2 (a) A pure waveform; and (b) a noisy waveform.

end of the nineteenth century, discovered that the random motion of the molecules of a gas had an energy directly related to temperature. This effect occurs not only in a gas but in any electronic circuitry which carries a current. High temperatures cause random movements of electrons that change smooth waveforms into rough ones as shown in fig. 7.2, an effect that designers of hi-fi equipment spend much time combating.

Hinton therefore used the name of Boltzmann to convey the idea that the energy of the state of a neural net could be given an uncertainty above and below that which may be calculated as shown for Hopfield nets in Chapter 6. The extent of this uncertainty is called, in line with Boltzmann physics, *temperature*. So, at zero temperature, the net is meant to behave exactly like the Hopfield model, while at higher temperatures an uncertainty proportional to the temperature is introduced into the activation function (see pages 96) of the net. While this helps it to escape from local minima it also prevents it from settling anywhere. Hinton suggested a regime which neatly overcomes this problem: start the net at a high temperature and 'cool' it down while it is running. This, it will be shown, ensures that the state of the net has the best chance of ending in the lowest minima related to given input data. We shall discuss this methodology, which goes under the name of *simulated annealing* and which has been used in other situations to compute problems with many variables (Kirkpatrick *et al.*, 1983).

The word *annealing* comes from yet another branch of engineering: metallurgy. It is the name given to the process of raising the temperature of a metal to near melting point and then lowering it, with the object of allowing the molecules of the metal to 'relax' and thus get rid of local stresses which may lead to metal failures. This process of 'relaxing' is, indeed, one of removing local pockets of stress energy in the metal and may be described as allowing the metal to escape from local elevated energy minima, and reach a 'relaxed' overall energy minimum.

Finally, in this chapter we will look at Hinton's proposals for new learning rules which attempt to create absolute energy minima. Perhaps the key achievement of these new rules is that they are capable of dealing with 'hidden' nodes, which are necessary if hard learning problems are to be solved. But first we shall put physical analogies aside and take a practical look at the way in which 'noise' may be introduced into a Hopfield net. That is, we shall describe the basic operation of a Boltzmann machine.

7.2 THE INTRODUCTION OF NOISE

We recall that the way things stand in a Hopfield net:

V_i becomes 1 if $\sum_{j\neq i} T_{ij}V_j > U_i$

V_i becomes 0 if $\sum_{j\neq i} T_{ij}V_j < U_i$

where V_i is the firing state of the neuron ($= 0$ when not firing and $= 1$ when firing)

U_i is the threshold of the neuron

and

$$\sum_{j\neq i} T_{ij}V_j - U_i$$

is the 'activation' (say $= A$) of the neuron, T_{ij} being the weight linking neuron i to neuron j.

This effect may be shown as a definite change in the firing probability

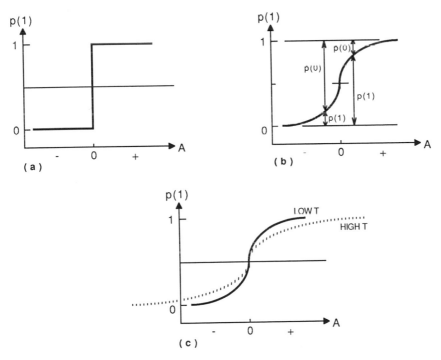

Fig. 7.3 The effect of 'temperature' on firing probability: (a) is a threshold function while (b) and (c) show versions of the Boltzmann firing probability function (BFPF).

p(1) for the neuron from $p(1) = 0$ (no chance of firing) when A is less than 0 to $p(1) = 1$ (certain firing) when A exceeds 0. This is seen in fig. 7.3(a). However, what is required to 'shake things up' is the situation shown in fig. 7.3(b) which suggests that for values of A that are less than 0 the neuron has a probability of firing p(1) which is not zero but approaches zero as A becomes more and more negative. Similarly, letting p(0) be the probability of the neuron *not* firing (where $p(0) = 1 - p(1)$), if A is greater than zero, there is a decreasing probability that the neuron will not fire as A increases.

What we have said about temperature suggests this sloping effect should be more pronounced at higher temperatures, as shown by the dotted line in fig. 7.3(c). Hinton suggested that a function known as a result of Boltzmann physics has precisely the characteristics required. This is equation (7.1):

$$p(1) = \frac{1}{1 + e^{-A/T}}$$

(7.1)

We shall refer to this as the Boltzmann firing probability function or BFPF. This function has been plotted in fig. 7.4 for temperatures of 0.5 and 0.25 (in arbitrary units, i.e. these are just numbers and not 'degrees Fahrenheit' or anything like that). It can be seen from this figure that the BFPF has precisely the desired features.

As an example of how this firing function works in altering the state transition diagram, we consider the Hopfield net shown in fig. 6.4 of Chapter 6. Here the parameters of the net are:

$$\begin{array}{lll} T_{12} = -0.5 & T_{13} = 0.4 & T_{23} = 0.5 \\ U_1 = -0.1 & U_2 = -0.2 & U_3 = +0.7 \end{array}$$

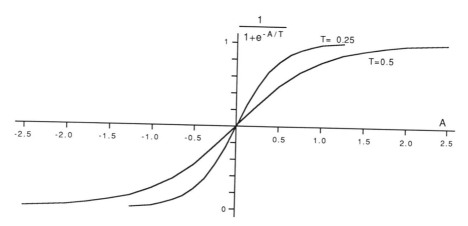

Fig. 7.4 The S-shaped Boltzmann firing probability function.

From these parameters the activation values for each of the three nodes may be calculated (A_1 for neuron 1, and so on). While this can be done for any state, in this case we shall choose $V_1V_2V_3 = 011$ for purposes of illustration:

$$A_1 = T_{12}V_2 + T_{13}V_3 - U_1 = -0.5 + 0.4 + 0.1 = 0$$
$$A_2 = T_{12}V_1 + T_{23}V_3 - U_2 = 0 + 0.5 + 0.2 = 0.7$$
$$A_3 = T_{13}V_1 + T_{23}V_2 - U_3 = -0.5 + 0.4 + 0.1 = -0.2$$

Now, equation (7.1) can be applied to each neuron in turn, using the value of A appropriate to that neuron. The results are tabulated in Table 7.1 for temperatures of 0.25 and 1 (again it is stressed that these are merely convenient numbers). Also we recall that p(1) is calculated by the application of the Boltzmann formula in (7.1), while p(0) is obtained simply from $p(0) = 1 - p(1)$.

From these values it is possible to calculate the transition probabilities to other states. The only states that can follow 011 are 011 itself and all the states that differ from 011 in the firing value of one neuron (recalling that only one neuron at a time can change its state). These states are 111, 001 and 010. In a general case, for an N-element net, transitions can occur to the state itself and N others.

The transition probabilities are calculated as follows. Say we consider a transition to state 111. This requires the first neuron to fire. The probability of this happening is p(1) for neuron 1. But, as this event has a one-in-three chance of occurring (each neuron has an equal probability of attempting to change at any one time and there are three neurons), the total probability of changing to 111 is: $p(1)_j/3$ where $p(1)_j$ is the probability of the jth neuron firing. Similarly $p(0)_j$ is the probability of the jth neuron not firing. Therefore if a state is reached through a change of firing in the jth neuron, the probability of reaching that state is $p(1)_j/3$, if V_j is 1 for that state and $p(0)_j/3$ if V_j is 0 for that state. This leads to a simple formula for determining the probability of transition to the state in which the jth neuron is expected to change:

$$[V_jp(1)_j + (1 - V_j)p(0)_j]/3$$

Table 7.1 Firing probabilities for the three neurons in state 011

Neuron Number	Temp. = 0.25		Temp. = 1.0	
	p(1)	p(0)	p(1)	p(0)
1	0.5	0.5	0.5	0.5
2	0.94	0.06	0.67	0.33
3	0.31	0.69	0.45	0.55

If V_j is 0 this evaluates to $p(0)_j/3$, while if V_j is 1 it evaluates to $p(1)_j/3$. Finally, the probability of not altering state at all is simply the remaining probability once all the possible changes have been accounted for. Formally stated, this is:

$$1 - \sum[V_j p(1)_j + (1 - V_j)p(0)_j]/3$$

The results of applying this formula in state 011 to each neuron in turn are shown for two temperatures in fig. 7.5 and compared with the transitions in the noiseless, Hopfield model. The thicker lines are an indication of the higher priorities. The higher temperature is seen to have the effect of bringing each of the non-returning transitions closer to one sixth (i.e. $(0.5)/3$) and the returning transitions slightly closer to 0.5.

Armed with these simple formulae, it becomes possible to redraw fig. 6.4 to take into account the Boltzmann transitions, and this is done

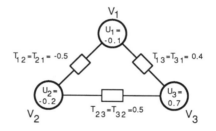

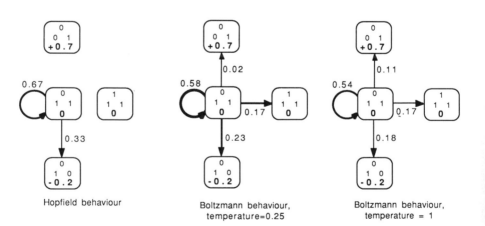

Fig. 7.5 Transition probabilities at different temperatures.

in fig. 7.6 for a temperature of 1. Despite the apparent messiness of this diagram, these new transitions (shown as shaded rather than solid arrows), clearly indicate that the noise due to temperature allows jumps *up* the energy values. For example, the state with the lowest energy level (010) not only retains a high probability (0.57) of returning to itself, but also has a probability of 0.15 of returning to states 011 and 000. It has an even lower probability (0.13) of reaching state 110. One of the consequences of the Boltzmann formulation also becomes quite clear: the greater the energy difference between one state and a possible subsequent state, the greater the probability of transition if the second state has a lower energy. If the transition is 'upwards', the energy 'gaps' are negative and, therefore, the greater they are, the less likely the transition becomes.

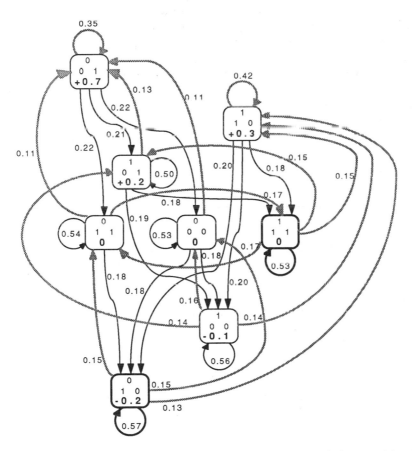

Fig. 7.6 The state diagram for the Boltzmann version of the machine in fig. 6.4 at a temperature of 1.

Diagrams such as fig. 7.6 are less than useful due to their complexity. Another way of displaying the complete picture of what the system is doing is by using a technique called the Markov chain.

7.3 MARKOV CHAINS

(This section discusses a tool which enables us to work out the probability of finding a Boltzmann machine in a particular state at a particular time. It may be skipped by those who are not keen to follow through the detail of an argument that uses a little knowledge of probability theory. A simple treatment may be found in Arthurs (1965).)

Given a set of events S_0, S_1 ... S_{m-1} and given a system for which these events follow one another with known probabilities $p(i, j)$ (the probability of state S_j following state S_i) the system may be represented fully by the m × m matrix of $p(i, j)$ values. This is known as a Markov chain and it can be used to work out the probability of the system being in a particular state at a particular time.

It is known that the probability of being in a state S_i at time t is $P_i(t)$, then the probability of being in some state j at time $t + 1$, $P_j(t + 1)$ (where, between t and $t + 1$, whatever mechanisms are involved in changing from one event to another have done their work) may be worked out by adding up all the probabilities of entering that state, taking into account the probability of being in the previous state.

To be precise:

$$P_j(t + 1) = \sum P_i(t)p(i, j). \tag{7.2}$$

Any probabilistic state transition diagram such as fig. 7.5 has all the requirements of a Markov chain. This is shown in Table 7.2 where states are labelled according to their binary number: e.g. $S_0 = 000$, $S_3 = 011$, etc.

To give an example, say that the probability at t = 0 of being in any state is 0.125 (that is one-eighth). The probability of the system being in, say, state S_2 is:

$$
\begin{aligned}
P_2(1) = {} & P_0(0)p(0,2) + P_1(0)p(1,2) + P_2(0)p(2,2) + P_3(0)p(3,2) + \\
& P_4(0)p(4,2) + P_5(0)p(5,2) + P_6(0)p(6,2) + P_7(0)p(7,2) \\
= {} & 0.125 \times 0.18 + 0.125 \times 0 + 0.125 \times 0.57 + 0.125 \times 0.18 + \\
& 0.125 \times 0 + 0.125 \times 0 + 0.125 \times 0.20 + 0.125 \times 0 \\
= {} & 0.125(0.18 + 0.57 + 0.18 + 0.20) \\
\\
= {} & 0.14125
\end{aligned}
$$

Table 7.2 Markov chain representation of fig. 7.5

Current State:		S_0	S_1	S_2	S_3	S_4	S_5	S_6	S_7
Next state									
S_0	0.53	0.22	0.15	0	0.16	0	0	0	
S_1	0.11	0.35	0	0.11	0	0.13	0	0	
S_2	0.18	0	0.57	0.18	0	0	0.20	0	
S_3	0	0.22	0.15	0.54	0	0	0	0.17	
S_4	0.18	0	0	0	0.56	0.19	0.20	0	
S_5	0	0.21	0	0	0.14	0.50	0	0.15	
S_6	0	0	0.13	0	0.14	0	0.42	0.15	
S_7	0	0	0	0.17	0	0.18	0.18	0.53	

The table contains the probability of going from a current state to a next state.

If the probability of being in state j at time t (i.e. $P_j(t)$) needs to be calculated, this is done by calculating $P_i(1)$ for all values of i, then $P_i(2)$ for all values of i, and so on until all values of $P_i(t-1)$ have been calculated, at which point $P_j(t)$ may be calculated. Textbooks on Markov chains, such as Arthurs (1965), describe ways in which these state probabilities behave in time as a function of specific characteristics of the Markov chain. These are useful techniques in the analysis of neural nets.

7.4 SIMULATED ANNEALING

Armed with the ability to calculate the probability of a net being in any given state at any given time it is possible to illustrate what happens as the temperature of the net is reduced. Again, this is done with the help of a Markov chain as shown in Table 7.3. Starting with equal probabilities of being in any state at time t = 0 (i.e. $P_i(0) = 0.125$ for all i) we allow the system to develop until t = 7 at a temperature of 1. It is noticed that for the last few steps at this temperature there is not much change in the probabilities. This is called *thermal equilibrium* in Hinton's papers.

Things only start changing if the temperature is changed, and this is done at t = 8 in Table 7.3 where the temperature is lowered to 0.25. Again thermal equilibrium is reached by t = 15. At this point we drop the temperature to 0 and look at the final likelihood of the net being in the three states that represent local minima for this system.

The point of all this is that, as expected intuitively earlier in this chapter, at the end of the annealing process the system is seen to finish in the stable states of the net with a probability related to their energy. In fig. 6.4 the lowest energy state, S_2, with an energy of -0.2, has the highest final probability, which is 0.494. S_4 is next, with an energy of

Table 7.3 Changes in probabilities of being in any particular state in advancing time and lowering temperature

State–Probability:		$P_0(t)$	$P_1(t)$	$P_2(t)$	$P_3(t)$	$P_4(t)$	$P_5(t)$	$P_6(t)$	$P_7(t)$
Temp.	Time t								
1.0	0	0.125	0.125	0.125	0.125	0.125	0.125	0.125	0.125
1.0	1	0.133	0.088	0.141	0.135	0.141	0.125	0.105	0.133
1.0	2	0.133	0.076	0.150	0.136	0.148	0.121	0.102	0.135
.	.	.	.	.	.	.	.	.	.
.	.	.	.	.	.	.	.	.	.
1.0	5	0.134	0.069	0.159	0.135	0.151	0.113	0.106	0.133
1.0	6	0.134	0.068	0.160	0.134	0.152	0.112	0.106	0.133
1.0	7	0.134	0.068	0.160	0.134	0.152	0.112	0.106	0.133
0.25	8	0.131	0.015	0.210	0.138	0.190	0.099	0.060	0.157
0.25	9	0.122	0.011	0.234	0.132	0.202	0.082	0.058	0.159
.	.	.	.	.	.	.	.	.	.
.	.	.	.	.	.	.	.	.	.
0.25	14	0.123	0.008	0.276	0.129	0.198	0.063	0.061	0.142
0.25	15	0.123	0.008	0.279	0.129	0.197	0.062	0.061	0.140
0	16	0.044	0.000	0.384	0.089	0.279	0.023	0.000	0.181
0	17	0.015	0.000	0.428	0.039	0.302	0.008	0.000	0.189
.	.	.	.	.	.	.	.	.	.
.	.	.	.	.	.	.	.	.	.
0	27	0.000	0.000	0.494	0.000	0.313	0.000	0.000	0.193
0	28	0.000	0.000	0.494	0.000	0.313	0.000	0.000	0.193

-0.1 and a probability of 0.313, while S_7 is the least probable stable state (0.193) and also the highest of the three in energy (0). By inspection of fig. 6.4 all the other states are clearly seen to be transient, in that once they have been left there is no way of returning to them. These latter states are confirmed to be transient in the simulated annealing Table 7.3 by the fact that their final probability is zero.

The Boltzmann version of the net in fig. 6.4 has not removed the 'false well' which was an accidental by-product of the way in which the weights and thresholds were calculated to provide the other two stable wells. What the Boltzmann approach *has* shown is that the probability of finishing in a particular state is heavily dependent on the energy of that state. This means that the training process must take careful control of the energies of the well states in the system. This is considered in the next section.

7.5 HIDDEN UNITS: A PROBLEM FOR TRAINING

The first useful assumption made by Hinton and Sejnowski in looking for ways of training Boltzmann machines is that not all units in a net are defined in the training set. Such hidden units are essential to solve the hard learning problem. We borrow one of Hinton's examples to illustrate why such units are necessary. Consider a net with three units and firing states V_1, V_2, V_3 as before. Let us say that there are four states which we wish to remain stable:

V_1	V_2	V_3
1	1	0
1	0	1
0	1	1
0	0	0

It is easily seen that each neuron in this arrangement is required to perform the parity function (i.e. fire when the number of ones in the input, i.e. the other two neurons, is odd). This is precisely the function that a 2-input McCulloch and Pitts node cannot perform. There is nothing in the Boltzmann firing arrangements that makes a difference to this deficiency. To get around this problem, we now add a fourth unit H (H for hidden) and arrange its firing pattern as shown below.

V_1	V_2	V_3	H
1	1	0	0
1	0	1	0
0	1	1	0
0	0	0	1

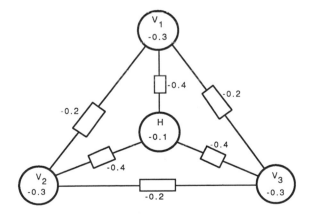

Fig. 7.7 Network with a hidden auxiliary unit.

A suggestion for the values of thresholds and connection strengths for H is shown in fig. 7.7. To check that this solution is correct, we calculate some activation values. Take, for instance, state $V_1V_2V_3H = 1100$, the activation values are:

$A_1 = -0.2 + 0.3 = +0.1$, so the next value of V_1 will be 1
$A_2 = -0.2 + 0.3 = +0.1$, so the next value of V_2 will be 1
$A_3 = -0.2 - 0.2 + 0.3 = -0.1$, so the next value of V_3 will be 0
$A_H = -0.4 - 0.4 + 0.1 = -0.7$, so the next value of H will be 0

This shows that state 1100 will repeat itself and is, therefore, stable. The same (through symmetry) goes for 1010 and 0011. Now we test state 0001.

$A_1 = -0.4 + 0.3 = -0.1$, so the next value of V_1 will be 0
$A_2 = -0.4 + 0.3 = -0.1$, so the next value of V_2 will be 0
$A_3 = -0.4 + 0.3 = -0.1$, so the next value of V_3 will be 0
$A_H = +0.1$, so the next value of H will be 1

Again this state is stable, showing that the action of the auxiliary unit has done its work.

The problem that having hidden units creates for training is that only the desired values for the *visible* units are known. The training procedure, which can only be based on information on whether the visible units are behaving correctly or not, must, somehow, ensure that the hidden units develop correct weights and thresholds. The techniques we have studied so far cannot achieve this, so we will now look at Hinton and Sejnowski's proposals for achieving successful training.

7.6 TRAINING THE BOLTZMANN MACHINE

Let us say that the net contains v visible units. These can have a total of 2^v possible states. Let us say that S_1, S_2, ..., S_a, ..., S_r are the training patterns required. They are specified only in terms of the values of the visible units. Generally, r will be less than 2^v. The training regime should specify not only the states themselves, but also the probability of their occurrence. The intention is to control the energy levels of the states of the net so that these states occur when the net runs freely with the same probability as they occur in training. Put another way, the training set represents an 'environment' which the net is meant to absorb and reproduce at its visible units when running freely. The hidden units provide an 'auxiliary engine' which helps to reproduce the environment at the visible units.

Formally, the environment (or the training set) is represented by a set of probabilities:

$$P^+(S_1), P^+(S_2) \ldots P^+(S_a) \ldots P^+(S_r)$$

The $^+$ sign is used to indicate that these are the desired probabilities which represent the environment. In contrast, we use the $^-$ sign to indicate the probabilities of the occurrence of the same patterns in the net when the net is allowed to run freely. These are:

$$P^-(S_1), P^-(S_2) \ldots P^-(S_a) \ldots P^-(S_r)$$

Clearly, it should be the objective of a training scheme to make these two sets the same. To this end, Hinton and Sejnowski have proposed that a useful measure of 'the distance' between these two sets is:

$$G = \sum_a P^+(S_a) \ln [P^+(S_a)/P^-(S_a)] \tag{7.3}$$

The natural logarithm (ln) in this equation will contribute zero if $P^+(S_a) = P^-(S_a)$. Also the first $P^+(S_a)$ term ensures that the more frequently occurring states have a greater effect in the overall sum. G can never be negative and becomes zero when the two sets of probabilities are identical. So, training should aim to reduce G to zero. It is here that Hinton and Sejnowski showed a very important result. We write this down formally first and explain it afterwards.

$$\frac{\partial G}{\partial w_{ij}} = -\frac{1}{T}(p_{ij}{}^' - p_{ij}{}^-) \tag{7.4}$$

$\partial G/\partial w_{ij}$ is the rate of change of G with a change in the weight w_{ij}.

This is seen to be proportional

first,

to $1/T$, T being the temperature in the Boltzmann sense

and second,

to $-(p_{ij}{}^+ - p_{ij}{}^-)$

where $p_{ij}{}^+$ is the average probability of the units on either side of the weight w_{ij} simultaneously firing with a 1 when the visible units of the net are driven by the environment, and $p_{ij}{}^-$ is the average probability of the units on either side of the weight w_{ij} simultaneously firing with a 1 when the net is free running.

The major significance of this discovery is that in order to reduce G by altering a particular weight, all that needs to be known is $[p_{ij}^+ - p_{ij}^-]$ which is 'local' information. So if this term is positive the weight to which the measurement 'belongs' can be increased by $k[p_{ij}^+ - p_{ij}^-]$, while if the term is negative the weight can be decreased by $k[p_{ij}^+ - p_{ij}^-]$. k (between 0 and 1) is a constant that has to be found by experiment. It is evident that if the process ends with G = 0 the net has learnt to reproduce the environmental state probabilities and is fully trained. Another major feature of this scheme is that it applies to both visible and hidden units. So the process of training sets up the 'auxiliary' or hidden engine in the net to deliver the required mimicking of the environment. We will now look at an example which shows how the quantities required for training are calculated and used.

7.7 AN EXAMPLE OF BOLTZMANN TRAINING

The example we have chosen is shown in fig. 7.8. The 'environment' consists of 00 and 11 appearing at $V_1 V_2$ with equal probability. In other words, V_1 and V_2 are required to communicate *via* the hidden unit H. The values of the two weights are arbitrarily chosen, as are the three values of zero for the thresholds. Using Markov chain methods it is possible to predict the distribution of states at thermal equilibrium for

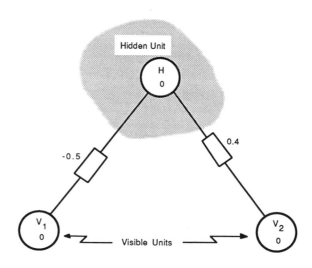

Fig. 7.8 A simple Boltzmann machine with one hidden unit.

Table 7.4a Final probabilities of being in any particular state

State-Probability:	$P_0(t)$	$P_1(t)$	$P_2(t)$	$P_3(t)$	$P_4(t)$	$P_5(t)$	$P_6(t)$	$P_7(t)$
Temp. 0.25	0.097	0.096	0.095	0.439	0.099	0.098	0.013	0.062

this net at a temperature of 0.25. This is shown in Table 7.4, where $P_j(t)$ is the probability of being in the jth state at time (t) (j being the binary value of $V_1 H V_2$ in that order, i.e. 011 = state 3).

To calculate the initial value of G we note that we have two values of 'a' in $P^+(S_a)$. The first of these is for V_1, V_2 = 00 and the other for V_1, V_2 = 11. Say that these are $P'(S_{00})$ and $P'(S_{11})$ respectively. We have said that these two states are equally probable in the environment, hence:

$$P^+(S_{00}) = P^+(S_{11}) = 0.5$$

Now, $P^-(S_{00})$ is the probability of the net delivering 00 at V_1, V_2 while free running. State 000 (S_0) and state 010 (S_2), have the desired values at the visible unit, hence (from Table 7.4):

$$P (S_{00}) = P_0(t) + P_2(t) = 0.097 + 0.095 = 0.192$$

Similarly, state 101 (S_5) and state 111 (S_7) have 11 at the visible units, and hence:

$$P^-(S_{11}) = P_5(t) + P_7(t) = 0.098 + 0.062 = 0.160$$

So, from equation (7.3),

$$G - P^+(S_{00}) \ln (P^+(S_{00})/P^-(S_{00})) + P^+(S_{11}) \ln (P^+(S_{11})/P^-(S_{11}))$$
$$= 0.5 \ln (0.5/0.192) + 0.5 \ln (0.5/0.160)$$
$$= 1.048.$$

To act upon the weights as indicated by equation (7.4) we need to calculate $[p_{ij}^+ - p_{ij}^-]$ for i,j = 1,H and H,2. The free running estimates can be obtained directly from the free running probabilities in Table 7.4 as

p_{1H}^- = the probability of V_1 and H being 1 at the same time
    = the probability of either 110 ($P_6(t)$) or 111 ($P_7(t)$) occurring
    = 0.013 + 0.062
    = 0.075

Similarly,

p_{H2}^{-} = the probability of H and V_2 being 1 at the same time
   = P3(t) or P7(t)
   = 0.439 + 0.062
   = 0.501

To obtain p_{1H}^{+} and p_{H2}^{+} it is necessary to 'rerun' the Markov chain but insisting that only the states that correspond to the 'clamping' can occur. For example, if V_1, V_2 is clamped to 00 the chain is started with $P_0(0) = P_2(0) = 0.50$ as only states 000 and 010 are allowed by the clamping. All the temporary values of state probabilities generated by the chain, say $P_0(1)'$ to $P_7(1)'$ are noted, and then the actual clamped values of the two possible states are calculated as:

$P_0(1) = P_0(1)' + P_1(1)' + P_4(1)' + P_5(1)'$
                    (i.e. all the states that have the unclamped H at 0)
$P_2(1) = P_2(1)' + P_3(1)' + P_6(1)' + P_7(1)'$
                    (i.e. all the states that have the unclamped H at 1)

Running the chain yields equilibrium values of $P_0(t)$ of 0.5 and $P_2(t)$ of 0.5.
This is done again for V_1, V_2 clamped to 11, yielding $P_5(t)$ of 0.606 and $P_7(t)$ of 0.394.
As we assume that the two clamping events occur with equal probability,

$p_{1H}^{+} = p_{H2}^{+} = P_7(t)/2 = 0.157$

(Clearly not all of the above procedure needs to be carried out to arrive at the result. It is included for completeness as it *would* have to be carried out in larger nets.) Now,

$\partial G/\partial w_{1H} = -(p_{1H}^{+} - p_{1H}^{-})/T$
              $= -(0.157 - 0.075)/0.25$
              $= -0.328$

Say we wish to remove one quarter of the value of G by changing w_{1H}. As $G = 1.048$ let ∂G be approximated by the required change -0.262. (For those expert in calculus, we are replacing ∂G by ΔG and replacing ∂w_{1H} by Δw_{1H}.)
The required change in w_{12} is:

$\Delta w_{1H} = \Delta G/-0.328 = 0.78$

Table 7.5 Final probabilities of being in any particular state (new weights)

State-Probability:	$P_0(t)$	$P_1(t)$	$P_2(t)$	$P_3(t)$	$P_4(t)$	$P_5(t)$	$P_6(t)$	$P_7(t)$
Temp. 0.25		0.113	0.109	0.111	0.025	0.111	0.109	0.345	0.078

Hence the new value of w_{1H} is $-0.5 + 0.78 = 0.28$.

Similarly the new value of w_{H2} calculated to remove another quarter of G is -0.36.

Now, 'running' the net with these weights yields a new set of probabilities as can be seen in Table 7.5.

The new value of G may be calculated as before. It turns out to be 0.893, a reduction of 15%. The reduction is much smaller than was intended simply due to the approximation of replacing ∂G by ΔG and replacing ∂w_{1H} by Δw_{1H}.

In fact, as things stand, it is impossible to reduce G to zero because no provision has been made to alter the neuron thresholds, and no solution exists for the value of thresholds set to zero as in this example.

7.8 A NON-MATHEMATICAL SUMMARY OF TRAINING

The last section has involved much use of mathematical notation, and it is worth standing back from this to give a general description of what is involved.

1. The aim is the adjustment of the weights including the hidden units.
2. The desired patterns at the visible units are clamped onto the net one by one (with the probabilities with which they are required to occur when the net is running freely).
3. During this clamping process the probabilities of both ends of each weight being 1 are noted.
4. The net is allowed to run freely and the probabilities of both ends of each weight being 1 are again noted.
5. The results of 3 and 4 are compared and the weights are adjusted in a way known to bring these results closer together.

This process is repeated until 3 and 4 are identical at which point we know that the net is behaving in the desired way. The quantity G is merely a handy way of representing the difference between 3 and 4, and Hinton's theory shows us how the weights should be altered to reduce G. This is used in 5 above.

7.9 COMMENTS ON BOLTZMANN MACHINES

The main characteristic of the Boltzmann machine is the fact that, when subjected to reducing amounts of noise, it has a final probability of resting in given states which is in direct proportion to Hopfield's calculation of the energy of those states. The key problem is to control the values of such energies by changing the weights. This has been shown to be a *gradient descent* optimization problem: that is, weights are adjusted to minimize the difference between the energies of given states and their desired energies. There is one important snag, however. Although the gradient descent method controls the energy of a given set of states it still does not remove the possibility of creating spurious local minima – it simply reduces the likelihood of their having lower energies than the trained ones.

EXERCISES FOR THE READER

Calculations on neural nets of advancing sophistication become difficult without some form of computational aid. To work out the results presented in this chapter the authors used a spreadsheet. These are particularly useful for simulating Markov chains. It is therefore recommended that some such aid be used in dealing with the exercises below. It is worth trying to predict what is likely to happen before doing the computation.

All of these exercises refer to fig. 7.8.

1. Having set up a computational aid, confirm the results obtained for the probabilities of occurrence of states and values of G.
2. The calculations in the text are carried out at a steady temperature of 0.25. What happens to G if the system is 'annealed' first with $T = 0.1$ and then $T = 0.01$?
3. Calculate G for weights as follows:

   $w_{1H} = 0.5$ and $w_{H2} = 0.5$

   $w_{1H} = -0.5$ and $w_{H2} = -0.5$

   and comment on the results.
4. Investigate the behaviour of the net with non-zero values of thresholds.

8

Error propagation

Hard learning problems occur in nets that are required to map a well-defined set of inputs into a well-defined set of outputs. They can generally be solved by the introduction of hidden units. Error back-propagation is the prescription originally suggested by Rumelhart, Hinton and Williams (1986) for dealing with the training of these hidden units. This algorithm has become one of the focal points of research in neural computing. Its operation is described and illustrated in this chapter.

8.1 HARD LEARNING REVISITED

The problem of hard learning as characterized by Minsky and Papert (1969) has been discussed in Chapter 3. Attention was drawn to the fact that a single-layer perceptron (or one layer of McCulloch and Pitts nodes) cannot perform simple functions such as parity. So far we have only seen one way of resolving this problem in the context of Boltzmann machines (Chapter 7), where, in a network of fully interconnected nodes, some were designated as hidden and others were designated as being capable of being clamped to desired values. Then, all the nodes including the hidden ones were trained by a gradient descent process in which weights were adjusted so as to make the probabilities of firing in the clamped state equal to those when the net is running free.

This 'solves' the hard learning problem, in the sense that the hidden units can provide the necessary auxiliary functions that hard learning problems require. The discussion centered on fig. 7.7, in Chapter 7, provides a reminder of the way in which such hidden units operate. The question raised in this chapter is whether the requirement of Boltzmann machines that all units should be connected to all others is a necessary prerequisite to the solution of the hard learning problem. The answer given originally by Rumelhart, Hinton and Williams (1986) is that this is not the case. They have shown that there is a form of network which is simpler than the fully interconnected net and in which one seeks to establish a relationship between a definite input and a definite output. This type of net has been defined in Chapter 1 as a feed-forward net (see fig. 1.2(ii)).

In fact, Minsky and Papert themselves argued that nets with one hidden layer could solve hard learning problems – if only one knew how to train the hidden layer. This argument has been rehearsed in Chapter 3 and is based on structures such as shown in fig. 3.9. A simplification of this structure is reproduced in fig. 8.1.

In Chapter 3 we drew attention to the fact that, to guarantee a result, the number of nodes in the hidden layer may have to be very large. However, this is not inevitably true and, in practice, a large number of hidden nodes may be tolerable.

It is accepted that structures as in fig. 8.1 may be very useful provided that a training methodology which is directed at hidden units can be found. Clearly such structures cannot 'free run' as they have no feedback among the units. In other words, given an input, the net must settle down to a set of values solely dependent on that input. So we will now look at a training method which controls the training of the hidden units by a process of propagation of measured errors from the output layer.

8.2 A NOTE ON FORMULATION

The proof of the validity of error back-propagation is essentially mathematical and relies on a knowledge of differential calculus. Rumelhart, Hinton and Williams (1986) give a detailed mathematical exposition; here we shall merely discuss the meaning and results of the technique. While mathematical notation cannot be avoided altogether, this will be accompanied by non-mathematical descriptions.

8.3 INTERNAL REPRESENTATIONS?

The hidden layer may be seen as the place in the net where the input

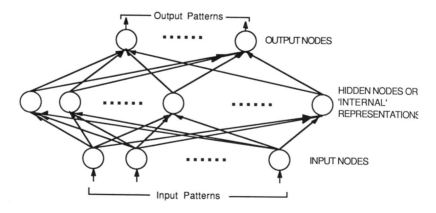

Fig. 8.1 Structure with one hidden layer.

data is partially labelled before the output layer needs to come to final decision. Hence this layer is said to be required to form 'internal representations' of the training set which are not provided by the trainer. For example, the network in fig. 8.2 solves the notorious parity problem for two inputs.

The left-hand hidden unit forms the representation 'Both input units are on' (B), while the right-hand hidden unit forms the representation 'Either input unit is on' (E). The output unit can then fire if 'E is on, but not B' which causes the whole system to fire if one but not both inputs are on, and this completes the parity function. The given weight and threshold values (θ) are seen to accomplish the required functions. So, the central problem is to discover a way of training which causes the hidden units to form suitable internal representations. Such training can only be based on observations of the state of the output and input units, not of the hidden units.

Here we quote the results found by Rumelhart, Hinton and Williams (1986) without going into the details of their proofs, which can be found in the original publication.

8.4 THE GENERALIZED DELTA RULE

(In this chapter we have used italics in the mathematical expressions in order to be consistent with Rumelhart, Hinton and Williams (1986).)

The training rules that we have seen so far have been specifically related to Hopfield models and Boltzmann machines.

In Hopfield models the training rules assume an abrupt change

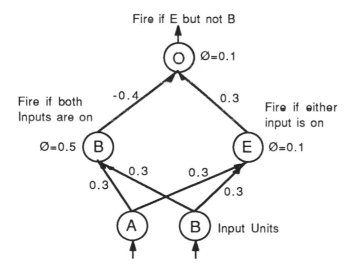

Fig. 8.2 Internal representations for the parity problem.

between the point at which the activation goes from negative to positive. We recall that the activation of the jth unit for the pth training example (a_{pj}, say) is given by taking the sum for all inputs i of the unit multiplied by the appropriate weight w_{ji} and adding to it the value of some threshold u_j. Whether an input is 0 or 1 is determined by the output o_{pi} of the ith unit connected to the jth unit. Putting this into a formula we have:

$$a_{pj} = \sum_{(for\ all\ i)} w_{ji}o_{pi} + u_j$$

The error, measured by the value of a_{pj} as compared to its desired value, is used to determine the weight changes.

In Boltzmann machines weight changes are determined according to a formula (equation (7.4), p. 125) which depends on the measurement of firing probabilities associated with a weight under two conditions:

(a) when the net is clamped according to the desired pattern, and
(b) when the net is free-running.

The object here is to find a way of altering weights for neural nodes that have an output function more broadly specified than the above:

$$o_{pj} = f_j(a_{pj})$$

In words, this states that the output of the jth node and pth input pattern is some, as yet unspecified, function f_j of the activation a_{pj}. That is, one attempts to deal with a whole class of neuron models for which the output rule can be specified in a general way and the generalized delta rule is a learning rule which applies to all these cases. But, more than this, the rule must be such as to deal with hidden units.

Remembering that feed-forward nets with input units, output units and hidden units are being considered, the Rumelhart *et al.* (1986) prescription is summarized by three statements.

1. For the pth presentation of an input/output pair for training, the change for the weight which joins the jth unit to its ith incoming connection ($\Delta_p w_{ji}$) is, as in the more traditional method, proportional to some computed error (∂_{pj}) for this jth unit. In mathematical form this can be expressed as:

$$\Delta_p w_{ji} = \beta \partial_{pj} o_{pi} \qquad (8.1)$$

where o_{pi} is the value of the ith incoming connection and β is a constant which determines the rate of learning.

CORTEX

Neural Networks Demonstration System

Supporting Back Error Propagation, McCulloch and Pitts, WISARD, Hopfield, Boltzmann, PLN and NPLN network types.

What they said about CORTEX:

"CORTEX is an excellent companion to 'An Introduction to Neural Computing'. It uses many of the examples given in the book and therefore supports the material in a direct way. Teachers may use it for demonstrations or laboratory experiments."
Professor Igor Aleksander, Imperial College London.

"The excellent display of a wide range of neural networks makes CORTEX an ideal teaching aid. I am currently using CORTEX to demonstrate neural networks in my third year Mathematical Biosystems course."
Professor John Taylor, Kings College London.

* Graphics: Hercules, CGA, EGA, VGA support * Mouse support * Maths coprocessor support *

The minimum hardware configuration to run CORTEX is as follows:
An IBM-PC/XT/AT/PS2 or a compatible computer.
A Disk Operating System (DOS) version 2.0 or later.
A minimum of 512 Kilobytes Random Access Memory (512K RAM).
A Hercules, CGA, EGA or VGA graphic display adapter.

The following hardware is optional:
A maths coprocessor to speed up floating point operations.
A mouse for faster and smoother operation.

Distributed outside North America by:
Unistat Ltd
PO Box 383, Highgate
London N6 5UP
ENGLAND
Tel: 44-(0)81-883 7155
Fax: 44-(0)81-444 9512

Distributed in North America by:
Adhoc Reading Systems Inc
28 Brunswick Woods Dr
East Brunswick
NJ 08816, USA
Tel: 201-254 7300
Fax: 201-254 7310

CORTEX

NEURAL NETWORKS DEMONSTRATION SYSTEM

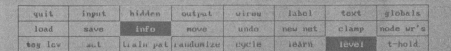

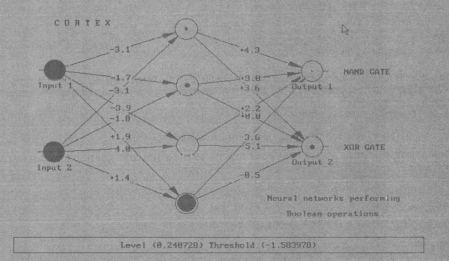

to accompany

An Introduction to Neural Computing
by Igor Alexander and Helen Morton

ok

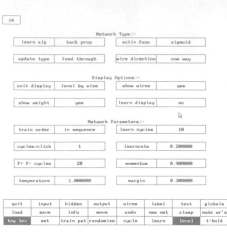

Network Type:-

| learn alg | back prop | | activ func | sigmoid |
| update type | feed through | | wire direction | one way |

Display Options:-

| unit display | level by size | | show wires | yes |
| show weight | yes | | learn display | no |

Network Parameters:-

train order	in sequence		learn cycles	18
cycles/click	1		learnrate	0.288888
P+ P- cycles	28		momentum	0.988888
temperature	1.888888		margin	0.388888

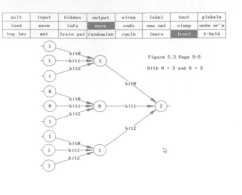

quit	input	hidden	output	wires	label	text	globals
load	save	info	move	undo	new net	clamp	node wr's
tog lev	set	train pat	randomize	cycle	learn	level	t-hold

Figure 5.3 Page 5-5

With M = 3 and K = 3

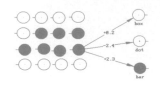

quit	input	hidden	output	wires	label	text	globals
load	save	info	move	undo	new net	clamp	node wr's
tog lev	set	train pat	randomize	cycle	learn	level	t-hold

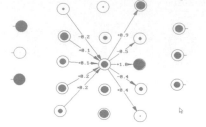

simple | mk-from | mk-to | clear-mk | new wir | done

quit	input	hidden	output	wires	label	text	globals
load	save	info	move	undo	new net	clamp	node wr's
tog lev	set	train pat	randomize	cycle	learn	level	t-hold

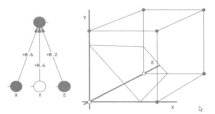

quit	input	hidden	output	wires	label	text	globals
load	save	info	move	undo	new net	clamp	node wr's
tog lev	set	train pat	randomize	cycle	learn	level	t-hold

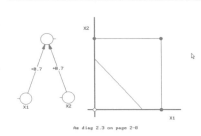

As diag 2.3 on page 2-8

quit	input	hidden	output	wires	label	text	globals
load	save	info	move	undo	new net	clamp	node wr's
tog lev	set	train pat	randomize	cycle	learn	level	t-hold

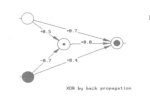

XOR by back propagation

Level (0.538648) Threshold (-0.271118)

quit	input	hidden	output	wires	label	text	globals
load	save	info	move	undo	new net	clamp	node wr's
tog lev	set	train pat	randomize	cycle	learn	level	t-hold

Parity Network

Fig 3.9 Page 3-14

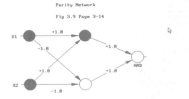

Level (0.888888) Threshold (1.588888)

quit	input	hidden	output	wires	label	text	globals
load	save	info	move	undo	new net	clamp	node wr's
tog lev	set	train pat	randomize	cycle	learn	level	t-hold

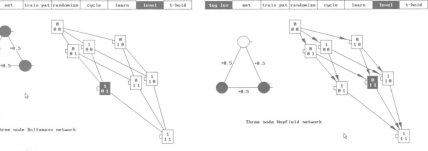

Three node Boltzmann network

Three node Hopfield network

quit	input	hidden	output	wires	label	text	globals
load	save	info	move	undo	new net	clamp	node wr's
tog lev	set	train pat	randomize	cycle	learn	level	t-hold

Figure 18.7 Page 18-19

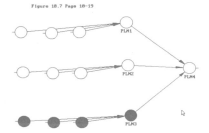

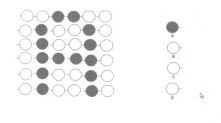

CORTEX neural network development system allows users to construct their own neural networks, define training patters, teach the network and then make it run.

Easy to use: CORTEX is fully mouse driven. You can construct a network, create the nodes, wire them up, set weights, levels and thresholds and label nodes simply by clicking on the relavent menu items.

Watch the network as it learns: During a network 'learning' phase there are three display options: i) single step, where you are prompted for a key press after each iteration of the training process, ii) view, where the patterns are presented and the weights change as you watch, and iii) no display, where the learning phase will proceed as fast as possible.

Special features: CORTEX contains energy level diagrams for Hopfield and Boltzman networks, and displays a geometrical interpretation of two and three input McCulloch and Pitts system as described in the book.

Seven network types supported are: McCulloch and Pitts (including 2D and 3D activation diagrams), WISARD, Hopfield and Boltzmann (both including energy level diagrams), back error propagation, PLN, NPLN.

Choice of ways to display activation levels: Activation levels of nodes may be represented in several different ways including numerically and by node size.

Load and save networks: Networks may be saved to disc along with all accompanying information, including any text and training patterns.

Demonstration networks included: Many example networks from the book, along with their training sets, are included.

Ideal for teaching: All the above features make CORTEX an ideal teaching aid.

But most of the work of Rumelhart *et al.* centres on the way in which the error ∂_{pj} may be computed even for hidden units. Hence the next two statements.

2. For output units, the error is calculated in a straightforward way based on a knowledge of a desired target output for the *j*th unit, t_{pj}. In fact the error is stated as:

$$\partial_{pj} = (t_{pj} - o_{pj})f'_j(a_{pj}) \tag{8.2}$$

The term $(t_{pj} - o_{pj})$ clearly indicates that the error is proportional to the difference between the actual output o_{pj} and the target output t_{pj}. The term $f'_j(a_{pj})$ means the 'rate of change of o_{pj} with respect to $f_j(a_{pj})$'. This last point is illustrated for a particular form of $f_j(a_{pi})$ in fig. 8.3.

Rumelhart *et al.* (1986) have shown that it is essential that $f'_j(a_{pj})$ be a smoothly increasing function with a_{pj}. In cases such as fig. 8.3 this causes greater weight-changing activity to take place for units where the output is less certain (i.e. close to 0.5, where the slope is steepest) than those in which it is more certain (i.e. close to 0 or 1).

3. If the unit is hidden, and its output is connected to *k* units, its error is defined as being proportional to the sum of the errors of all these

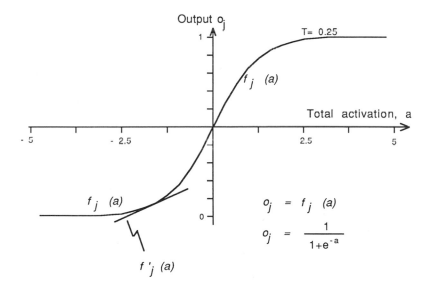

Fig. 8.3 Examples of $f_j(a)$ and $f'_j(a)$.

k units as modified by the weights connecting these units. In symbols:

$$\partial_{pj} = \left(\sum_{(for\ all\ k)} \partial_{pk}w_{kj}\right)f'_{j}(a_{pj}) \tag{8.3}$$

With these ideas in mind we note that training implies two steps. First is the 'forward' step during which the input is applied and allowed to propagate to the output. The error values of the output units are calculated and compared to the targets for such units (which must be known). During the second, 'backward', phase these errors are propagated backwards and weight changes made. To be precise, once the output error has been calculated, the weight changes in the output layer can then be made using (8.2) and (8.1). This fixes the error values for the previous layer (using (8.3)) and the weight changes can be made using (8.1) in the first inner layer. This procedure may be propagated backwards until the weights in the input unit are adjusted. This is then followed by another forward step and a further backward step, and so on. The work of Rumelhart *et al.* shows that an overall output error defined as half the sum of the squares of all the output errors, or in symbols:

$$E_p = 0.5 \sum_{(for\ all\ j)} (t_{pj} - o_{pi})^2$$

is minimized by the two-step error back-propagation procedure. All this can be illustrated by means of a simple example. But to do this we must first say a little more about the activation function used by Rumelhart *et al.*

8.5 A CONVENIENT ACTIVATION FUNCTION

Rumelhart and his colleagues have suggested than an S-shaped function as shown in fig. 8.3 is useful in this sort of work – such as:

$$o_{pj} = \frac{1}{1 + e^{-a_{pj}}} \tag{8.4}$$

where

$$a_{pj} = \sum_{(for\ all\ i)} w_{ji}o_{pj} + u_j \tag{8.5}$$

as seen earlier.

A useful property of this formulation is that $f'_{j}(a_{pj})$ (which is $\partial o_{pj}/\partial a_{pj}$) has a simple form:

$$f'_j(a_{pj}) = o_{pj}(1 - o_{pj}) \tag{8.6}$$

This simplifies the weight adjustment rules:

for output nodes, (8.2) becomes, $\partial_{pj} = (t_{pj} - o_{pj})o_{pj}(1 - o_{pj})$ (8.7)

for hidden nodes, (8.3) becomes, $\partial_{pj} = \left(\sum_{(\text{for all } k)} \partial_{pk} w_{kj} \right) o_{pj}(1 - o_{pj})$

$$\tag{8.8}$$

We now follow an example to illustrate the application of these learning rules.

8.6 EXAMPLE: COMMUNICATION IN A LINE OF NODES

One of the simplest possible networks has been chosen for this example. This is shown in fig. 8.4. We have used Rumelhart's convention that the input to the net is represented as a node which can be set to fire (output 1) or not fire (output 0) by an outside agent. The task for the network is for the output node to respond in an inverted way: 0 when the input is 1, and 1 when the input is 0. The task of the training algorithm is to find values of w_1, u_1, w_2 and u_2 that satisfy this task requirement.

The first thing we note is that, so far, there has been no mention of methods for adjusting biases such as u_1 and u_2. This can be done by treating them as incoming weights coming from a unit whose output is always 1.

The next observation is that the assumed firing rule for the neurons, as shown in fig. 8.3, requires that their output should always be a number in the continuous range from 0 to 1. That is, 0 and 1 are extreme limiting conditions. This means that if the error back-propagation learning algorithm is used to try to achieve output targets of 0 and 1, these might only be reached with an infinite amount of training. So, where the specification says that the output should be 0

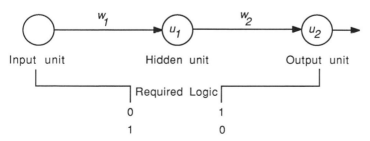

Fig. 8.4 A communication network.

and 1 in response to 1 and 0 respectively at the input, it is likely that only output values such as 0.2 and 0.8, respectively, might be achieved within a reasonable amount of training time.

It is interesting to speculate about the nature of the solution to this problem. Clearly either the hidden unit learns to act as an invertor (output low when input high, and *vice versa*) with the output unit 'following' the hidden node (output and input doing roughly the same thing), or the hidden unit follows the input with the output unit doing the inversion. Taking the first of these possibilities, a suitable set of values might be $w_1 = -4$, $u_1 = 2$, $w_2 = 4$ and $u_2 = -2$. So when the overall input is low, say 0, the total activation of the hidden unit is 2 due to the bias. Looking back at fig. 8.3, a unit with a total activation of 2 shows that the output of the hidden unit is high.

In fact, using equation (8.4), with the input unit at 0 the output of the hidden unit (with its own activation at 2) may be calculated from:

$$o = \frac{1}{1 + e^{-2}}$$

$$= 0.88$$

However, if the input unit is 1, the hidden unit activation turns out to be $-4 + 2 = -2$, which using (8.4) as above turns out to be 0.11. So the hidden unit is indeed acting as an invertor.

The activation of the output unit for the above two cases respectively for an input of 0.88 becomes:

$$(4 \times 0.88) - 2 = 1.52$$

and for an input of 0.11 it becomes

$$(4 \times 0.11) - 2 = -1.56$$

Using the activation function (8.4) again, the two activations of the output unit lead to overall outputs of:

0.82 when the input unit is 0 and
0.17 when the input unit is 1

So, the output node is clearly acting as a follower and the overall task has been approximated taking 0.82 as 1 and 0.17 as 0.

Now we apply the training algorithm to see how it could reach a similar solution. It is essential that all weights and biases have randomly chosen initial values. It is known that should the system start with equal weights and be required to learn differing weight values, it can never learn. The reason for this is (taking just the hidden units connected to the output unit) is that equal error signals would be sent to these weights and they could never adopt different values. Rumelhart *et al.* call the process of starting with differing weights *symmetry breaking*.

So the initial weights arbitrarily chosen for this example are:

$$w_1 = -0.2, u_1 = -0.3, w_2 = 0.2 \text{ and } u_2 = 0.1$$

Before training we calculate the overall error made by the net, defining this as the sum of the squares of the error made with the input at 0 and the error made with the input at 1, i.e.:

$$\text{Overall error} = (\text{Error}_0)^2 + (\text{Error}_1)^2 \tag{8.9}$$

With the input at 0 (we call this *case 0*), the activation of the hidden unit is just -0.3 due to u_1.

Using the formula (8.4) we have:

$O_{(for\ unit\ 1\ and\ case\ 0)}$

$$= \frac{1}{1 + e^{0.3}}$$

$$= 0.426$$

This causes the activation of the output unit to be (output of unit 1) $\times w_2 + u_2$ that is

$$0.426 \times 0.2 + 0.1 = 0.185$$

So

$O_{(for\ unit\ 2\ and\ case\ 0)}$

$$= \frac{1}{1 + e^{-0.185}}$$

$$= 0.546$$

Comparing this with the desired output of 1 gives:

$$\text{Error}_0 = 1 - 0.546$$
$$= 0.454$$

A similar calculation for the overall input at 1 (i.e. case 1) gives us:

$$\text{Error}_1 = -0.544$$

This allows us to calculate the initial overall error as:

$$(\text{Error}_0)^2 + (\text{Error}_1)^2 = (0.454)^2 + (-0.544)^2 = 0.502$$

We now begin to apply the algorithm letting the learning rate be, somewhat arbitrarily, $\beta = 1$.

A training cycle consists of the application first of input 0 and target output 1 (say, p = 0), and second, of the application of input 1 and target output 0 (p = 1).

We recall that formula (8.1) is:

$$\Delta_p w_{ji} = \beta \partial_{pj} o_{pi}$$

Also from (8.7):

$$\partial_{pj} = (t_{pj} - o_{pj}) o_{pj} (1 - o_{pj})$$

To calculate the required increment on w_2 for p = 0 we note that for the above equations:

$$o_{pj} = o_{02}$$
$$w_{ji} = w_2$$
$$(t_{pj} - o_{pj}) = \text{Error}_0$$
$$o_{pi} = o_{01}$$

So,

$$\partial_{pj} = \text{Error}_0 \times o_{02} (1 - o_{02})$$

And, finally,

$$\begin{aligned} \Delta_0 w_2 &= \text{Error}_0 \times o_{02}(1 - o_{02}) \times o_{01} \\ &= 0.454 \times 0.546(1 - 0.546) \times 0.426 \end{aligned}$$

$$\begin{aligned} &\qquad (o_{01} \text{ is calculated by applying (8.4) to} \\ &\qquad\qquad\qquad \text{the hidden unit with an input of 0)} \end{aligned}$$

$$= 0.0478$$

Similarly we can calculate the increment to u_2:

$$\begin{aligned} \Delta_0 u_2 &= \text{Error}_0 \times o_{02}(1 - o_{02}) \times 1 \\ &= 0.111 \end{aligned}$$

Part of the error back-propagation algorithm is that the new weights of the output unit be calculated first and then used in the calculations for the adjustments to earlier units. This applies every time one takes a propagation step backwards.

So, the new value of w_2 is 0.2478 (or 0.248 to retain the previous level of 3-figure accuracy) and this may be used for adjusting the parameters of the hidden unit.

$$\Delta_0 w_1 = \text{Error}_0 \times o_{01}(1 - o_{01}) \times \text{Input} \times w_2 \quad \text{(from (8.8) and (8.1))}$$
$$= 0 \text{ (because the input is 0)}$$
$$\Delta_0 u_1 = \text{Error}_0 \times o_{01}(1 - o_{01}) \times 1 \times w_2$$
$$= 0.0275$$

The new u_1 is $-0.3 + 0.0275 = -0.273$ (rounding to three-figure accuracy).

Repeating this for the input at 1 and the output target at 0, the parameters are again incremented, completing the first training cycle. Out of interest, we calculated the overall error and discovered it to be 0.500, which is 0.002 less than the original value. This seems to be little progress for much calculation, however it serves to verify that the training formulae leads to the reduction of overall error but does so in small steps. In fact, it took 126 cycles of the above calculation to reach an overall error of 0.0513 with the net outputting 0.856 when the input is 0 and 0.175 when the input is 1. The parameter values at this point in the calculations are:

$$w_1 = -6.05, \, u_1 = 2.65, \, w_2 = 3.68 \text{ and } u_2 = -1.66$$

These values are not dissimilar to those obtained by design earlier in this section. So this example has enabled us to understand the detail of the computations involved in error back-propagation, and we can now look at some areas to which Rumelhart and his colleagues applied the technique.

8.7 PARITY

Clearly the greatest temptation in finding problems on which to test error back-propagation is to consider some of the tasks identified as being 'hard' by Minsky and Papert (see Chapter 3). Parity (outputting a 1 when the input pattern contains an odd number of 1s) is classical among such problems. It is possible to show that a simple structure with

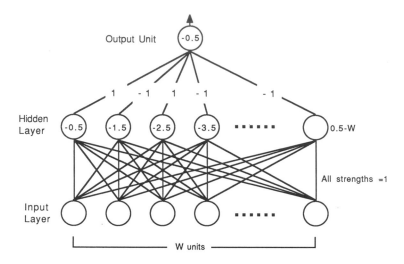

Fig. 8.5 A network that computes parity.

one hidden layer with only W hidden units for a W-input problem is capable of doing the task. This is shown in fig. 8.5.

In this arrangement the input units are in the bottom row and these are all assumed to be clamped, some on, some off. The next row up is the hidden layer where each unit is connected to all the input units. It is assumed that all connections from the input layer to the hidden layer have connection strengths of +1. Working from left to right, the first hidden unit responds if at least one input unit is at 1, the second if at least two and the gth unit if at least g input units are 1. Therefore, the hidden units come on one by one, from left to right, as the number of firing input units is increased. As the weights to the output unit are alternatively valued +1, −1, +1 . . . and if the number of input units that are firing is even, the activation of the output unit will be zero (since the number of positively weighted inputs is equal to the negatively weighted ones.) However, if the number of firing input units is odd the total activation of the output unit is +1, which causes the output to fire.

Rumelhart and his colleagues have trained a system by error back-propagation with W = 4 and $\beta = 0.5$. It took on average 2825 presentations of each of the sixteen input patterns to reach a solution similar to the one above. The internal representation learnt by the hidden units is to recognize unequivocally the number of input units which are on, and to do so independently of which inputs are on.

8.8 OTHER HARD PROBLEMS

Rumelhart *et al.* demonstrated error back-propagation on several other hard learning tasks. Two of these are mentioned below as they are often quoted in work on neural computing. The reader is advised to read the original publication to discover the details of these tasks.

8.8.1 The encoding problem

This uses a net with W input units fully connected to a single layer of Log_2W hidden units which, in turn, is fully connected to an output layer with W units. The task is simple: the input patterns and output patterns consist of all arrangements with only one 1 and the rest 0. For example, if W = 10, the input and output patterns are 1000000000, 0100000000, 0010000000, . . ., 0000000001. So the hidden units have an opportunity of developing the Log_2W binary codes that are required to represent W numbers. The system is trained to associate an input pattern with exactly the same output pattern. A successful demonstration of a system with W = 8 is quoted. Curiously, the hidden units used intermediate values (such as 0.5) in the discovery of the solution.

8.8.2 Symmetry

Here the task is to detect whether a pattern on W input units (W is even in this case) is symmetrical about the middle of the pattern. For example, 001100 is symmetrical while 111011 is not. The type of solution found is shown in fig. 8.6. All symmetrical patterns activate the hidden units with a value of zero. They have negative biases so their outputs will be off. The output will be on as the bias on the output unit is positive. But all non-symmetrical patterns lead to one of the hidden

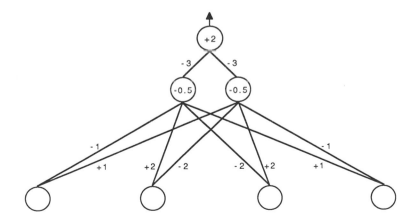

Fig. 8.6 A network that detects symmetry.

units coming on which turns off the output unit. Rumelhart and his colleagues found that a system for patterns of length six learnt this type of solution in 1208 presentations of all 32 possible patterns. Interestingly, systems for strings of any length require only two hidden units. The weights in the hidden unit arrange themselves in 1:2:4:8 . . . patterns.

8.9 RECURRENT NETS

Having developed the back-propagation algorithm which can clearly be applied to feed-forward networks (i.e. nets without feedback), it becomes proper to ask whether the same training method may be applied to nets which incorporate some feedback loops. Rumelhart and his colleagues argue that there is a sense in which the error back-propagation scheme may be applied to networks that contain feedback. This is best seen by considering the simple net of fig. 8.7.

It is well known in the analysis of digital systems that, given a specific time span, a feedback network may be represented by a feed-forward system with a repeating set of parameters. The actual net in fig. 8.7 may be represented by the repeating or 'recursive' equivalent structure as shown. This means that, given a set of weight and bias parameters, and setting the two units in the actual net to some state S at time t-2, by time t the units will be in the same state as would be the t-th layer of

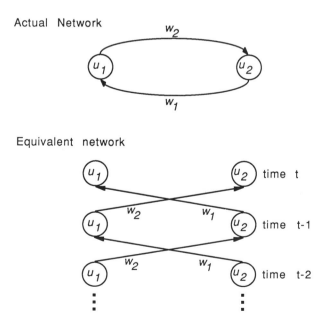

Fig. 8.7 Space equivalent of a net with feedback.

the equivalent net with the (t-2)th layer seen as a set of input units in state S.

Assume, for example, that the net is required to enter state 00 if started in 00 and state 11 if started in 11. This can be thought of as applying the error back-propagation to a 2-layer net which is trained on the input/output pairs: 00/00; 11/11. The solution is something like:

$$w_1 = 1, w_2 = 1, u_1 = -0.1, u_2 = -0.1.$$

Two questions arise: what is the meaning of 'hidden units' and how does one deal with the situation where the back-propagation algorithm indicates different weight changes for what is essentially the same weight. We answer these only briefly, referring to Rumelhart *et al.* (1986) for a full explanation. Hidden units occur in time when the starting state of a structure with feedback is known, and a desired state several steps ahead in time is known. Then the intermediate steps are treated as hidden units. In fig. 8.7, for example, the state at time t-2 may be treated as the setting of input units, the state at time t as a target, so the state at time t-1 is placed in the role of a hidden unit and may be treated as such in the application of the error back-propagation rule.

On the second question, Rumelhart *et al.* indicate that, as the calculation for weight changes proceeds backward in time, the calculated increments for each physical weight are simply added to the weights as the calculation proceeds.

8.10 SUMMARY

The main attraction of the error back-propagation technique is that it is applicable to a much wider variety of networks than are Boltzmann methods. This has made the algorithm one of the focal points of research on neural computing. It is constantly being revised and improved, so the contents of this chapter merely provide an introduction to the fundamental version of a useful algorithm which will undergo many improvements as time goes by.

EXERCISES FOR THE READER

1. It is difficult to apply the error back-propagation algorithm without some form of computational aid, so the main exercise for the reader may be to construct such an aid. Spreadsheets are very useful in this context.
2. Using the recursive structure of fig. 8.7 with the weights as calculated

to keep 00 and 11 stable, work out what happens if the net is started in 01 or 10.

3. Using the same system as in exercise 2, why is it not possible to cause 01 and 10 to become 11 while retaining a stable state for 00?

4. Show that the problem encountered in exercise 3 is solved by adding new connections to the net. (The connections go from the output of each unit back to the input of the same unit.)

9

Variations

Here we describe three of the other major contributions to neural computing – the unsupervised learning methods of Kohonen (1984, 1988 and 1989), the unsupervised learning systems that go under the heading of 'competitive learning', and Hinton's suggestions for the role of neurons that have 'multiplicative' properties (Hinton, 1981). The first two are designed to discover the existence of natural groupings within data presented to the net, while the last scheme helps in situations where visual data is rotated or moved within the field of view in some other way.

9.1 WHAT VARIATIONS?

So far, we have considered the development of neural computing as a progression, from the McCulloch and Pitts models, the rough perceptrons, WISARD-like systems, Hopfield's content-addressing and Hinton's Boltzmann machines, to error back-propagation. Among many variations we have not explored, three departures have been selected for description in this chapter because they illustrate important properties not seen so far. The first two (unsupervised learning and competitive learning) are descriptions of nets that react to common features in a stream of data on which they are trained – unlike the systems described so far which always have clearly defined data on which the systems can be trained (e.g. 'this is the letter A', or 'this pattern should form a stable image in the net'). These unsupervised learning methods have an important role to play in systems such as speech recognizers.

The third variation suggests a role for neurons that do not quite conform to the McCulloch and Pitts model but are known to exist in living systems. These are called 'multiplicative' since they react to the product of the activation of pairs of synapses. These neurons are required in systems which can learn to recognize patterns even when they have been rotated or moved within the field of view.

9.2 UNSUPERVISED LEARNING

In much of what we have seen of neural computing so far, it has been assumed that data for both inputs and outputs of nets is available. In perceptron systems (see Chapters 2 and 3), the classification of training patterns is provided in the sense that one particular neuron is taught to respond to patterns belonging to one particular class. This is also done in WISARD-type systems (see Chapter 5). In the case of Hopfield systems (Chapter 6) and Boltzmann machines (Chapter 7), a pattern that is to remain stable in the net provides both input and output data to which the net adapts. In error back-propagation (Chapter 8) target patterns are given for input patterns so that the system can calculate the errors from which the weight-adjustment algorithm operates.

But there are both biological and technical reasons for asking whether a net could 'make sense of' streams of data when the way in which such data should be classified is not specified. The phrase 'make sense of', when translated into technical terms, implies that the system discovers for itself the features of the data. In biological systems the early stages of both vision and hearing extract features in a prewired way. In vision it is known that groups of adjacent cells respond to visual features such as edges or bars, while in hearing, the cochlea (the sound sensing canal in the ear) separates the frequency content of sounds by causing adjoining areas of cells to fire only if certain frequencies are present in the sound. For example, if a musical scale is played on a violin, each note emits a sound pressure wave of different frequency and causes different cells connected to the cochlea to fire. Similar notes cause adjacent cells to fire, so an increasing scale causes a line of cells to fire one after another.

It could be argued that these living systems have evolved to extract such features simply through repeated exposures to the environment. The fact that an environment is full of trees and horizons requires the development, it is argued, of simple cells that respond to such features. In hearing, sounds are characterized by the presence or absence of simple frequencies. The pronounced phonetic vowel 'aah' has a different combination of frequencies from the vowel 'ee'.

The features mentioned so far have become 'built-in' to the nervous system through evolution. However the ability to cause different parts of a neural system to fire in the presence of more complex but persistent features of the environment through learning, but without the agency of a teacher or trainer, is obviously an important feature of a living learning system. This is called unsupervised learning. In technological terms there are obvious advantages to be gained by developing devices which group items of data according to frequently occurring features without the intervention of a teacher.

9.3 ORDERED MAPS

Teuvo Kohonen of Helsinki University in Finland is one of Europe's foremost contributors to neural computing. He has largely directed his attention towards techniques for unsupervised learning with associative properties (Kohonen, 1984/88). These techniques involve nets that learn to respond in different parts to differences in input signal. They are called *ordered maps*. He has applied his method mainly to speech recognition, and has built several successful practical systems. To illustrate the method of unsupervised learning and ordered maps we first introduce an example based on a highly simplified and modified version of Kohonen's method, and then explain the actual features of the method proper.

The scheme is illustrated in fig. 9.1. It consists of 16 3-input 'neurons'. These neurons all receive the same 3-bit input message. It is assumed that the 'environment' of which the net must learn the features without being supervised consists of patterns 001 and 111. We represent such patterns as three boxes so that a binary string (t, l, r) is shown as the state (white for 0 and black for 1) of the *t*op box, then the bottom *l*eft box and then the bottom *r*ight box.

The neurons perform a very simple function: they have 'weights' like the neurons we have seen so far, but these weights assume values of only 0 or 1. Each neuron has three weights, corresponding to the binary features of the environment (t, l, r). These weights act in a slightly different way from those encountered previously: the output of the neuron is merely the sum of all inputs (t, l, r) for which the value of the weight is the same as that of the input. In other words the neuron responds with a number 0, 1, 2 or 3 depending on how many input values match the weight values. Now, the weights of the neuron are represented in fig. 9.1 in exactly the same format as the input: three boxes. So taking neuron number 1 in fig. 9.1(a) its initial 'weight pattern' is 011. From this, its response to all possible inputs can be calculated. For example, the response to input 000 is 1, to 100 it is 0, to 011 it is 3 and to 111 it is 2.

To start with, the neuron weights are set arbitrarily as shown in fig. 9.1(a). The initial response to the two patterns that we have called the environment (001, 111), is also shown in (a) and (b). The objective of *self-training* in the system is for the system itself to allocate areas within the network which, through firing in response to patterns in the environment, distinguish between such events. The first step is to identify a neuron which, without any training, responds strongly to the first environmental pattern 001. Neuron 2 is one of the two which responds with the maximum value of 3 to this pattern. It is selected arbitrarily as being the 'response focus' for this pattern.

Training consists of first defining a 'neighbourhood' around the response focus. Here we define this as containing the four neurons that are 'next door' or 'next door but one' to the focus. This means that neurons 0, 1, 3 and 4 are in the neighbourhood of neuron 2. The second

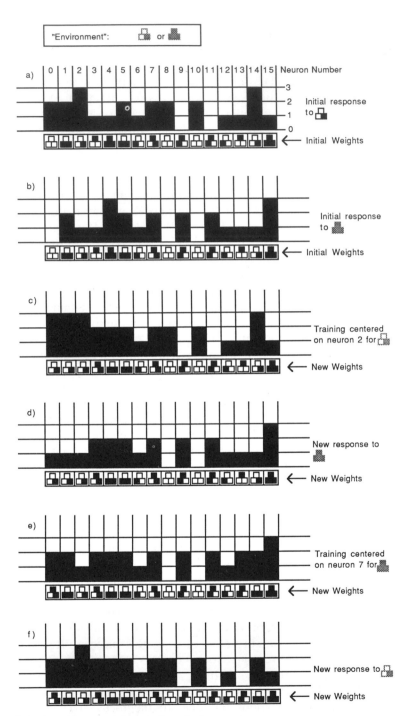

Fig. 9.1 A self-organizing ordered map.

step is to alter the weights of the neurons in the neighbourhood so as to strengthen the firing. This is done so as to increment the response by one step: that is, just one weight is changed thus improving the match between weight and input by one. So, for example, the weights of neuron 0 are changed from 000 to 001 which changes its response to input 001 from 2 to 3. The summary of changes for the entire neighbourhood is listed below.

Neuron 0 changes from 000 to 001 altering response from 2 to 3;
Neuron 1 changes from 011 to 001 altering response from 2 to 3;
Neuron 2 does not change as it is giving maximum response;
Neuron 3 changes from 100 to 101 altering response from 1 to 2;
Neuron 4 changes from 111 to 011 altering response from 1 to 2.

If the response of a neuron is initially 2, there is just one possible way in which the weight changes can be made; but if the response is 1 there are two possible weight changes that will increase the response, and where the response is 0 there would be three choices. In our example we choose one of these possibilities arbitrarily. Having set the weights for the first environmental pattern, we now turn our attention to the second environmental pattern, 111. The new response is shown, in fig. 9.1(d) and it is seen that the focus is unequivocally neuron 15.

To apply the training algorithm, we now need to define a neighbourhood for this neuron which seems to be a bit close to the end of the line. So as not to have to make special rules which cater for 'edge effects' in such nets we simply assert that the two ends of the line of neurons are adjacent. So the neighbourhood of neuron 15 contains neurons 13, 14, 1 and 2. We can now apply the algorithm with the effects as shown below.

Neuron no. 13 changes from 100 to 110 altering response from 1 to 2;
Neuron no. 14 changes from 001 to 011 altering response from 1 to 2;
Neuron no. 15 does not change as it is giving maximum response;
Neuron no. 1 changes from 001 to 101 altering response from 1 to 2;
Neuron no. 2 changes from 001 to 011 altering response from 1 to 2.

By going back to the 001 environment now that the system has been trained on both (fig. 9.1(f)) it can be seen that the net has learned to do just what was required of it. It has selected neuron 2 as signalling the presence of environment 001 by being the only neuron to give a response of 3 to this input pattern, and similarly, as seen in fig. 9.1(e), it has dedicated neuron 15 to identifying environment 111.

So the central principle is for the net to learn to respond in a different place for inputs that are different. Kohonen has extended this notion into two dimensions (rather than the one which exists in the above example).

9.4 KOHONEN'S 'TOPOLOGY-PRESERVING' MAPS

This work has been largely directed towards speech recognition (Kohonen, 1989). It converts speech utterances into 15 frequency components. This in itself may require some explanation.

Electrical engineers have shown that complex signals such as those resulting from speech uttered into a microphone may be broken down into the sum of many 'pure' sounds with different intensities. A pure sound is something like a very clean note played on a violin, and rough sounds such as 'grr' or 'sh' may be represented by an agglomeration of pure sounds. Pure sounds can be 'filtered out' by electronic circuits, which are called *filters*. So, Kohonen's scheme (in common with many other methods of speech analysis) starts with 15 such filters, and utterances such as '*ah*' or '*k*' (called *phonemes*) are represented by 15 variables x_1, x_2, ..., x_{15}. Each of these variables is a number which represents the intensity at the output of one filter. For example, if these numbers are in the range 0–100, a sound such as 'sssss . . .' which has much high frequency content may generate values for x_1, x_2, ..., x_{14}, x_{15} which are (say): 0, 0, 0, 0, 0, 0, 0, 0, 0, 12, 21, 55, 66, 78, 90.

However, a sound such as 'uuuu . . .' (as in ho*o*p) has much low frequency content and may generate values such as 32, 55, 93, 30, 55, 10, 0, 0, 0, 0, 0, 0, 0, 0, 0. In mathematical language, these lists of 15 numbers are *vectors*. The usual notation for such a vector is $\mathbf{x}(t)$. The time index (t) has been included as, in general, it is assumed that this vector varies with time and that time is controlled by a clock. For example at time $t = 1$ the sound might be 'sssss . . .' and:

$$\mathbf{x}(1) = 0, 0, 0, 0, 0, 0, 0, 0, 0, 12, 21, 55, 66, 78, 90$$

While at time $t = 2$ the sound might be 'uuuu . . .' giving:

$$\mathbf{x}(2) = 32, 55, 93, 30, 55, 10, 0, 0, 0, 0, 0, 0, 0, 0, 0$$

In this scheme, the system is said to be synchronous with $t = 0, 1, 2, \ldots$.

Kohonen uses a 96 neuron net, 8 rows of 12 neurons organized in a 'hexagonal' pattern as shown in fig. 9.2.

In the simplified example of fig. 9.1 each neuron received a 3-number vector where the numbers were 0 or 1. Here all neurons receive the current 15-number vector where the numbers are real and not binary

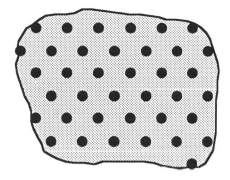

Fig. 9.2 Part of a hexagonal arrangement of neurons.

(i.e. the inputs have continuous values). So, to match these inputs, each neuron has a 15-value weight vector $\mathbf{m}(t) = m_1, m_2, \ldots, m_{15}$. The weights are different from those in fig. 9.1 in that they again have numerical rather than binary values. The process starts with the weights of the neurons being set to arbitrary, randomly selected values. Given the first training vector $\mathbf{x}(0)$, the first task is to find the neuron with the best matching weight. This is done by calculating the vector difference between the input and each of the weights as follows:

$$/x_1(0) - m_1(0)/ + /x_2(0) - m_2(0)/ + \ldots + /x_{15}(0) - m_{15}(0)/$$
$$= /\mathbf{x}(0) - \mathbf{m}(0)/$$

where $/a - b/$ is the absolute difference between a and b (that is if a is 3 and b is 5, $/a - b/$ is 2: the negative sign is ignored). $/\mathbf{x}(0) - \mathbf{m}(0)/$ is called the *Euclidean distance* between $\mathbf{x}(0)$ and $\mathbf{m}(0)$. So the focus neuron, c, is found for which the Euclidean distance from the first input vector is a minimum.

In contrast with our simple example in fig. 9.1, Kohonen's adaptation rule is time dependent in two ways. First, the neighbourhood of the focus neuron is made to shrink with time. Second, the amount by which the weights in the neighbourhood are changed is made to decrease with time. This ensures that the weights of the focus unit are the most affected, and there is a decrease in effect as one moves away from the focus.

An interesting property of this method is that, being trained on spoken words, the foci specialize on phonemes so that similar phonemes are close together and dissimilar ones far apart. This is why such nets are said to learn to become ordered maps. Figure 9.3 shows the way in which the net specialized to phonemes of spoken Finnish.

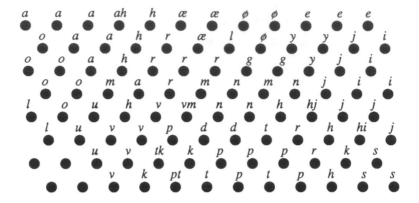

Fig. 9.3 An ordered map for Finnish phonemes.

So, if a word is spoken into a system it causes neurons to fire in a sequence which appears as a trajectory on the ordered map. The type of trajectory which results from a spoken word is illustrated in fig. 9.4 where it can be seen that the operating point of the net changes from phoneme to phoneme, with a little uncertainty in between.

The central feature of this arrangement is that the same word spoken on different occasions will cause the system to follow roughly the same trajectory. Kohonen (1989) briefly describes the way in which such trajectories may be recognized by conventional computation using a personal computer and some auxiliary boards. The major advantage is that the trajectories have been developed by the net itself in a way

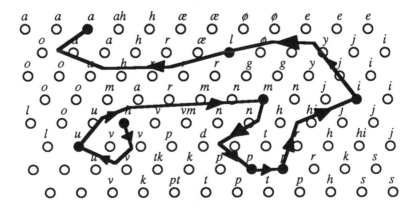

Fig. 9.4 A trajectory for the Finnish word /*humppila*/ (the activated units are shown as full dots).

optimal to the net. This emphasizes the benefits of unsupervised learning in neural computing.

9.5 COMPETITIVE LEARNING

One of the features of the ordered maps we have seen in the first part of this chapter is that, in some sense, different parts of the net are 'in competition' with each other. In the early stages of learning, one neuron 'wins' the competition and claims a territory around itself. In competitive learning almost the opposite goes on: once a unit wins the competition it inhibits others in its neighbourhood from firing. The scheme was studied by some leading figures in neural computing in the 1970s: Chris von der Malsburg (1973) in Germany, Kunihiko Fukushima (1975) in Japan and Stephen Grossberg (1976) in the USA.

A group of M cells within which such inhibition occurs is called an *inhibitory cluster*, and it has the property of decoding a distributed pattern into a one-in-M firing pattern. A scheme with two competitive layers is shown in fig. 9.5. Each cell in a layer is connected to all the cells in the previous layer. In the illustration, in the first competitive layer, the value of M for the inhibitory clusters is 4, while it is 3 in the second competitive layer. Every unit simply sums the value of the active (= 1) weights leading to it. In some versions of this scheme it is convenient to ensure that the sum of *all* the weights leading to the unit is unity. Within an inhibitory cluster only one element, the one with the highest input sum, is allowed to become active (= 1, all the others being 0).

Training is done within the inhibitory clusters and is merely a matter of shifting weight from the inactive inputs to the active ones in some predefined increments. Generally the sum of the weights leading to a unit is kept constant and is the same for all units. This is best illustrated

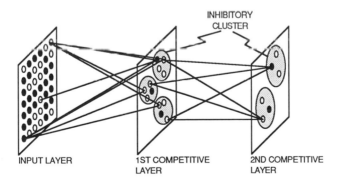

Fig. 9.5 A multi-layer competitive system.

by an example. Figure 9.6 shows a simple competitive learning arrangement with a 1×4 binary input pattern and a single inhibitory layer which contains only two units. The initial value of the weights is shown in (a). The system is exposed to the pattern as shown (which in the text we refer to as 1100). Unit A responds according to the sum of its active weights (i.e. weights with an input of 1) which is $2 + 2 = 4$, while unit B responds with $2 + 3 = 5$. So B wins the competition and the response of the unit is regarded as B.

In general, the response of the system is either A or B or, on occasions, the two in equal parts, which we shall label I (for indeterminate).

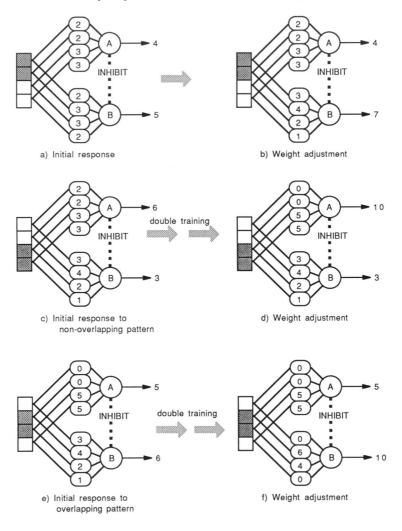

Fig. 9.6 Illustration of competitive learning.

Table 9.1 Untrained response of the competitive net with weights as in fig. 9.6(a)

Indeterminate inputs	A-responding inputs	B-responding inputs
0000	0001	0100
0010	0011	0110
0101	1001	1100
0111	1011	1110
1000		
1010		
1101		
1111		

This can be expressed as a 3-way division of all the 16 possible inputs into groups for which the response is either I, A, or B. For the initial setting of the weights as in (a) of fig. 9.6, this division is listed in Table 9.1.

There is not much one can say about this table: as one might expect, the division is apparently arbitrary due to the arbitrary setting of the weights. One effect should, however, be noticed: the response to 0000 and 1111 will be indeterminate irrespective of the setting of the weights. In the case of 0000 the input to all units will always be 0 while in the case of 1111 the total input will always be 10, which is the chosen value for the sum of the weights of each unit.

We now train the system on pattern 1100. As we have seen the response is B, and therefore only the weights of B are adjusted. We increase each of the active weights, from 2 to 3 and from 3 to 4, respectively, decreasing the inactive weights from 2 to 1, and 3 to 2. This leads to the new weight configuration as in fig. 9.6(b). Again, we can list the division of all the input patterns into their three classes as in Table 9.2.

Table 9.2 Trained response of the competitive net with weights as in fig. 9.6(b)

Indeterminate inputs	A-responding inputs	B-responding inputs
0000	0001	0100
0101	0010	0110
1010	0011	1000
1111	0111	1100
	1001	1101
	1011	1110

It is now evident that the system has classified as B all the patterns that have more 1s in the top half of the pattern in the figure (or left in the text) and as A where this greater number is in the bottom (or right) half. Evenly balanced patterns are either classified as I, or arbitrarily, as B or A. So, the competitive learning net, just by seeing one pattern with a strong feature in the top (or left) side, has learnt to distinguish between patterns with this top-bottom imbalance. This may be confirmed by looking at fig. 9.6(d) which is the result of training twice on 0011 which causes unit A to alter its weights in confirmation of the split which has already been learnt.

In fact, the division of patterns remains exactly the same as in Table 9.2, with the weights of unit A being more heavily committed to the division. But what if further training were to take place, say on pattern 0110? Double training leads to the set of weights shown in fig. 9.6(f) and the consequent division of input patterns as shown in Table 9.3.

The way in which this scheme has absorbed the training information leads it to be very sensitive to the presence or absence of a 1 in the second position from the top (left) in the input pattern, A almost always responding to the absence and B to the presence. The exceptions are 0111 and 1000 which are indeterminate.

The exponents of competitive learning argue that the scheme is an unsupervised way of extracting features or 'structure' from the set of patterns used for training. The 'structure' in the training leading to fig. 9.6(d) is the 'top-bottom' property while, given the additional training leading to fig. 9.6(f), the 'structure' becomes the presence or absence of the second bit. But there are pitfalls with this methodology: much depends on the initial value of the weights and in some tasks the appropriate number of layers of competitive learning required to achieve adequate performance and their inner structure can only be ascertained by experimentation. The reader is referred to Rumelhart and Zipser's

Table 9.3 Trained response of the competitive net with weights as in fig. 9.6(f)

Indeterminate inputs	A-responding inputs	B-responding inputs
0000	0001	0100
0111	0010	0101
1000	0011	0110
1111	1001	1100
	1010	1101
	1011	1110

Chapter 5 in Rumelhart and McClelland (1986) for a detailed analysis and discussion of competitive learning.

9.6 OTHER VARIATIONS

The last part of this chapter relates to the possible existence of synapses that interact with one another as suggested by Crick and Asanuma (1986). Figure 9.7(a) shows a sketch of an arrangement of synapses sometimes found in the brain. It is thought that firing on both synapses is required to activate the neuron. Say that the synaptic weight of synapse 1 is w_1 and that of 2 is w_2. Also say that the firing on axon 1 is represented as I_1, and firing on axon 2 as I_2. Then the activation of the combination is:

$$I_1 \times w_1 \times I_2 \times w_2$$

This is called a 'multiplicative' arrangement as the effect of the one synapse is multiplied by the effect of another. To simplify things, say that the only values that I_1, w_1, I_2 and w_2 can have are 0 and 1, then all four variables must be 1 for the activation to be 1. As far as learning goes, if both axons are at 1 and the activation of the combination has to be increased to aid the neuron to fire, it is assumed that both weights go to 1. It should be noted that after such learning, both axons have to be active for the activation to be 'felt' by the neuron. This arrangement is shown in diagrammatic form in fig. 9.7(b), the filled triangle being the multiplicative combination described above. In logical terms, the two axons may be thought of as forming an AND gate.

Hinton (1981) has suggested that this arrangement can be used in a neural net which recognizes stylized letters irrespective of their orientation. This arrangement is shown in fig. 9.8. The lowest level contains neurons that fire if they recognize the presence of individual features in

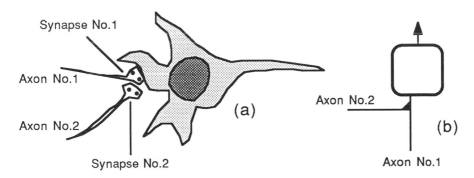

Fig. 9.7 A 'multiplicative' synaptic arrangement.

the image as shown. These are called *retinocentric* units. The middle layer, before any training takes place, is assumed to have every unit connected to every unit in the first layer. (In the figure only the relevant connections are shown.) However each output unit (at the top of the diagram) is assumed to be connected only to a separate specialized group of units. First we will describe how the system learns with the letters in an upright position and then show how the learning is extended so that the letters will continue to be recognized should they be twisted either to the left or to the right by 90°.

Training first takes place with the inputs in an untwisted position. Imagine that the letters are Scrabble tiles held in the hand of the learner. In a living system it is assumed that a part of the learner's brain which senses the state of the appropriate muscles will generate signals which indicate that the tile is not twisted.

In the artificial system of fig. 9.8 we simply assert that a *no-twist* neuron as shown in the group at the left is firing and that the system is 'looking at' the letter T on the Scrabble tile. We show all active units during this part of learning in grey. The retinocentric units are assumed to require no learning. The two on the left will fire, as they respond to the features contained in the T. It is further assumed that the left-hand unit in the top layer is required to fire for the letter T. Initially, the special units in the middle layer are assumed to fire in direct response to their corresponding input units (i.e. the ones directly below them). The

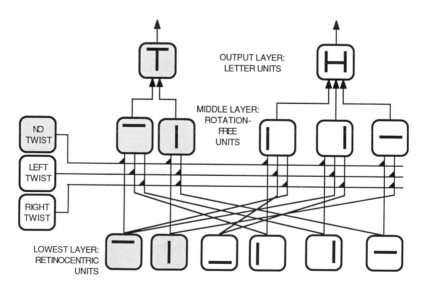

Fig. 9.8 Learning to recognize letter patterns: the state when T is upright.

effect of learning is for the synaptic connection to be made as represented by the filled triangle between the no-twist input and the input to the middle layer from the first layer. If the same is done for the H, the middle layer will have learnt the features of the upright characters.

Say that now the learner turns a tile (say, T) round to the left. The no-twist neuron ceases firing and the left-twist neuron takes over. Without giving an explanation of how this might happen, we assert that the output units keep their feature units in the middle layer firing (because the meaning of the tile has not changed). Then additional multiplicative synapses will be made with the left-twist neuron. This state of things is indicated in grey in fig. 9.9. Similar learning could take place with the tiles twisted to the right.

When learning is complete, the system may be thought to perform a search by letting the twist neurons fire one by one until a recognition is achieved. Incorrect matches do not provide sufficient activation for any of the output units, while correct ones identify not only the letter but also its orientation.

This is undoubtedly an interesting idea, and it is generally accepted that such systems merit much further research.

9.7 SUMMARY

Neural computing is an expanding paradigm. There is much new work which provides additional insights on the major themes discussed in this

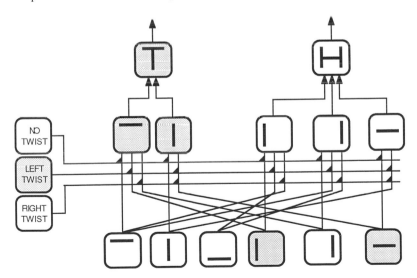

Fig. 9.9 Learning to recognize letter patterns: the state when T is twisted 90° to the left.

book. We have not attempted to cover all such variations. Our aim in selecting the three areas discussed in this chapter has been to highlight variations that embody the important principles of unsupervised/ competitive learning and the application of neurons with multiplicative properties. Anyone embarking on the design of a neural computer or program needs to know of these concepts.

EXERCISES FOR THE READER

1. In fig. 9.1, the initial choice of neuron 2 as the focus for training on pattern 001 was arbitrary. It could have been neuron 14. Work out how the net develops if the second choice is made.
2. In the system of fig. 9.6 it has been said that behaviour is much dependent on the initial choice of weights. Repeat the training as carried out in this example but start with a set of weights 6, 1, 2, 1 and 1, 4, 3, 2 and comment on the result.
3. Given the alternatives of a perceptron-like system, a Boltzmann machine and unsupervised learning (or competitive learning), discuss the factors that influence the choice of technique. In your discussion refer to examples of clearly defined data on which the system can be trained.
4. Referring to fig. 9.8, show that the letters are not recognized with the wrong-twist neuron firing. (Calculate the activation at all the units for twisted H and T letters with the wrong twist neurons firing, assuming that all weights have a value of 1 and that the thresholds are such as to require all the inputs to fire for the unit to fire.) What happens if an upside-down T is presented?

10

Logical memory neurons

Neural nodes may be described by their truth tables. Varying the weights changes the truth tables. In this chapter we consider systems in which the training algorithms act directly on stored truth tables, thus eliminating the need to utilize weights. The advantage of these 'weight-less' systems is that they are implementable as networks of random-access memories. We define several typical structures for such devices, including units called probabilistic logic nodes (PLNs) which are RAMs that store the probability of firing of the node. Synchronous and asynchronous systems are discussed and it is seen that the latter behave much like Hopfield, Boltzmann and error back-propagation models.

10.1 WHAT IS A LOGICAL MEMORY NEURON?

The notion of using a random access memory (RAM) device as a neural node has been introduced in Chapter 5. We recall that the analogy centres on the fact that the address terminals of the RAM device can act as the neural inputs and the data-output terminals as the neural outputs of a node. Since the content of the RAM defines the logical function of the node, we will call neural models based on RAM 'logical memory neurons'. In Chapter 5 it has also been seen how a perceptron-like device (the WISARD) can be constructed using RAM. The WISARD is a practical, working, learning pattern recognizer. Now we will take up this line of reasoning again and show how the notion can be extended to cover ground very similar to that discussed in Chapters 6–8: the design of dynamic nets with content-addressable emergent properties (Hopfield and Boltzmann models) and of feed-forward systems which learn to transform patterns through error back-propagation.

The motivation for this work has been threefold. First, as in the case of the WISARD, the memory/logical approach lends itself to fast implementation using conventional silicon memory techniques. Second, this approach is amenable to simple analysis that is commonly used for logic circuits. Third, the memory/logical model allows one to study biological systems which apply to neural node functions that are more complex than the MCP.

The possibility of overcoming the hard learning problem using memory/logical methods was first proposed by one of the authors (Aleksander, 1978). And, in 1983, the existence of Hopfield-like content-addressable emergent properties was shown to apply to the memory/logical paradigm (Aleksander, 1983). More recently, it has been shown that error back-propagation has its counterpart in fast, probabilistic versions of memory/logic systems known as probabilistic logic nodes (PLNs) (Aleksander, 1988).

We intend to clarify the terminology before working through these developments, using simple examples and relating them to what we have discovered so far about neural computing from the preceding chapters.

10.2 DEFINITIONS AND TERMS

A RAM neuron is the most basic type of logical memory neuron for the design of networks of logical memory neurons or, more concisely, *logical neural nets*. A RAM neuron is the node defined in Chapter 5 (page 71). It receives N binary inputs at the address terminals (X_1 to X_N) and produces one binary output at the 'data-out' terminal (F_j for the jth neuron in a net). Training is achieved by supplying the desired output values of 0 or 1 at the 'data-in' terminals for given input patterns, while the writing mechanism of the RAM device is energized ('write-enabled' in computer designer's jargon). Logical neural nets have well defined *learning phases* when the elements of the net are write-enabled and changes occur in the stored content of the RAM device. In contrast, there are *running phases* during which the writing mechanisms are disabled and the net is carrying out computational tasks based on previously learned material. A conventional RAM device which stores M bits per word, is viewed as M RAM neurons with their inputs receiving the same data, while each of the M outputs can learn independent responses to this data. A glance at fig. 5.2 in Chapter 5 should clarify these issues.

In this work we shall refer to *canonical* (in the dictionary sense of 'standard' or 'accepted') forms of network. These are standard networks of logic neural nodes of some broadly specified structure (the RAM neuron is an example of the simplest form of such structures). In these standard networks the main variable is the value of N, the number of inputs per node, all nodes in the canonical net having the same number of inputs. Again referring back to Chapter 5, the WISARD discriminator scheme (page 82), designed for a particular size of input image and a given number of image classes, is a canonical in the above sense. We have seen that the only parameter to affect the performance of the WISARD, given a training set, is the value of N.

Logical neural nets may be run either synchronously, with all nodes making a new attempt at firing in response to a clock pulse, or asynchronously, with nodes firing at random but making a known average of W attempts per unit time. The latter is precisely the arrangement assumed in the Hopfield and Boltzmann nets of Chapters 6 and 7.

A *probabilistic logic node* (PLN) differs from the RAM neuron in the sense that a q-bit number (rather than a single bit) is now stored at the addressed location in a RAM. The content of this location is turned (by means we shall discuss later) into the probability of firing (i.e. generating a 1) at the overall output of the node. Say that q is 3, then the binary numbers 0 to 7 can be stored in each location of the RAM. One way of regarding the actual number stored may be as a direct representation of the firing probability, i.e. treating the number as a fraction of 7. So a stored 2 would cause the output to fire with a probability of 2/7, and so on. This is not the only way of organizing PLNs and others will be discussed later when we shall return to such devices in more detail.

A *N-connected canonical net* is a net containing a number R of nodes (RAM neurons or PLNs) with N inputs per node. The minimum value of R is $N + 1$, it is accepted in neural net studies that it is not useful to connect the output of a node back to its own input as this would create the possibility of nodes remaining stuck in a state from which they cannot exit. The net with $R = N + 1$ has the output of each node connected to one input of every other node. Such a net is called a *fully connected canonical net*. The general N-connected canonical net, where $R > N + 1$, is therefore partially connected and requires a specification (e.g. random or ordered in some way) for the interconnections. Figure 10.1 illustrates some of these concepts.

A *pyramid* is a network of cells as shown in fig. 10.2. We note a simple relationship between the width W, depth D and number of inputs per cell, N:

$$W = N^D \ (N \text{ and } D \text{ are integers})$$

Therefore, for a given input width (or given depth) the pyramid is seen to be canonical, in the sense that its definition depends only on N.

Armed with these definitions we shall now look at examples of the behaviour of some canonical networks.

10.3 A FULLY CONNECTED ASYNCHRONOUS RAM-NEURON NET

We consider a 3-node fully connected RAM-neuron net. This structure is precisely the one shown in fig. 10.1(a). We assume an arbitrary

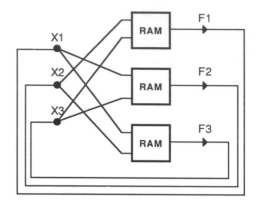

a)   Fully 2-connected net with R=3

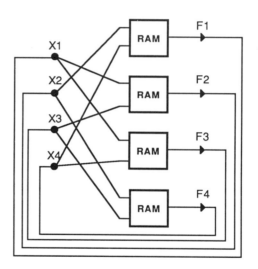

b)   Randomly 2-connected net with R=4 and the added restriction that each output shall be connected to exactly two inputs.

Fig. 10.1 Examples of canonical nets.

content of the RAMs shown as the following truth tables:

Input	X_2	0	0	1	1
Input	X_3	0	1	0	1
Output	F_1	0	0	1	0

We now assume that the operation of the net is asynchronous. This means that, given a state (i.e. a pattern of 0s and 1s at F_1, F_2 and F_3),

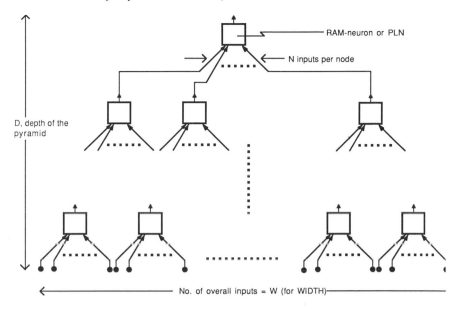

Fig. 10.2 A pyramid.

Input	X_1	0	0	1	1
Input	X_3	0	1	0	1
Output	F_2	1	1	0	0
Input	X_1	0	0	1	1
Input	X_2	0	1	0	1
Output	F_3	1	0	0	1

only one of the three nodes of the net can change at one time, and consequently, there can be at most three states that follow the given state and which occur with equal probability. Which state follows, depends on which of F_1, F_2 or F_3 is read first. So the following states are found by assuming that only one of the nodes at any one time allows its memory location to be interrogated. Doing this for each of the three nodes gives us the three possible 'next states' each occurring with equal probability.

As an example let us take $F_1F_2F_3 = 000$.

If F_1 interrogates its memory, as the input is $X_2X_3 = 00$, the value of F_1 remains at 0 according to the truth table, and there is a re-entry into state 000 with, so far, a probability of 1/3.

If F_2 interrogates its memory, as the input is $X_1X_3 = 00$, the value of F_2 changes from 0 to 1 according to the truth table, and there is an entry into state 010 with, so far, a probability of 1/3.

Finally, if F_3 interrogates its memory, as the input is $X_1X_2 = 00$, the value of F_3 changes from 0 to 1 according to the truth table, and there is an entry into state 001 with, so far, a probability of 1/3.

This procedure allows us to calculate all the transition probabilities, and to represent the result as a Markov chain, very similar to that resulting from the Boltzmann machine in Chapter 7 (pages 120–1). The complete Markov chain is shown in Table 10.1.

Using the techniques of Chapter 7 this representation allows us to compute the final probabilities of being in any state (e.g. $P_0(t)$ for state 0). These are listed in Table 10.2.

In order to make comparisons with Boltzmann machines we can now

Table 10.1 Markov chain representation of the 3-RAM asynchronous net. States are represented by their binary number, e.g. $S_0 = 000$, $S_3 = 011$, etc. The table contains the probability of going from a current state to a next state.

Current state:	S_0	S_1	S_2	S_3	S_4	S_5	S_6	S_7
Next state								
S_0	1/3	0	0	0	1/3	0	0	0
S_1	1/3	2/3	0	0	0	1/3	0	0
S_2	1/3	0	2/3	1/3	0	0	0	0
S_3	0	1/3	1/3	2/3	0	0	0	1/3
S_4	0	0	0	0	2/3	1/3	1/3	0
S_5	0	0	0	0	0	1/3	0	1/3
S_6	0	0	0	0	0	0	1/3	0
S_7	0	0	0	0	0	0	1/3	1/3

Table 10.2 Final probabilities of being in any particular state

State-probability	$P_0(t)$	$P_1(t)$	$P_2(t)$	$P_3(t)$	$P_4(t)$	$P_5(t)$	$P_6(t)$	$P_7(t)$
t = 18	0.084	0.083	0.250	0.166	0.167	0	0.167	0.083

define an energy associated with the states by using the Boltzmann formula:

$$p = 1/(1 + e^{-KE})$$

to relate some energy E to some probability p, K being an arbitrary constant.

Starting with this idea we need to make several adjustments.

1. For convenience, we make K = 1.
2. The Boltzmann formula relates energy increase to probability increase (this is a 'kinetic' energy in physics) whereas here we need to relate the 'stored' energy of a state (or 'potential energy' using the physics analogy) to probability. The higher the probability of occurrence of a state the lower its 'stored' energy. So, we let $P_j(t) = 1 - p$ ($= 1 - 1/(1 + e^{-KE})$) in order to relate high probabilities to low energies.
3. It is quite possible, in our general formulation, for $P_j(t)$ to be 0 or 1. In the above relationship between E and p this would imply values of E of $+\infty$ and $-\infty$ respectively. As we are trying to infer energy from probability of occurrence of a state, we can limit E (arbitrarily) to lie between -5 and $+5$.

   It turns out that when $(1 - p)$ is 0.00667, then E is $+5$,

   also when $(1 - p)$ is 0.99333, then E is -5.

We now modify $P_j(t)$ slightly to $P_j(t)'$ using the formula:

$$P_j(t)' = 0.00667 + (0.99333 - 0.00667) \times P_j(t) \qquad (10.1)$$
$$= 0.00667 + 0.98666 \times P_j(t)$$

which has the property of making

$$P_j(t)' = 0.00667 \text{ (i.e. E} = +5) \text{ when } P_j(t) = 0, \text{ and}$$
$$P_j(t)' = 0.99333 \text{ (i.e. E} = -5) \text{ when } P_j(t) = 1$$

So, given a value for $P_j(t)$, we find the corresponding $P_j(t)'$ from (10.1) and use it in the formula $P_j(t)' = 1 - 1/(1 + e^{-F}j)$ which, when solved for E_j gives:

$$E_j = \ln(1 - P_j(t)') - \ln(P_j(t)') \qquad (10.2)$$

(ln stands for 'natural logarithm', that is, logarithm to the base 'e').

Using these relationships we can calculate the energy of all states as in Table 10.3 and draw the state/energy diagram as in fig. 10.3.

Table 10.3 Energies related to final probabilities

State-energy:	E_0	E_1	E_2	E_3	E_4	E_5	E_6	E_7
Energy value:	2.3	2.3	1	1.6	1.6	5	1.6	2.3

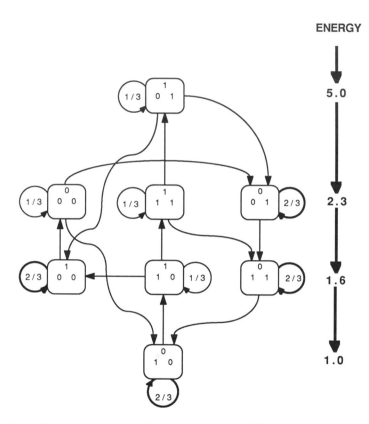

Fig. 10.3 The state energy diagram for the RAM-neuron net.

It can easily be appreciated that, to a rough first approximation, the energy of a state depends on the difference between the total probability of entering a state and the total probability of leaving it. States that have no probability of being left are *local minima* (there are none in fig. 10.3). Armed with these notions we can now describe a simple training algorithm.

10.4 TRAINING ASYNCHRONOUS RAM-NEURON NETS

The object of training, as usual, is to create energy minima, preferably globally rather than merely locally. The direct way of achieving this is to clamp the net into the desired state while supplying the desired state itself to the 'data-in' terminals. Taking the example of fig. 10.1 again and assuming that we wish to train the net to remain stable on patterns 000 and 111, the feedback loops would be clamped first to 000 with 000 supplied to the 'data-in' terminals of the RAMs (not shown in fig. 10.1 – see fig. 5.1 in Chapter 5 for the detail). The writing mechanism of the RAM is energized, ensuring that 000 at the X terminals will result in 000 at these terminals for all firing attempts of the net. The same can be made true for 111. Assuming that, before the training commenced, the contents of the RAMs were those described at the beginning of the previous section and which led to the behaviour in fig. 10.3, it is instructive to note below how the contents change as a result of training the net to be stable on 000 and 111. The changes are denoted by a bold number **0** or **1**.

Input	X_2	0	0	1	1
Input	X_3	0	1	0	1
		---	---	---	---
Output	F_1	0	0	1	**1**

Input	X_1	0	0	1	1
Input	X_3	0	1	0	1
		---	---	---	---
Output	F_2	**0**	1	0	**1**

Input	X_1	0	0	1	1
Input	X_2	0	1	0	1
		---	---	---	---
Output	F_3	**0**	0	0	1

As might be expected, this has a considerable effect on the Markov transition probabilities and these are shown in Table 10.4. Again, changes are shown by bold entries.

The net effect of training is clear: not only have the trained states been left with no exits (i.e. they are local minima), but also the number of entries to them from other states has been increased. This is due to the way in which a change in a truth table affects several states and, with this form of training, is likely to encourage transitions to the training states.

In fact, fig. 10.4 shows the remarkable effect that the training has had on the state/energy relationships in the network.

So far it has been demonstrated that the RAM-neuron net behaves in much the same way as nets of the Hopfield or Boltzmann kind. The major advantage is the very direct form of training which has been

Table 10.4 Markov chain representation of the trained 3-RAM asynchronous net

Current state:	S_0	S_1	S_2	S_3	S_4	S_5	S_6	S_7
Next state								
S_0	**3/3**	**1/3**	**1/3**	0	1/3	0	0	0
S_1	**0**	**1/3**	0	0	0	1/3	0	0
S_2	0	0	**1/3**	1/3	0	0	0	0
S_3	0	1/3	**1/3**	**1/3**	0	0	0	**0**
S_4	0	0	0	0	**2/3**	1/3	1/3	0
S_5	0	0	0	0	0	**0**	0	**0**
S_6	0	0	0	0	0	0	1/3	0
S_7	0	0	0	**1/3**	0	**1/3**	1/3	**3/3**

shown to create the desired energy wells. However, much of the activity of the net which is not related to the trained states is a function of initial arbitrary settings of the truth tables in the RAM-neuron net, and this is analogous to initial arbitrary settings of weights in the Hopfield and Boltzmann models. Indeed, despite the obvious lowering of the energy

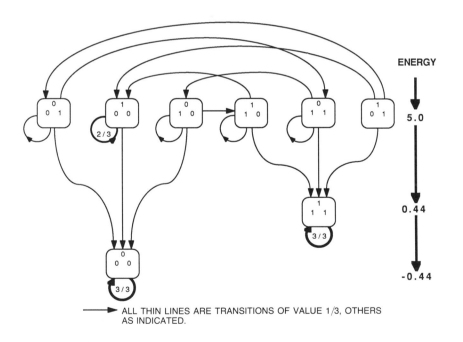

ALL THIN LINES ARE TRANSITIONS OF VALUE 1/3, OTHERS AS INDICATED.

Fig. 10.4 State/energy diagram of the trained asynchronous RAM-neuron net.

due to training, the actual energies of the trained states and the difference between them in the above example are solely due to the initial arbitrary content of the RAM memories. Uncontrolled false minima could be part of such arbitrariness. Soon we shall show that canonical nets made of probabilistic logic nodes have characteristics that more closely represent the training. But first, we shall briefly deal with synchronous versions of RAM-neuron nets.

10.5 SYNCHRONOUS RAM-NEURON NETS

With synchronous nets the truth tables stored in the RAM neurons completely determine the successors of each network state. There can be only one successor state for each current state. Taking the network of fig. 10.1 with the arbitrary truth tables given earlier we can calculate the successor state of each state. For example if $X_1X_2X_3 = 000$, $F_1F_2F_3$ may be read off the truth tables as being 011. This can be repeated for each of the eight states resulting in the state diagram shown in fig. 10.5(a). Such systems are known as *finite state, deterministic automata*: finite state, because the number of states is finite in number (precisely 2^N for N nodes); deterministic, because the successor state is completely determined by the current state. The word *automaton* comes from a branch of computer science theory which relates state structures to physical circuits (see Aleksander and Hanna, 1978).

Despite the deterministic nature of these systems, a probability of the net being in any particular state, and hence an energy, may be associated with each state. As before, the assumption is that the system can start in any of the eight states with equal probability. In fig. 10.5(a) it is clear that at some arbitrary point in time greater than 8 (the maximum length of any chain of states) the system has equal probabilities of $1/5$ being in any of the five states S_0, S_3, S_2, S_6 and S_5. Equation (10.2) can be applied to these probabilities giving an energy of approximately 1.4 for each of these states. As there is at this point a probability of zero of being in states S_1, S_7 and S_4, these states have a maximum energy of 5. A slightly different way of looking at these probabilities may be to ask what is the probability of being in any cycle. Deterministic automata such as these, with only one successor state for each state, must always complete a sequence by being in a cycle of one or more states. In the example of fig. 10.5(a) the probability of being in the S_0, S_3, S_2, S_6, S_5 cycle is unity after at most two time steps. Hence a minimum energy of -5 may be associated with the entire cycle. We call this the *cycle energy*.

Training, again, is a simple matter: the pattern for the desired stable state is merely applied to the data-in terminals of the RAMs in fig. 10.1, and the same pattern is put on the input (address terminals while the

Examples of the binary coding for states used in this figure and in fig 10.6:

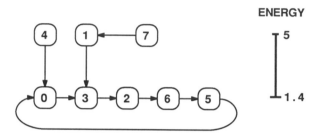

(a) Untrained response

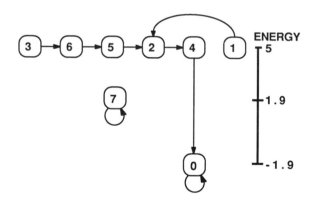

(b) Trained response

Fig. 10.5 The synchronous behaviour of the RAM-neuron in fig. 10.1.

writing mechanism for the RAMs is energized. In fig. 10.5 this has been done for states S_0 and S_7. There is only one state in each cycle, so the objective of training has achieved the creation of local minima. But we shall now show that, curiously, the two states acquire different probabilities.

First, we note that the state energy is the same as the cycle energy in these cases as there is only one state in each cycle. The probability of being in either cycle is proportional to the number of starting states that lead to the cycle. So the probability for S_0 is 7/8 as seven out of eight states lead to it (giving an energy of -1.9 from equation (10.2)). By the same argument, the probability of S_7 is only 1/8 (energy of $+1.9$). It is clear that, although the learned local minima have been properly created by training, their entry states, and hence overall energy, are a function of the arbitrary initial setting of the truth tables as was the case in the asynchronous system. While this problem does not invalidate the techniques of using canonical RAM-neuron systems, it will be demonstrated that it may be alleviated by using probabilistic logic nodes.

10.6 FULLY CONNECTED PLN NETS

We recall that a probabilistic logic node (PLN) has been defined as a RAM-neuron which, instead of storing just 0 or 1 for each input pattern j, stores Pj which is a string of bits which encode a number between 0 and 1 representing the probability of firing (i.e. producing a 1). As an example we can again consider exactly the same structure as in fig. 10.1(a), but this time the nodes are PLNs. Let us say that the RAMs that constitute the PLNs only store three messages: 0 when the neuron always outputs 0, 1 when the neuron always outputs 1 and 'd' when the neuron outputs 0 and 1 randomly with equal probability.

The key property of such devices is that, through storing 'd', the neuron has the ability to 'say' 'I don't know'. Therefore, before any training takes place, all the nodes in a net are set to 'd'. The initial Markov chain for such systems is easily imagined. If the system is synchronous, the probability of any legitimate transition between one state and its successor between any two states is the same and is equal to $1/2^N$ for an N-element net. This means that all states start off at the same energy, corresponding to the above probability. Should the net be asynchronous, given state S, transitions can only take place to other states that differ from S in only one variable (of which there are N) or back to S itself. The probability of transition to any state other than S is $(1/N) \times (1/2)$ (which is $1/2N$), as $(1/N)$ is the probability of a particular node attempting to fire, while $(1/2)$ is the probability of a change in the state of that particular neuron. Consequently, the probability of transition back to S is given by:

$$1 - (\text{sum of probabilities of transitions to non-}S\text{ states})$$

$$= 1 - N \times (1/2N)$$

$$= 1/2$$

So, staying with the asynchronous case, as all states have the same transition probability patterns before any training takes place, the 2^N

states have equal probability of occurrence and therefore all have equal energy, corresponding to the probability of $1/2^N$.

Taking now the specific case of a 3-element fully connected PLN net (in the format shown in fig. 10.1(a)), imagine that training, as in the case of RAM-neurons, consists of setting the address terminals and the data-in terminals to the 0/1 pattern of the desired stable state. Then, whether the system is synchronous or not, all RAMs will contain 0 stored at their 00 inputs (they are 2-input RAMs), 1 at the 11 inputs and 'd' for all other cases. In the synchronous case the 000 and 111 states will be stable (note a state consists of the output of the three neurons). Transitions for other states may be calculated as follows. Take $X_1X_2X_3 = 001$, $F_1F_2F_3$ is dd0 as only F_3 'recognizes' its 00 input as 0, while F_1 and F_2 each have an input of 10 which addresses the 'd' message. This means that there are transitions to states 000, 100, 010, and 110 with equal probability (of $1/4$). The resulting state diagram for a synchronous network is seen in fig. 10.6(a).

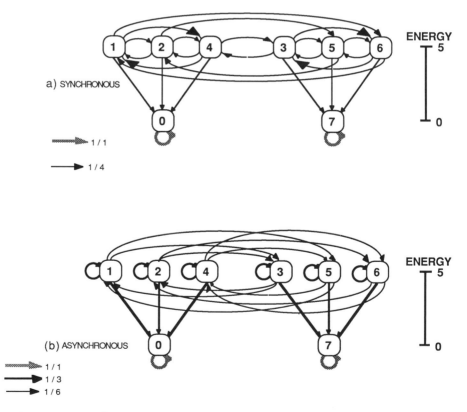

Fig. 10.6 State/energy diagrams for fully connected nets of PLNs.

The asynchronous behaviour is slightly different (fig. 10.6b). Taking again $X_1X_2X_3 = 001$, $F_1F_2F_3 = $ dd0 as before. If F_1 attempts to fire (probability of $1/3$), states 001 and 101 are equally likely (probability of $1/6$ each). If F_2 attempts to fire (probability of $1/3$), states 001 and 011 are equally likely (probability of $1/6$ each). If F_3 attempts to fire (probability of $1/3$), state 000 will follow. Despite the broad similarity to the synchronous case, the asynchronous scheme has one significant difference. Take state 1 (001). In the synchronous case the network has a probability of $1/3$ of entering its appropriate stable state (000 in this case, being the more similar of the two), while the probability of drifting off elsewhere is $2/3$. In the asynchronous case, realizing that the return to the same state does not affect the argument, it is seen that the probability of entering the appropriate state is the same ($1/3$) as that of 'drifting off' to other states. The fact that this difference exists prompts us to look a little more closely and more generally at the way the trained states act as 'attractors' of transitions from similar states.

10.7 ATTRACTORS

The question is whether the creation of stable states through the training of a fully connected PLN net makes those states attractors of transitions from similar states. Consider the general case of an N-element net. Say that it is trained to make the all-0 pattern stable. Now consider what happens if the system is started in a state which has all 0s except one. Say that the kth neuron is in the 1 state.

In the synchronous case, all the neurons except the kth are addressed by a string of 0s with a single 1 in their midst. This finds a 'd' stored at all addresses but one, and a 0 at the kth neuron. The next state will then have a 0 at the kth neuron and arbitrary values at all the other neurons. This means that about half the neurons will output a 1. So the next state will be even less like the trained state than the state with only one 1. Therefore the training has not created an attractor and transitions to the trained state are purely accidental. Before saying how one gets around this problem, it is interesting to consider the asynchronous case trained on the same pattern.

In the asynchronous case, only one neuron output can change at any one time. The addressing is the same as before so that when a neuron attempts to fire, all except the kth neuron will output a 0 with 50% probability. This means that half of the states with only one disruption will enter the trained state. So, even if the trained state is not a perfect attractor, it is much more successful than the synchronous case.

It has been shown in Aleksander (1988) that the way to overcome the problem in the synchronous case is to 'clamp' the desired output while the feedback connections are subjected to small amounts of noise. Here it is worth pointing out that the problem is less severe for nets that are not fully connected because a single disruption finds fewer neurons with a 'd'.

The major difficulty with fully connected PLN networks is that their memory cost escalates exponentially with size of net. For an $N + 1$ node net, $2N$ storage locations are required in each. In the final canonical case considered in this chapter, it will be shown that a very similar performance can be obtained at lower cost through the use of PLN pyramids.

10.8 PLN PYRAMIDS: TRAINING ALGORITHMS

The structure of a pyramid has been shown in fig. 10.2. Here we consider only pyramids that contain PLNs. We also start by assuming that the PLNs are of the three-message variety, storing 0, 1, or 'd'. The key fact about a pyramid is that, inherently, it will contain hidden units. This means that an error is known only for the output of the entire pyramid, rather than for each PLN, and it is therefore necessary to find a way of training the intermediate layers. An untrained PLN pyramid will output 0s and 1s with equal probability in response to any input pattern as all the nodes contain only 'd' values. This means that it starts with 50% error. The following steps constitute a training algorithm for a single pyramid:

1. Identify the training set. This must consist first of a set, Z0, say, of input patterns for which the response is to be 0, so $Z0 = (z0_1, z0_2, \ldots)$. Similarly we can define the set for which the pyramid must respond with a 1, that is, $Z1 = (z1_1, z1_2, \ldots)$.
2. Select a training regime. This refers to any specific way in which the two sets above are to be presented to the net. For example, the two sets could be applied in random order, interleaved, or one after the other, and so on. In general the fully learned solution may not depend on the selected regime. However, in quoting experimental results it is always worth stating the regime, in case it had an influence. The regime usually refers only to one presentation of the two sets. For repetition arrangements see part 4 of this algorithm.
3. For the first (or, in general, next) training pattern applied to the input, if the output is consistently right (e.g. remains at j for a pattern that belongs to Z_j), do nothing. If the output is varying in time between 0 and 1, as soon as it becomes right, examine the current output of all nodes and store it. This means that all the nodes whose input currently addresses a 'd' will have the 'd' replaced by their current output (which, as a result of the 'd', has been arbitrarily

selected). If the output is consistently wrong, all nodes that output a consistent output (i.e. do not have their 'd' addressed) have the content of their stored location returned to 'd'.
4. Repeat applying the training patterns according to the regime until no errors are detected or the error rate reaches an irreducible minimum.

The best way of seeing how this scheme works is to look at a specific example. Figure 10.7 shows a two-layer pyramid of 3-input PLNs, with, consequently, nine inputs. These inputs are arranged as a 3×3 matrix and the training regime being shown in the figure is interleaved as:

$$z1_1, z0_1, z1_2, z0_2, z1_3, z0_3$$

It should be noted that the values allocated to the contents of PLNs 1, 2 and 3 (the layer of hidden units) are largely arbitrary, and the solution is easily found. The example contains no instance of consistent error. In general, this algorithm will find appropriate values in the hidden layer and hence not fall prey to 'hard learning' difficulties. More taxing tasks (i.e. the problem of detecting parity) are discussed in Aleksander (1989).

Clearly, should the PLNs store more than three messages the training algorithm would need to be modified. Step 3 above might read something like:

3. For the first (or, in general, next) training pattern applied to the input, if the output is consistently right (e.g. remains at j for a pattern that belongs to Z_j), do nothing. If the output is varying in time between 0 and 1, as soon as it becomes right examine the current output of all nodes and 'encourage' the current output. This means that if the addressed location contains a probability of firing greater than 0.5, increase it by some amount ∂, while if it is less than 0.5, decrease it by ∂. If the output is consistently wrong, all nodes that give a consistent output (i.e. do not have their 'd' addressed) have the content of their stored location 'discouraged' by altering it towards 0.5 by an amount ∂.

Myers (1989) discusses optimal ways of selecting values of ∂.

10.9 PLN PYRAMIDS: GENERALIZATION

After training, the pyramid responds either with a constant 1, a constant 0, or a mixture of the two with an average ratio of one to the other. Taking a general pyramid with N-input nodes, a depth D and a width W

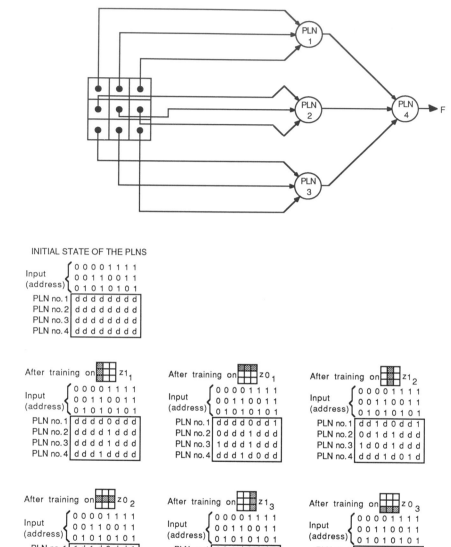

Fig. 10.7 Development of PLN stores with training.

(see fig. 10.2), we can get a measure of generalization by considering what happens if the pyramid has been trained on only one input pattern (say all-1 to respond with 1). We also assume that the nodes have three-message codes at their storage locations. In what follows we predict the response to a pattern that has just one 0 in a string of 1s in order to assess the effect of net parameters (specifically N) on this response.

The input layer contains W/N nodes, and in one of these nodes the 'd' will be addressed, while the other nodes will respond in the way they have been trained. Therefore 50% of the time the response at this first layer will be as for the all-1 input ('right') and the other 50% of the time it will differ at only one point. By the same argument, the response of the second layer will be as trained while the first layer is 'right'. It will also be 'right' for 50% of the time that the first layer is 'wrong'. Therefore the second layer is right $1 - (0.5)^2$ of the time. As this argument is progressively applied to layers towards the output of the pyramid, it may be seen that the output of the pyramid will produce a 1 with a probability of:

$$1 - (0.5)^D.$$

For a given W, D depends on N as D = ln W/ln N (from W = N^D). For example, taking W = 256, D and the response for different values of N are shown below:

$N = 2$	D = 8	Response = 99.6%
$N = 4$	D = 4	Response – 93.8%
$N = 16$	D = 2	Response = 75.0%

If the number of 0s in the test pattern is increased, by the time this number is about W/N and each input node is likely to find 'd' at its addresses, the total response will fall to 50%. In the above example, this fall to 50% response will happen for approximately:

128	0s when $N =$	2;
64	0s when $N =$	4;
16	0s when $N =$	16;

So, for a fixed W, the higher the value of N, the more sharply 'tuned' to the training set the pyramid will be. While this is similar to the WISARD discriminator (Chapter 5), the pyramid has a characteristic that distinguishes it strongly from the discriminator: it is possible to make the pyramid very sensitive to small differences. For example it is possible to make the pyramid fire 100% 1 for the all-1 input pattern and 100% 0 (i.e. 0% 1) for an all-1-except-for-a-single-0 pattern. This theme will be revisited in the exercises at the end of this chapter.

10.10 FULLY CONNECTED PYRAMID NETS

Here we consider the final canonical form: a fully connected net for which each node is a pyramid. The idea is illustrated in fig. 10.8 for a 3×3 system. Note that, respecting the idea that a node in a fully connected net should not be connected to itself, the nine nodes each require eight inputs. Hence N, W, D for each pyramid is 2, 8, 3 in this case. Imagine that the system has been trained so as to maintain the all-1 input stable.

Tested on all-1 except for one 0 (as before), in the synchronous case, the $1 - (0.5)^D$ rule with $D = 3$ tells us that the probability of the output of any pyramid firing with a 1 is 87.5% (i.e. 7/8). So the probability of the disrupted state being followed by the trained state is $(0.875)^8$, that is, about 34% (note that the ninth output is guaranteed to output a 1 as

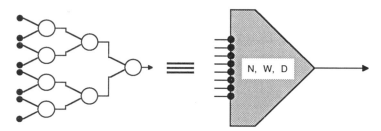

Symbol for a pyramid

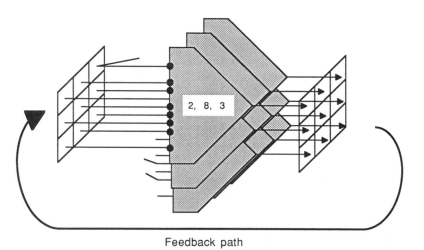

Feedback path

Fig. 10.8 A fully connected pyramid net.

it is blind to the disruption). The probability of just one output being disrupted in the state following the first may be calculated to be 39% and (since the probability of transitions with more than one disrupted output is $100 - 34 - 39 = 27\%$) this must be the most likely event. Thus, as in the case of fully connected PLN nets, training creates local minima, but they are not attractors. To overcome this use can be made of noise as was mentioned earlier.

In the asynchronous case, as only one node can change at any one time, the overall probability of falling into the trained state is actually 87.5%, with the rest (12.5%) leading to another state that has only one disturbed point. So at the next point in time, the probability of entering the trained state is $(87.5 + 0.875 \times 12.5)\% = 98.4\%$. In other words the probability of entering the trained state increases with time, showing that the training algorithm indeed creates attractors.

10.11 COST

It was said earlier that one of the reasons for working with pyramids of PLNs was in response to the number of required storage locations which increases exponentially with the size of the net. If one is to make such systems in VLSI, the number of storage locations determines the amount of silicon area required and hence chip cost. It is possible to show that the total number, $T(N, D)$, of nodes in a pyramid with parameters N and D is:

$$T(N, D) = (N^{D+1} - 1)/(N - 1) \tag{10.3}$$

Given some W it is possible to calculate the variation of the number of storage locations for different values of N (and, hence, D). For example if $W = 16$ and $N = 2$ (and hence $D = 4$), $T(N, D)$ is 15 and the number of storage locations per node is 2^2, that is, 4. Hence the total number of storage locations (say C) required is $4 \times 15 - 60$. We can tabulate some of these values below, all for $W = 16$:

$N = 2$ $C = 60$
$N = 4$ $C = 80$
$N = 16$ $C = 65\,536$

The last of these corresponds to the case where one PLN with 16 inputs is used. This provides a comparison between storage costs of PLN and pyramid systems. So it is clear that the pyramid concept allows the neural net designer an opportunity of selecting a value of N which gives an appropriate amount of generalization (which decreases with N) and reduces cost (which markedly increases with N).

10.12 SUMMARY

The use of memory devices as neurons as described in this chapter could be described as the design of neural nets without weights. Weight variation has been replaced by updating procedures for the content of the memory neurons and it has been shown that the central characteristics of Hopfield nets (seeking of energy minima at run time), Boltzmann machines (training of hidden units, escape from local minima) and error back-propagation (learning from errors), have been retained. Indeed the last of these exploits error learning by methods that are more direct and faster than error back-propagation. The methodology offers additional optimization parameters such as directness of implementation using digital logic techniques, choice of synchronous or asynchronous operation (asynchronous systems are fundamentally stable, synchronous ones require a scheme of noise reduction in training, but can provide a richer set of state changes) and the use of probabilistic outputs from the nodes.

At a theoretical level, the analysis using Markov chains provides a simple link between the state transition diagram of a logic/memory net and the energy concepts that are used for weight-based systems.

EXERCISES FOR THE READER

1. For the fully connected RAM-neuron network in fig. 10.1(a) and with the initial memory contents as stated in the chapter (page 166) develop the Markov chains, the state diagrams and the energies of all the states. (Assume that the system is trained on states 110, 101 and 011.) Do this for both synchronous and asynchronous operation, contrasting the two.
2. Repeat exercise 1 for the same network, which this time contains PLNs rather than RAMs. Are there significant differences in comparison with the RAM-neuron net?
3. What would happen if, in addition to the above, the nets in (1) and (2) above were subsequently trained on the 111 state? What are the consequences of this result on the operation of nets of this kind?
4. Work out how the trained net of fig. 10.7 responds to the patterns shown below:

Fig. 10.9 3 × 3 Test patterns.

Comment on the generalization of the pyramid.
5. Assume that the pyramid in fig. 10.7 is trained (from scratch) to

respond with a 1 to the all-1 pattern. It is then trained to respond with 0 to all-9 patterns that have just one 0, the rest being 1s. Can the net then be further trained to respond with a 1 to the all-0 pattern? How does this compare with McCulloch and Pitts nodes?

6. Discover the energies of states for the net in fig. 10.8 for both the synchronous and asynchronous case. Be warned, this is virtually impossible to do with pencil and paper, a computer will be required. Start by defining the 512-state Markov chain.

11

Speech, language and vision

Much of the excitement of studying neural nets lies in their potential in applications for which solutions have not been found through conventional computing. These tasks are in the 'understanding' of perceptual inputs such as speech and vision. In this chapter we first look at the way in which utterances can be assembled into meaningful phrases and such phrases related to stored knowledge of scenarios (such as being in a restaurant, a bank or catching a subway train). Work on vision which includes the ability of giving selective attention to parts of a seen pattern is also reviewed.

11.1 THE NATURE OF NEURAL COMPUTING APPLICATIONS

Neural computing is a developing field of study and is being eagerly watched for signs that it can be applied to hitherto unattained computing goals. There are dangers in expecting too much too soon. However, even at this early stage, it is becoming clear that the impact of neural nets is likely to be in areas of artificial perception – making sense of speech, language and visual images. This is where the promises of going beyond the capabilities of conventional programming arise, simply because conventional programming requires an algorithm which, in turn, requires a full analysis of the problem. But because the mechanisms used by humans when they carry out these tasks are not fully understood, satisfactory algorithms cannot be devised. The expectation is that neural nets will build up such solutions through being trained on appropriate input/output relationships. In a sense, an analysis of the solutions found by these nets provides an explanation of the mechanisms that are involved.

Against this, it can be argued that neural nets can be simulated by conventional programming, therefore neural nets are just another programming style. Although this statement is quite true, it misses the point that the learned knowledge residing in a trained neural net together with the structure of the successful net constitute an explanation of the mechanisms involved. Not only can this solution be used where no solutions existed before, but also the learned contents of the successful net can be studied to provide insights into the nature of the task itself. Probably, since 'conventional programming' implies running simulations of nets on slow serial machines, actual parallel systems will have to be built to make use of these solutions in practice.

Perceptual tasks are areas in which living organisms still set the standards of competence. It is therefore the case that early applications of neural computing back two horses: first the aim to throw light on possible perceptual mechanisms in living organisms and, secondly, to improve artificial mechanisms through the understanding which has been gained. This does not close the door on applications that are totally unrelated to living systems; but it does explain why the modelling of behaviour in living organisms is so dominant in early application studies in neural computing. In this chapter we shall review such studies, giving precedence to those investigations that are likely to lead to competent artificial systems.

Among much research in the area of perceptual processing, we have chosen to describe the work of three teams. The first is the TRACE model which assembles phonemes into meaningful phrases. This was developed in the USA by Jay MacClelland at Carnegie-Mellon University, in Pittsburgh. The second is a language understanding system which accesses 'scripts' as studied by Noel Sharkey and his colleagues at Essex and Exeter Universities in the UK (Sharkey, 1988). The third is the vision understanding system of Kunihiko Fukushima of the NHK Science and Technical Research Laboratories in Tokyo, Japan (Fukushima, 1988a). Fukushima's system not only recognizes highly distorted versions of its training patterns, but, in a version that contains feedback, exhibits properties of selective attention.

11.2 FROM HEARD UTTERANCES TO THE RECOGNITION OF WORDS

One factor that makes the recognition of speech difficult is that the actual signals transmitted by the speaker are just triggers for what is stored in the receiver's memory. Human memory seems capable of putting together the whole from parts of a signal that is spread out in time. In neural processing this means that sequences of sounds must eventually activate single areas of the net. The letters c-a-t must activate a different part of the net from c-a-p. An arrangement called TRACE has been proposed by McClelland and Elman (1986) which demonstrates one neural architecture which is capable of just this kind of behaviour. The scheme is shown in fig. 11.1. This is a highly simplified version of

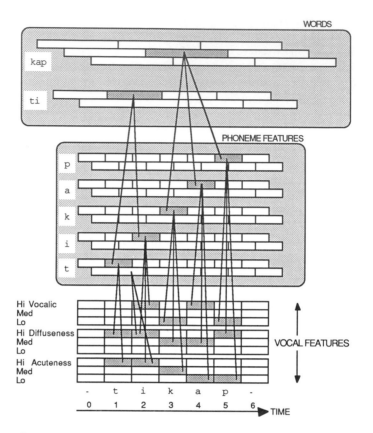

Fig. 11.1 A simplification of the TRACE model.

the original design which enables us to concentrate on the principles involved.

There are three layers. The lowest layer contains measurements taken from the raw signal (from a microphone, say) of speech utterances. The detail of how these features are computed is beyond the scope of this description – a simplified version of the method is given. The whole example is designed to illustrate how the words in the phrase 'tea cup' may be extracted from the sound. The central features are the phonemes (in this case /t i k a p/) and the first task of the system is to identify these phonemes from a stream of measurements in the lowest level of the net.

The phoneme /t/ for example, is characterized by a high degree of acuteness (sudden onset of the sound) and diffuseness (roughly, the amount of air blast used in the pronunciation of the sound) and no vocalic (voiced sound from the vocal chords). The lowest layer can be thought of as a stream along which these detected features flow in time, the most recent features being at the left and the oldest ones being at the right. The mechanics of how this flow is ensured is not of concern here. Suffice it to say that an engineer would use devices called *shift registers* to provide the temporary storage required for the flow. The essence of the arrangement is that it turns features that exist in time into records that can be processed in space. The figure shows the state of this arrangement at one particular moment in time, at a later moment the contents of the lowest layer will have shifted towards the left.

In the middle layer there are as many groups of units as there are phonemes, and these units have adapted to detect specific features. For example, the active unit shown for the phoneme /t/ is active since it has, at the moment of time for which the snapshot of fig. 11.1 was taken, correctly detected the features in the lower level that characterize that phoneme. The key feature of the arrangement is that for each unit in the /t/ group there is a similar connection to the first layer (virtually under the feature, not shown in the figure) so that at the next instant in time, a unit to the right of the one that is firing as shown, will fire. Therefore in the central layer the pattern of recognized phonemes will flow from left to right.

At the top layer, detectors become activated by sequences of phonemes, for example the group /ti/ is shown as being activated, identifying the word 'tea'. A second group detects the word 'cup' and consequently this layer must contain as many groups of detectors as there are words to be recognized by the system. So far, only the key elements that enable the net to group together those features that occur in time in order to perform the recognition have been described. But the designers of TRACE have added some subtleties of neural engineering which remain to be described. These are shown in fig. 11.2.

The first additional set of connections is inhibitory between alternative decisions within each layer. This makes the action within each layer competitive in precisely the way that was described in Chapter 9. The second is a little more subtle. It is known that sound features that are identical as far as their physical characteristics are concerned, and hence trigger identical patterns in the lowest level in the TRACE scheme, are perceived by people in different ways.

For example, while the /g/ sound in bag and the /k/ sound in back are perceived as being quite distinct they are interchangeable in words such as gift and kiss (that is /g i f t/ and /k i f/ lead subjects to hear the same thing at the beginning of the word). In technical terms the perception of phonemes at the middle layer needs to be context-dependent if it is to model this property. That means that the recognition of a phoneme is influenced by those that come before and after it. McClelland and Elman engineered this by modifying the connections

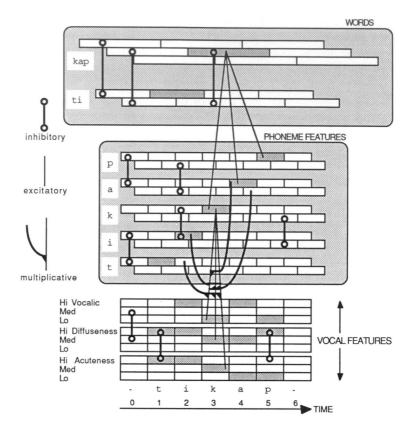

Fig. 11.2 Additional neural connections in the TRACE model.

between the feature and phoneme levels by means of multiplicative connections such as described in Chapter 9. As fig. 11.2 shows these connections are made from neighbouring phoneme identifications providing the neighbouring context dependence. The results with TRACE show that the last two neural engineering additions improve the recognition performance of the system. It leaves open the question of whether they are in play in living systems.

11.3 'UNDERSTANDING' THE WORDS

There is undeniably more to the appropriate reaction to spoken language than the recognition of spoken words through spatially differentiated firing in a net as described above. If you were to say to a colleague at work, 'Let's go and have a hamburger at lunchtime,' your colleague is likely to reply not only to the question, but to the prediction of what the question implies for her. She is likely to have a mental picture of the nearest hamburger restaurant, the range of hamburgers and other items it sells, the actions that are needed to get there and the atmosphere she will find when she does. So she may say something like 'that's fine,' having sized up and found agreeable the entire mental scenario. On the other hand she may respond: 'I'd rather not, the smell of fried chips puts me off, and I don't have the time to go all that distance in any case.'

This ability of brains to recall scene-descriptive knowledge from cues arising in a conversation has been of much concern among the advocates of artificial intelligence. Probably the most often quoted work in this area is that of Schank and Abelson (1977) who suggested that cues in speech bring into 'active' memory an appropriate script, within which sense is made of the words which have been heard and appropriate responses are formulated. The difficulty with this idea is that it neither provides a hint as to how the brain so rapidly selects and moves through such scripts as a conversation unfolds, nor does it give a robot designer a lead on the way he could use the notion in the design of language-understanding systems that would allow robots to be instructed through a verbal interaction with a human operator.

This, therefore, becomes an ideal task for those interested in neural nets. The rapid access to script-like firing patterns in a net from cues in a conversation seems to be part of the emergent properties of a neural net. Noel Sharkey and his colleagues in the University of Exeter (and formerly at the University of Essex) in the UK have looked closely at this possibility, and we review some of their proposals and experiments here (Sharkey, 1989).

In script-like models it is generally accepted that there is a hierarchy of elements. At the top level there are major scenarios (called *schemata* or *scripts*). Sharkey used five such scripts:

cashing a cheque
going to see a film
catching a plane
taking the subway
shopping in a supermarket.

Each script is made up of *scenes*; for example, 'Taking a subway' contains the scenes: (being at the) station entrance, ticket counter, train, seat, arrival platform, ticket control, exit of subway. It so happens that some scenes are shared by various schemata (e.g. ticket counters occur when you go to see a film, catch a plane, or take a subway), while others belong to only one scene. The way that Sharkey has suggested that such items may be represented in a neural net is shown in fig. 11.3.

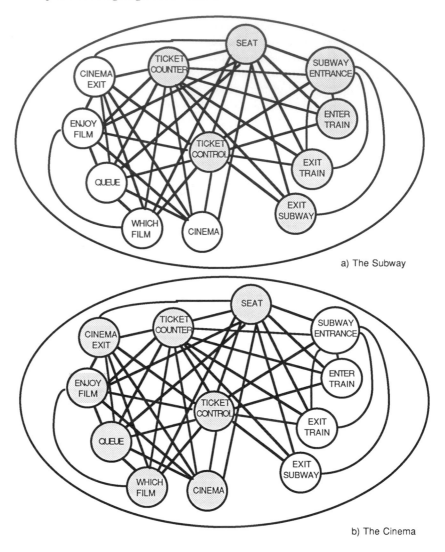

Fig. 11.3 A neural net for two schemata.

Only two of the schemata are shown: 'Going to see a film' ('The cinema', for short), and 'Taking the subway.' There is one node per scene and the schema is represented by an active group of nodes (firing). It should be noted that the two schemata shown have three scenes in common.

Details of neural engineering in this case are, first, that the net has a Hopfield-like character, in the sense that all units are connected to all others and there are no hidden units. Not all the connections are shown because matters have been arranged so that scenes that never co-occur have negatively weighted connections, and only the positively-weighted ones are shown in the figure. Second, the nodes themselves have s-shaped activation functions as described in Chapters 7 and 8. Third, a 'pulsing' system has been devised. This starts from the assumption that the system is asynchronous and that only one unit can change its firing state at one time. When a unit 'comes on' (changes from 0 to 1) this is seen as an impulse which shuts off all its neighbours that are connected by negative weights. This scheme avoids annealing and accelerates the entry into energy minima. Training is accomplished using the standard delta rule as described for Hopfield nets in Chapter 6.

The net used by Sharkey contained 25 neurons representing 25 scenes with varying degrees of overlap. These represented the five schemata described above. He showed first that an unambiguous initial clamp (i.e. one that belongs to only one schema) rapidly recalls the complete schema. But most important is Sharkey's further result that, having settled into one schema, the system nevertheless is capable of moving very quickly into another in response to new inputs, given an unambiguous scene from the second schema. This may provide the basis for an explanation of the way in which a human being tracks the content of a conversation that provides cues from different schemata in rapid succession. An example might be: 'Let's go and see a film. We'll take the subway and eat afterwards'. Three schemata need to be activated in rapid succession to explain what might constitute 'understanding' in the recipient.

11.3.1 Actions

Sharkey has also performed two additional experiments in this area. In the first, he associated *actions* with the schemata. For example a scene such as 'ticket counter' may have central actions associated with it: 'hand over money' and 'pick up tickets'. There are also secondary actions such as 'receive change' and 'thank the seller'. In Sharkey's scheme 72 actions were represented at a lower level in the net as shown in fig. 11.4.

The representation is a model of what has been observed by psychologists: memory of a schema consists of scenes and supporting actions (Galambos and Rips, 1982). The latter come into play not only when trying to understand what someone is saying, but also when the subject is in an environment which he recognizes as a known schema and then has to decide what actions to take. For each scene, Sharkey identified one action as being central, one secondary and others tertiary. These are used in training by giving the system more exposures to the central action features than the secondary ones, and even fewer exposures to

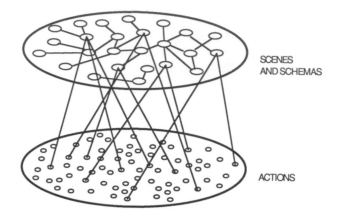

SCENES
AND SCHEMAS

ACTIONS

Fig. 11.4 Actions and schemata.

the tertiary ones. The connections between action neurons and schema neurons are bidirectional.

Tests on the system showed that, given a central action as a starting clamp, the appropriate scene would be retrieved. Then, if the system is allowed to run further, all the actions for that scene are retrieved as well as the other scenes in the appropriate schema. Eventually the entire complex of the schema and all the attendant actions are retrieved.

But this is merely a jumble of activated features in the net. It is the sorting out of these into the appropriate time sequences which is the subject of Sharkey's last experiment.

11.3.2 Timing

A simplified version of Sharkey's suggestion for ordering the recall of actions as a time sequence is shown in fig. 11.5. It consists of a combination of a schema/scene net with an action net (now labelled 'actions at time t') similar to that in fig. 11.4, to which has been added a replica of the action net labelled 'actions at time t + 1'.

So, an action, say at time t (in the 'action at time t' net), together with a stable schema (unchanging in time), produce the next action and generate it in the 'action at time t + 1' net. On the arrival of a clock pulse, the content of the 'action at time t + 1' net is shifted to the 'action at time t' net through a circuit that has been labelled 'unit time delay'. This means that the content of the lower action net is normally one unit of time behind the content of the upper action net.

Initially the system was trained to associate the first action clamped on the t + 1 action net of a schema with the schema clamped on the schema net. Then the action was fed back to the t action net and the system was trained with the second action on the t + 1 action net. This

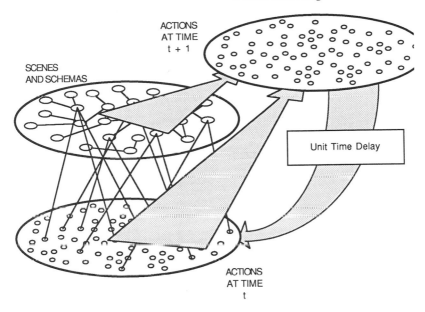

Fig. 11.5 Sequence recall.

was repeated until all the actions were exhausted. The entire process was then repeated for another schema, and so on for all the schemata.

When tested, the system generated (from the t action net) the appropriate taught sequence of actions with the schema net acting as a 'context memory'. The effect of having a particular schema constant in the context memory while the action sequence is being recalled is that an action X at time t in schema A activates the t + 1 net differently from the same action X in context (schema) B. So the action following X becomes determined by the schema context. This has the advantage that if certain actions are common to several schemata they can be chained differently depending on the context. For example, in the context of being in a bank, the action 'receive money' may follow the action 'write out a cheque', whereas in the context of a cinema, it may be the action 'receive tickets' which follows the action 'write out a cheque'.

Sharkey goes on to show that if the combination of the t-action net and the schema net are allowed to generalize, the less central actions become active in the t-action net. This gives the system the ability to output a much more detailed set of actions than those that are input to it in the first place. This, too, is an effect observed in human beings. For example if you were to ask a friend to identify the restaurant where you are going to meet, he might simply say, 'the George and Dragon in the High Street'. Were he to think that you are not familiar with the

area he might give a much more detailed explanation: 'Come out of
your office, cross the Brompton Road and take the No. 9 bus. Get off
at the corner of . . . then walk a few yards and the George and Dragon
is on your left.' The point is that the more detailed set of actions lies in
memory and actions which can be recalled and output at any of several
levels of detail which can be determined by the speaker. Sharkey's
model does this, but has to be externally controlled by the setting of
thresholds in the t-action net.

There is a great deal of work to be done on refining and developing
models in this area. Nevertheless, Sharkey's work on schemata and
action recall provides a valuable model of the way in which a neural net
could react appropriately to natural language.

11.4 MULTI-LAYER IMAGE RECOGNITION: THE NEOCOGNITRON

Another major target for neural nets is the identification of images. This
task has already been used in this book as a vehicle for explaining the
behaviour of many neural nets, and the WISARD system (discussed in
Chapter 5) is a neurally-based pattern recognizer. In this chapter we
discuss another pattern recognizer, the Neocognitron designed by Kunihiko Fukushima of the NHK Science and Technical Laboratories of
Japan (Fukushima, 1988). This work illustrates clearly the advantages
that can be obtained from the use of multi-layering in neural nets. Part
of the arrangement is shown in fig. 11.6.

The input layer holds the binary image. Subsequent layers are
organized in pairs, an S-layer followed by a C-layer. The S-layer has
units which are trained to respond to specific features in the previous
layer. Parts of the S-layer are also specialized for a particular type of
feature. For example, all the units in the central part of the S_1 layer
respond to vertical bars in a 3×3 patch by signalling the position of this
feature. The top part responds to horizontal bars and another part to
diagonals, and so on . . . . The C part of each layer merely allows for
some spatial displacement of the sought-for feature. Again the units
look at a 3×3 patch on the S layer, but this time they respond if they
find an active unit within this 3×3 window. These C-functions are
preprogrammed and have the effect of 'spreading' the discovery of a
feature, and thereby facilitating the task for the next layer.

Subsequently layers such as S_2 look for combinations of features in
the C_1 layer. For example, the part of S_2 shown in fig. 11.6 responds to
the combination of a horizontal and a vertical bar present in the input.
Fukushima's system was designed to recognize handwritten numerals. It
contains four pairs of layers. The action of its C-layers is illustrated in
fig. 11.7 where the type and position of the features identified is shown.

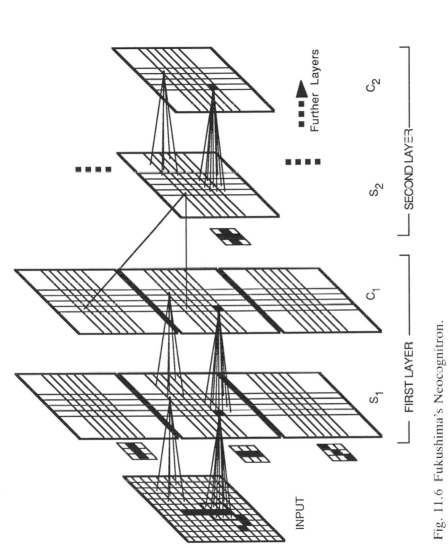

Fig. 11.6 Fukushima's Neocognitron.

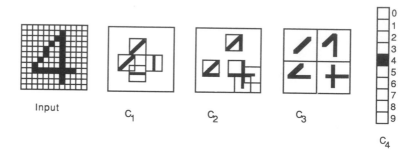

Fig. 11.7 Action of the C-layers in the Neocognitron.

Fukushima's system operates on a 19×19 binary input image. He has described training schemes that are either supervised or unsupervised. The latter is based on techniques similar to those of Kohonen described in Chapter 9. Systems are trained layer by layer with important features of the images being identified by a human. This process is described in some detail in Fukushima (1988). The structure of this system provides a high degree of accurate generalization, and examples of training patterns and resulting generalization are shown in fig. 11.8.

It is clear from Fukushima's results that the method of layering the network in which each layer recognizes ever more complex features gives some important cues to the way that recognition independent of

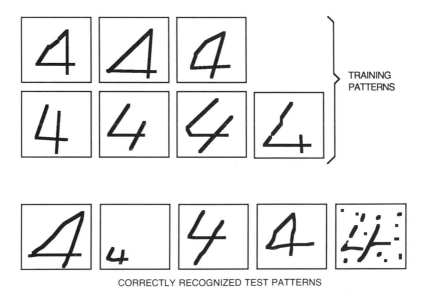

Fig. 11.8 Showing the power of the generalization of the Neocognitron.

distortion might take place in natural neural nets. This is a property that can also stand artificial systems in good stead.

Fukushima did not stop his consideration of multi-layer nets with feed-forward structures. In 1986 he proposed closing the loop with a return net, and not only discovered the emergent property of pattern completion (as in Hopfield nets) but also showed that feedback can lead to what he called 'selective attention' (Fukushima, 1988b). Without going into any of the details, the principle of his net is shown in fig. 11.9. The forward path shown in (a) is like that of the original Neocognitron. The feedback path works backwards from the image at the recognition layer and attempts to reconstruct the original form of the recognized image. But the feedback process interacts with the forward path so that the process of reconstruction aids the process of recognition.

If an ambiguous image is presented to the input layer as shown in (b), and the recognition layer operates on a competitive basis, it will attempt to signal the recognition of only one alternative. The feedback path

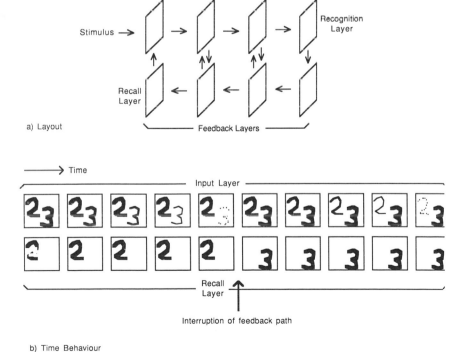

Fig. 11.9 Feedback and selective attention in the Neocognitron.

therefore tries to reconstruct one of the alternatives only, and facilitates only the chosen alternative in the forward path. The effect is shown on the input layer where the recognized alternative is facilitated and the one that it not recognized 'faded' by a process of cellular inhibition. The system is bistable: which of the alternatives is recognized at any moment is arbitrary. So, should the feedback path be interrupted at the time shown in (b), the system can flip to the other alternative, and will do so arbitrarily. If the system is run with interruptions of the feedback path, it will sometimes settle with one alternative in the recall layer and sometimes with the other. Fukushima labels this process *selective attention*. It is analogous to the similarly labelled process in humans.

11.5 SUMMARY

The experimental applications highlighted in this chapter have shown progress in areas where neural computing is likely to be more effective than conventional programming: areas which involve the 'understanding' of sensory information. It has been seen that two major mechanisms are at work in all these schemes: layering and feedback. In each case as one progresses through the layers the net reacts to more complex combinations of features. The feedback, on the other hand, enhances the temporal processes which in the case of word recognition and image recognition lead to selectivity in the net's reaction, while in the case of language understanding it leads to time-ordered recall. It is anticipated that, in the future, much of the function of the brain will be unravelled through an understanding of the interaction of layering and feedback. Again, it is worth noting that an understanding of these mechanisms is of equal importance to the engineer. The examples seen in this chapter are, indeed, good instances of 'neural engineering'.

EXERCISES FOR THE READER

Short of developing simulations of the systems described in this chapter, there is little in the way of an educational exercise from which the reader could benefit. It is suggested however that the reader should read the original publications which form the basis for this chapter, and ponder on the way in which layering and feedback appear to be the fundamental architectural properties that are common to the three perceptual tasks which are being modelled.

12

Future directions

In the final chapter of this book we try to provide some perspective on the role of neural networks in the general area of computing. Taking the view that neural computing is complementary to conventional computing, we suggest a hybrid architecture that combines the two methods. This also contains a 'sensory' neural layer where no learning takes place, but in which speech and vision signals can be processed so as to facilitate the work of a learning or 'cognitive' net. We review the work of Carver Mead (1989) who has developed several analog sensory nets of this kind.

We then survey some unsolved problems which need to be researched before the hybrid architecture can be properly applied, and end with a speculative list of applications which could benefit from neural computing.

12.1 THE NEED FOR PERSPECTIVE

The very fact that neural computing is attracting a vast amount of research attention makes it important to develop a long term perspective by identifying some targets which are ambitious, but worth achieving. In the final chapter of this book this is what we shall attempt to do. Being a multi-disciplinary field, neural computing has targets in many domains: neurophysiologists may seek to find a better background from which to explain their experimental findings, mathematicians may look for improved techniques for solving complex systems of equations, physicists may look for good models of the behaviour of materials. But here we shall concentrate on just one possibility which is in the domain of computing: the opportunity for making machinery which, in some applications, is more competent than that which is normally available.

As we have seen in Chapter 11, there is much promise in the development of neural nets for the understanding of speech, language and visual input. We shall refer to these as cognitive processing tasks, using the word 'cognition' as defined in the *Oxford English Dictionary* ('the act of, or faculty of knowing') to stress that cognitive processing carried out by neural nets depends heavily on acquired knowledge or experience. Cognitive tasks have been the target for much of artificial intelligence work based on pre-programming, but this has resulted in only limited successes. Neural nets hold the promise of some further achievement.

So our aim in this chapter is to describe a framework, perhaps only an approach, which may lead further. This is centered on the combination of neural nets with conventional computing. The neural part of such a hybrid divides further into, first, 'sensory' levels of signal processing and, second, the net which performs cognitive tasks using the results fed into it by the first part. The sensory part will be considered closely, as this has not featured in other parts of the book. With this architectural combination in mind, we shall discuss some as yet unsolved problems and then we speculate on application areas that may benefit from the neural computing approach.

12.2 A GENERAL NEURAL ARCHITECTURE

During the time that a concept is in the early stages of development it is fashionable to suggest that the idea is so powerful that it will replace all that went before it. So it was with artificial intelligence and expert systems, and so it seems to be with neural computing. It is possible to read, not only in the daily press but also in the technical press and in some learned journals, how the power of neural computers will over-shadow conventional computing. The view taken here is that this is almost certainly not going to be so. Instead, neural computing is likely to act as a powerful addition to the armoury of techniques currently available in conventional computing. We believe that the two method-ologies working together hold the greatest promise, and it is this notion which leads to the speculative architecture shown in fig. 12.1.

There are three major parts to this architecture:

a sensory neural level
a cognitive neural level and
a conventional computing level

Peripheral connections are made to appropriate video cameras, micro-phones and other electronic sensors on the input side. On the output side, the system may have the ability to connect to robot arms, voice synthesizers, graphics screens and so on. The conventional computing level of the system would have provision for conventional communica-tion with the user: keyboard, mouse, display screen and the like.

We will look first at the accurate translation of sensory information into symbols. We shall then consider the way in which the three parts of this system might interact. But first, we distinguish between the sensory neural level and the cognitive level.

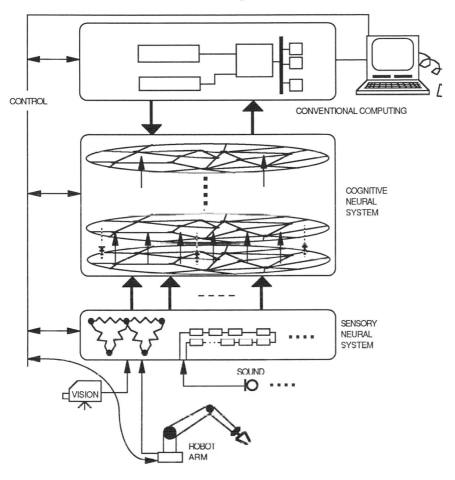

Fig. 12.1 A general architecture, incorporating neural nets.

The main difference between these two lies in the fact that the sensory level contains fixed processing equipment that does not learn but is helpful in distinguishing between different forms of input. For example, in vision this equipment distinguishes between lines of different orientations or responds differently for the movement of a line in different directions. This is useful in the sense that, if a visual scene has to be interpreted by some cognitive apparatus, this apparatus can operate on features recognized at this early stage. This makes the task for the cognitive apparatus easier.

For example, say that part of a system is required to detect the presence or the absence of rectangular boxes. The task is rendered easier if the sensory layer presents the same features to the cognitive layer irrespective of the lighting angle in the scene. So, the sensory machinery may be neural, but is fixed in terms of the tasks it performs. By contrast, it is in the cognitive system that all the learning and adaptation must take place. Figure 12.2 shows an idealized view of this distinction. The sensory neural system in this case extracts the edges and produces a 'sketch' which is independent of lighting conditions. The task for the cognitive system is to associate the frame-like image produced by the sensory system with the statement, 'It's a box'. This means that what has to be learnt by the cognitive neural system is the same even if the input images are very different, and it is in this sense that the task of the cognitive system is made easier by the sensory neural system. We shall now look at these two types of system a little more closely, starting with sensory neural systems.

12.3 SENSORY NEURAL SYSTEMS

The main contributor to the design of sensory neural systems is Carver Mead of the California Institute of Technology. His approach is to

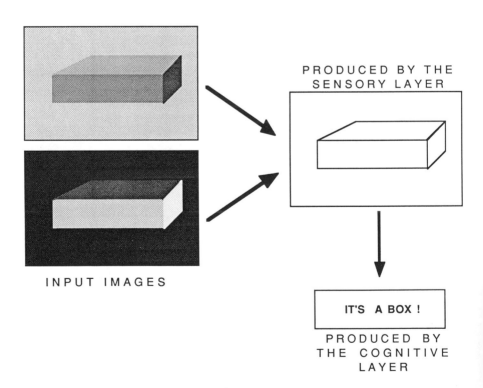

Fig. 12.2 Division of tasks between sensory and cognitive systems.

model the early stages of perceptual signal processing in a manner that closely resembles what is known of similar processing in living organisms. The approach highlights the power of analog silicon circuitry and his work is detailed in a book (Mead, 1989). Here we shall discuss some of the achievements of this technology and relate it to the generic architecture of fig. 12.1.

Carver Mead and his colleagues have produced four analog silicon systems of note:

SeeHear: a light-source detecting aid for the blind;
an optical motion sensor;
a silicon retina;
an electronic cochlea.

To get a measure of these developments we shall look at the first two of these in some detail, and then consider electronic retinas and cochleas only very briefly.

12.3.1 SeeHear

The principle of this aid, which is intended to help blind persons locate light sources, is shown in fig. 12.3. The blind person is equipped with a

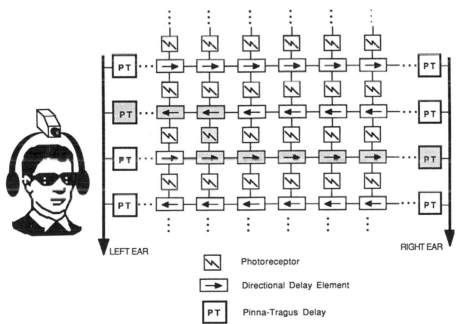

Fig. 12.3 The SeeHear system.

camera-and-headphones arrangement so that the position of the light source is detected with respect to the position of the head. Two principles of hearing are used as a basis for this aid: stereophonic direction detection, and the detection of elevation, known as the pinna-tragus effect.

Stereophonic detection is known to depend on two factors:

1. If the source of sound is off-centre with respect to the head, the signal arriving at each ear will have slightly further to travel to one ear than to the other. This means that it will be slightly delayed in one ear with respect to the other. The brain is capable of using this cue to interpret the direction of such sounds.
2. There is a 'head shadow' effect as an off-centre sound which reaches the further ear has to travel through the material of the head, and may be slightly muffled by this.

All that needs to be said about *elevation* is that pinna is the scalloped part of the ear and the tragus is the little mound in front of it as shown in fig. 12.4. The way that a sound bounces between these two, and becomes modified as a result, provides the brain with a cue regarding the elevation of the incoming sound wave.

Returning to fig. 12.3 we give a simplified description of the operation of the chip it depicts. Assume that an intense, small light source is in the field of view. The first task of the chip is to cause a photoreceptor to respond to this and emit a signal at an audible frequency. This signal propagates through directional delay elements and reaches the lines which are eventually connected to the two earpieces with an overall delay dependent on the horizontal position of the active light sensor, which is a function of the direction of the 'seen' light source. So, if the

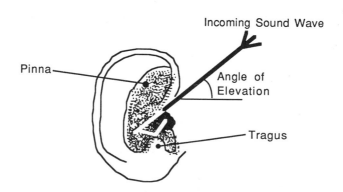

Fig. 12.4 The pinna-tragus assumption of elevation detection.

vision signal were central, the sound would arrive at the two ears with the same delay, that is, with no relative delay between the ears. However, were the light source detected closer to the left edge of the chip it would reach the left ear before the right ear giving the impression of a sound which is coming from the left.

The 'head shadow' effect is built into the characteristics of the signal delay elements to enhance the impression of directionality. In a similar way, light sources detected at different levels of elevation are given their appropriate pinna-tragus characteristics by the devices shown at the edges of the chip. It should be emphasized that the design of this chip is of considerable complexity and sophistication. Here we have merely described its major mechanisms in a very simplified way. Full details may be found in Mead (1989).

Although the success reported with this arrangement is only moderate (the localization can take place only with large displacements), the technique has much potential for further development through the use of VLSI technology for low-level neural processing tasks in the sensory domain.

12.3.2 Motion detection

Living organisms are known to be particularly sensitive to the motion of objects in their field of view. Carver Mead developed an array-like light-sensitive chip which continuously output a pair of signals indicating the coordinates of the velocity of an object focused onto the field of view of the chip. One of the principles of applied mathematics is that if a point moves from x,y position (on a two-dimensional plane) at time 0 to position x',y' at time t, the velocity in direction x is $(x' - x)/t$ and the velocity in the y direction is $(y' - y)/t$. These two quantities fully define the velocity of the object. In trigonometric form, the magnitude of the velocity is $\sqrt{[(x' - x)^2 + (y' - y)^2]}/t$ and its direction has a gradient of $(y' - y):(x' - x)$ to the x (horizontal) direction (this is an angle of $\arcsin[(y' - y)/(x' - x)]$).

This is fine for a point but becomes more complex for an object in motion as shown in fig. 12.5. This shows an object and its displacement in time t. Eventually, an array of sensors will be used to calculate its real velocity. At the moment we show how this can be done with just the two sensors in the figure. Leaving aside for the moment what the sensors actually do, a difficulty arises from the fact that each sensor has only a limited view of what has happened in time t. To make things clear, we have positioned the sensors so that they track points on the edge of the object starting from the bottom left side of the sensor.

This point could have moved to a range of positions of which three are shown for each sensor. The uncertainty is resolved (as shown at the

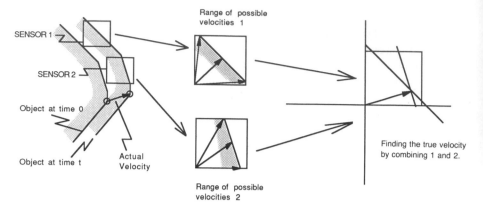

Fig. 12.5 Combining the uncertainty of two sensors to calculate velocity.

right of the figure) by combining the views from the two sensors and selecting the velocity arrow on which both sensors agree. This is the principle on which Carver Mead's velocity sensing array operates: getting an opinion from many sensors and finding a value on which they agree.

We now need to show how the principle may be turned into action for a circuit and we remain with the above example containing just two sensors. A circuit is shown in fig. 12.6. The sensors do a little more than just sensing. Effectively they sense the position of the edge of the displaced object and (this is the clever bit) they can be given as input a

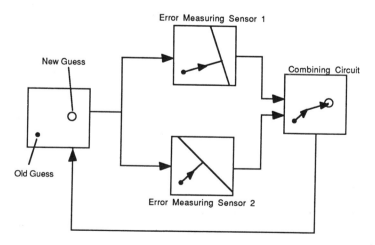

Fig. 12.6 A circuit for measuring velocity.

guess of where the head of the velocity arrow might lie. In response they output an error which is the magnitude and direction of the shortest distance to the edge which they have sensed. The two sensors receive the same guess, and each gives an opinion of the error. Component **B** combines all these opinions and generates a signal which indicates how the guess could be modified to reduce all these errors. The guess for the velocity comes from component **A** in the first place, so the output from component **B** is fed back to **A** which issues a better guess and the whole system settles down to a point at which the sensors signal no, or minimum, error. (It may not be possible to reduce the error completely to zero due to the inaccuracy of the sensors themselves.) Component **A** also generates the signal which indicates the agreed velocity.

What we have described above is merely a principle whereby a feedback circuit can keep track of the velocity of objects with appropriately positioned sensors. But because it is not possible to position sensors so conveniently with respect to the shape of the object, Carver Mead used an array of 64 sensors arranged in an 8 × 8 pattern loosely based on the principle described above. The array is designed to react not only to edges of objects but to any changes of intensity of the image.

12.3.3 Electronic retina and cochlea

The objective of going into some detail in the discussion of Mead's work in the above paragraphs, is to show that the practical knowledge exists to process sensory data with neural-like silicon technology. In addition to the chips described so far, Mead has designed and built a model of a living retina: 'A thin sheet of neural tissue that partially lines the orb of the eye'. The artificial version is a network of resistors with processing elements at the nodes. The behaviour of the model is very much like that of the living eye: it is largely insensitive to lighting conditions, but it is highly sensitive to variations (edges) in intensity patterns in the field of view.

The electronic cochlea too is a close model of its living counterpart. The natural version, a part of the inner ear, is a snail-shaped, rolled, narrowing, tube and is the receptor for sound waves. It measures both the intensity and the frequency content of sound waves. Any given frequency is translated into vibration at a specific position in the tube, stimulating nerve endings at that point which leads to the sensation of hearing the sound and identifying its pitch. The magnitude of the vibration is an indication of the intensity of the sound.

Mead's concluding comments on the electronic cochlea include:

... It converts time-domain information into spatially encoded information by spreading out signals in space according to their time scale. ... The silicon model of this travelling-wave structure exhibits behaviors that bear an uncanny resemblance to those of the living system.

The philosophical question raised by such work is whether, in the context of making usable machines, it is necessary to mimic quite so closely the functions of living organisms. We would argue, purely on the basis of the desirability of the architecture shown in fig. 12.1, that for the time being, anyway, the lower sensory level has to be as lifelike as possible. After all, the neural part of that architecture is designed to improve human–machine interaction and therefore should, perhaps, be capable of dealing with visual and auditory symbols in a human-like way. Particularly in speech, it is likely that the symbols have evolved to suit human hearing, as well as possible, hence artificial mechanisms should benefit from being human-like.

From here on we return to the general architecture and assume that the sensory neural system is capable of performing the major task of turning raw sensory information into signals that are appropriate for processing at the cognitive neural level. It is the control and operation of the latter that is the ultimate challenge for neural computer designers.

12.4 THE COGNITIVE PROCESSING CHALLENGE

The major challenge for neural computer designers is the need to coordinate various neural processes each of which is known to be feasible. We illustrate this with some specific tasks (which are described as challenges rather than recipes for a solution).

12.4.1 Is it a box?

Earlier we suggested that the cognitive layer would be responsible for taking the line features shown in fig. 12.2 which were produced by a sensory layer and exclaiming: 'It's a box.' Here we break down the cognitive task and reveal some of its components in order to illustrate how the cognitive neural system in fig. 12.1 might work in concert with both the sensory system and the conventional computing part of the overall architecture. First, as shown in fig. 12.7, part of the cognitive net needs to perform a pattern completion exercise. This could occur in the manner of schemata discussed in Chapter 11. The features of the image activate a box-like schema at some layer L in the cognitive neural system (fig. 12.7(a)). Other arrangements of features may activate a pyramid-like schema in the same layer (fig. 12.7(b)). The stable 'box'

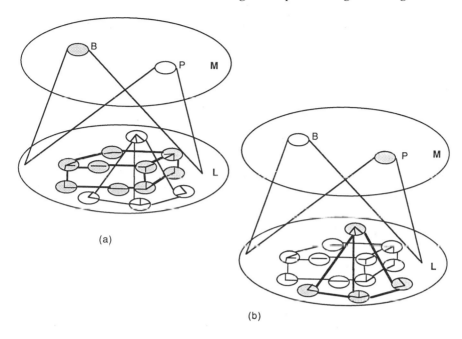

Fig. 12.7 Schemata for the recognition of image features.

schema in (a) leads to a localized identification at some B-neuron in a higher layer (M) while another recognition (of the pyramid, say) may lead to the activation of some P-neuron in layer M. It now remains to be said how such a recognition can be turned into an answer to the spoken phrase, 'What do you see?'.

At the lower levels of cognitive processing, it is clear that several recognition activities must be going on in parallel. Such activities are related to the different senses: while part of the neural circuitry decodes what the eye 'sees' as in fig. 12.7, another must be devoted to the extraction of meaning from what the ear 'hears'. Calling again on the method of schemata, but now on the speech understanding side, the elements 'what', 'you' and 'see' could be thought of as forming a stable schema at one layer which, at a higher layer, is interpreted by the activation of one (or a few) units as 'introspective description (voiced sequence) required on the vision side of the net'.

In such a layer within the net, other localized representations may be:

'introspective description required on the auditory (tactile, . . .) side,'
'movement required of the robot arm to coordinates x,y,z,'

'voice utterance required in response to state of vision side of the net,'
etc. . . . .

In a living organism, this process of localized interpretation in a higher net of a stable schema in a lower net must eventually lead to the appropriate actions in the organism. (Note: some of the 'actions' could be internal, such as 'thinking about an event'.) In a man-made machine, however, there comes a point at which conventional processes of computation could be triggered off by the state of the neural net. For example, the state 'introspective description (voiced sequence) required on the vision side of the net' is a clear instruction which could be interpreted by a conventional computer and a voice synthesizer. The machine would 'address' the upper vision layer, discover that 'box' is activated, interpret 'introspective description required' as an instruction to output, *via* the voice synthesizer, the phrase 'it's a ⟨content of vision layer⟩'.

It should be stressed that these mechanisms and interactions between conventional and neural structures are highly speculative and may make useful topics for future research in neural computing.

12.4.2 'To get to Covent Garden, change at Green Park'

In Chapter 11 (fig. 11.5 in particular) we described Noel Sharkey's suggestion for generating an appropriate description of a sequence of actions under the control of a stable schema (e.g. the actions required by the schema of catching a train). This is an example of 'temporal neural processing': it requires the recall of sequences of events and the actions that would change such sequences. This aspect of neural computing is still very much in its infancy, and is a fruitful area for further research.

Temporal processing includes the ability of living neural systems to enable living organisms to predict sequences of events on the basis of past experience. A central and general question is how sequences of actions leading to given outcomes (like, 'If you change to the eastbound Piccadilly line at Green Park you will first get to Piccadilly Circus and then Covent Garden') are learnt and recalled by humans. Such ability to predict events on the basis of past experience is the focus of some psychological theories of personality (different people have different experiences and hence different personalities) and the behaviour of individuals (behaviour being dictated by the prediction of future events from individual knowledge) (Kelly, 1955). The accurate prediction of events is helpful not only in order to find one's way around the London underground when there are no maps to be seen, but, more importantly, it underlies some of the ability of individuals to survive.

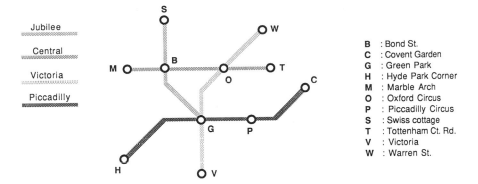

Fig. 12.8 A simplified map of the London underground.

To illustrate what may be needed, we continue with the example of the underground journey. Consider part of the London underground map shown in fig. 12.8. Say that a fully interconnected layer in a cognitive net is capable of learning a sequence of states by 'being' in a state, and being trained to change to the next. These states could be names of underground stations. So if the state of the net is P, it could learn that the next state will be C, in the sense that if the net is clamped to P and released, it will change to C. However, a characteristic of such a layer is that one state can only lead to another specific state. Therefore merely labelling states as stations would lead to confusion, as there are many states that can follow G in our example – something else is also needed.

Clearly, the net has to store context as a 'state' (e.g. 'I am on the Victoria line at O and I am trying to get to C') to determine the next state (which should be 'I am at G changing to the Piccadilly line towards P trying to get to C'). The way in which these sequences are learnt by exploration rather than the memorization of a map is one of the open questions in neural computing. That is, the problem is not how such knowledge may be represented in neural nets (Sharkey and others provide sensible suggestions for that), but how this knowledge could get there, particularly through exploration. The challenge therefore is for a neural net to gather sufficient experience to be able to answer questions such as 'How do I get from Victoria to Covent Garden?'

Eamon Fulcher at Imperial College, London (Fulcher, 1989), discusses the implications of the fact that animals learn backwards from goals (as in experiments where the animal has to learn to find its way around a maze in order to gain a reward). In neural net terms he suggests that while part of a net learns the links between temporal events backwards in time, another should retain a memory of the final outcome or 'goal'. So, we imagine one layer of the structure of the cognitive neural system in fig. 12.1 as being divided into two sectors, a 'context' sector and a 'place/action' sector. The key to this approach is that the 'goal' of a sequence is very much like the 'context' in Sharkey's work. The learning would go as follows.

At the early stages of learning the organism would learn single steps such as: 'If I am at Piccadilly Circus (P) and am going east on the Piccadilly line I get to Covent garden (C) next'. The layer of the cognitive neural net would represent this as:

	Context/goal	:	Place/action	
	C	:	P	East on Piccadilly
leads to	C	:	C	Goal achieved

At some later time in learning the state transition that needs to be learned is:

	Context/goal	:	Place/action	
	C	:	G	East on Piccadilly
leads to	C	:	P	East on Piccadilly

Continuing in this way, the following state transitions could be learned:

	Context/goal	:	Place/action	
	C	:	V	Initial state
leads to	C	:	V	North on Victoria
leads to	C	:	G	North on Victoria
leads to	C	:	G	Change to East on Piccadilly
leads to	C	:	G	East on Piccadilly
leads to	C	:	P	East on Piccadilly
leads to	C	:	C	Goal achieved

In other words, it is crucial that the learning should be done in the context of goals. So, in the context of going to Swiss Cottage (S), instead of:

leads to	C	:	G	Change to East on Piccadilly

we would have

leads to	S	:	G	Change North on Jubilee

which gets around the ambiguity surrounding G.

Research still needs to be done on mechanisms that lead to such learning.

12.4.3 'Was that mushroom rotten?'

A similar problem arises when an organism receives information from an environment at unpredictable points in time. For example a mushroom-eating creature depends for its survival on telling the difference between poisonous and good mushrooms. Poisonous mushrooms are as tasty as others, but produce stomach aches at unpredictable times after they have been eaten. Catherine Myers at Imperial College, London, has shown how 'windows of memory' held in reverberating nets can sort out this kind of problem (Myers, 1989b). This reinforces the notion that the future development of neural net applications depends on how well they can be made to learn to predict and control a wide variety of environments.

12.5 FUTURE APPLICATIONS

The nature of neural computing is so general that, given enough research and development, it may become a standard part of every computer. Perhaps the architecture suggested in fig. 12.1 will form the basis of what will, in the future, be found in all computing machines. But more important may be low-cost special devices that are enabled by the central strength of neural nets to absorb the knowledge required to interpret vision speech and language, and the ability to coordinate speech output and, possibly, movement in robots. The relationship between large systems, as in fig. 12.1, and such applications may be the same as that which exists between the general-purpose computing machine and the chip which controls a washing machine. They both use the same computing principles, but one is general while the other is closely tailored to a specific application. Here we look, with a heavy dose of imagination (which assumes that most of the problems we raised in the last section have been solved), at the tailored applications which may benefit from neural computing.

12.5.1 The home

In many settings, but particularly in the home, surveillance and security may benefit. Distinguishing between the smoke of a cigarette and the early detection of a dangerous fire is an example of a security task which is hard to achieve at present. The detection of an intruder as opposed to a member of the family is also a difficult, but worthwhile target. The interrogation of a home 'security monitor' from afar by means of a telephone is done at present, but with very crude sensing methods. Neural computing could not only provide a way of increasing the 'intelligence' of the sensors, but also of increasing the intelligence of the interaction that one might have while interrogating such devices.

Care for the disabled and the aged is an important target. The blind may be aided by being able to query the status of objects using their voice, and getting audible reactions. For example:

Person: 'What is the current oven setting?'
Oven: 'Mark 4 but not up to this temperature yet'.
Person: 'Please set it to gas mark 5 and ring the bell when it has reached that temperature'.
Oven: 'I have understood that you want me to set myself to gas mark 5 and I shall ring the bell when that temperature has been reached'.

While a conventional computing chip could do all the measurements required in the above example, the capacity of a neural net would be needed to understand and generate the linguistic input and output.

The deaf could be aided by intelligent displays. The development of automatic translators from speech into visible signs could be enabled by neural techniques. 'Reminding devices' for the aged and those with memory disorders become feasible, so do automatic monitoring aids for all those who may be out of social contact in their homes. Clearly the aged and the disabled need support when they leave their homes too, presenting a worthwhile target for the development of portable, miniaturized neural devices. Such applications have been suggested in the past as being within the range of conventional computing. This is partly true, but the ability to recognize events 'seen' through television cameras, to accept spoken questions and to answer them lies outside of conventional computing alone, but seems feasible for a combination of the conventional and the neural.

The opportunities for entertainment and the use of television channels also abound: language-driven tele-shopping ('show me what the Afghan carpet you are selling for £1200 looks like . . . closer please . . .') is just one example. Also those interested in computer games will be quick at spotting the opportunities for direct interaction with the players through language rather than joysticks.

12.5.2 Production aids for industry

This is the classical area for which automatic machines have been developed and could be improved by neural networks: the use of vision for automatic quality control and inspection, robot guidance and the inspection of inaccessible areas (as in nuclear power plants). Clearly, much has already been achieved with pre-programmed algorithms, but the possibility of fine tuning on detailed images by an unskilled operator using natural language not only appears to be an effective way of automating processes, but would also serve to bring lesser-skilled operators into closer touch with high-technology equipment.

Another area that could benefit in a similar way is the monitoring of the health of machines from the sounds that they make. Some of this is already being done with conventional methods. Neural nets, however, open up the opportunity of teaching the recognition machinery from examples when the features of the sounds which determine the health of the machine cannot be pre-specified for translation into an algorithm.

At the management level, neural techniques could be helpful in optimizing production schedules in the face of complex constraints.

12.5.3 Communications

The use of voice to control communication services (for example, automatic directory interrogation) is being developed now by the world's major communication companies. This effort will benefit from neural techniques which will make it possible to use linguistic constructions far in advance of the single-word triggers for simple pre-programmed actions which are being used now. These communication examples include the use of face expression identification techniques for low-cost videophones, which, again, relies heavily on the knowledge-storing abilities that neural nets can offer.

There is also scope for much imaginative thinking in the provision of personal communication facilities tailored to individuals: enabling doctors to keep in touch with their patients (without either having to learn to type), lawyers with their clients, parents with their children.

12.5.4 Medicine

Conventional computing has been helpful in providing diagnostic aids, graphic visualization through reconstruction of scanned images, and the enhancement of medical images in general. But other areas, such as the detection of pathological occurrences in images of cervical smears or breast images for automatic screening, have not been as successful as one would like. The main reason for this is that humans doing these tasks use experience and knowledge which cannot be easily expressed in terms of rules for conventional computers. Neural nets may well provide the medium in which such knowledge can be stored and accessed.

12.5.5 Finance

Activities such as risk assessment rely considerably on the knowledge and experience of the assessor. This is one area in which software that emulates modestly sized nets is already being used to try to capture the decisions made by good assessors. Feed-forward networks are trained on their actual decisions. This sector of application is likely to grow, as the decisions will require ever more subtle storage of experience and hence larger and better-structured neural nets.

12.5.6 Other applications

Defence organizations are clearly taking much interest in neural net techniques which could provide fast reactions from computing machinery used for the guidance of missiles and vehicles. Also, the technique is seen as being helpful with high-sensitivity security and surveillance problems, reconnaissance tasks, and many others. Guidance is of importance in civil applications too, ranging from prosaic tasks such as the cleaning of supermarket floors to the on-board assessment of traffic conditions in cars, with the possibility of automatic accident avoidance equipment. Here too, the speed and knowledge-storage capacity of neural nets is likely to allow progress to be greater than could be achieved with conventional computing alone.

While on the subject of transport, planning of railway routes, air traffic control and similar tasks could benefit from the transfer of human experience into neural nets, with the obvious advantage of avoiding human errors which may be due to fatigue and overload.

In the office, the use of voice in the control of word processors has been suggested for some time as a suitable application for conventional expert systems. However attempts to build such systems have not come to full fruition due to the explosion in the required number of rules and exceptions to rules. Nets with stored experience again offer hope in this area. But looking beyond the translation of speech to text, the possibility of developing letter-writing machines which take minimal instructions from their users, and compile full letters seems an interesting possibility.

12.6 A FINAL WORD

When looking at the above list of potential improvements in computing machinery there is a danger that we will assume that these are merely a matter of automatic development. It is worth recalling, however, that neural computing has only recently started to be understood sufficiently to allow planning for some new machine designs and much remains to be established with scientific precision and discovered through imaginative insights.

The core of what remains to be done will involve the development of rules and tools for the use and design of neural systems. These will be based on this gradual emergence of understanding of neural net behaviour. Thereafter serious progress towards applications can only be made once appropriate machines with large, flexibly reconfigurable physical (as opposed to emulated) neural strutures become available.

Comments on the exercises for the reader

Introduction

1. In a conventional computer, 'memory' has the form of a filing cabinet with numbered filing slots called 'addresses'. Facts and data are stored at these addresses, and it is the responsibility of the program to keep track of the addresses at which such data are held. The steps of the program itself are memorized in adjacent pockets of the filing cabinet, care being taken that this is done in a different memory 'area' (part of the filing cabinet) from the data. The computer works by being given the starting address of the program, executing the steps one by one, picking on data as required by some of these steps, and then halting when this essential step is reached in the program.

   In human beings the word 'memory' refers to an altogether different and greater range of phenomena. It is implied in phrases such as 'putting a name to a face', 'remembering one's childhood', 'remembering the price of a bar of chocolate'. Much of human memory has also to do with actions: 'knowing how to reply to a fast service at tennis', 'remembering to move stage left while reciting a particular line in Hamlet'. So human memory is more akin to the execution of some complex program on a computer. In the brain such 'programs' seem to be executed at very high speed and are unlikely to be the result of operations carried out with a filing-cabinet-like mechanism.

2. The computer with the filing-cabinet memory requires very precise instructions, or rules, which distinguish the stored image of one face from another. It is difficult for the programmer to work out beforehand what such rules should be. Although face recognition programs exist, they are not very successful and therefore this is considered to be a hard (not impossible) task for conventional computers.

   In the brain the recognition of a face occurs at great speed and it is something that humans feel is 'easy' and 'natural'. A possible reason for this is that the neural nets of the brain are highly tuned to known faces and easily triggered into retrieving this information: an example of experience-based systems being better suited to a task than program-based ones.

3. The issue is one of performance. It is quite true that any neural net could be simulated on a large enough conventional computer. However the serial simulation of the highly parallel process that neural nets are, could lead to extremely long execution times. The main advantage of a specially constructed parallel neural net is that its ability to retrieve complex, experientially acquired data would capitalize on one of the properties of such nets: the ability to retrieve in relatively few steps of operation. In a simulation, this advantage would be lost.

4. It is quite true that neural nets may not be capable of 'explaining' their 'method' for retrieving information. But this may not matter in cases such as rapid recognition of speech and vision signals. Human beings are not able to give such explanations either. However, as neural technology develops, using nets to give descriptions of experientially acquired knowledge is likely to become commonplace (examples are given in Chapter 11).

Chapter 1

1. Without the firing rule, F1 is 0 for input 101 only, 1 for input 111 only and $ for other inputs; F2 is 0 for input 111 only, 1 for input 010 only and $ for other inputs; F3 is 0 for input 101 only, 1 for input 010 only and $ for other inputs ($ being the 0/1 condition explained in the text).

So for (a): F1,F2,F3 = $ 1 1
    for (b): F1,F2,F3 = 0 0 $
    for (c): F1,F2,F3 = $ $ $

That is, the responses are as follows:

for (a) the response is 011 or 111
for (b) the response is 000 or 001
for (c) the response is any pattern

These are much less 'knowledgeable' responses than those using the learning rule, in the sense that there is no generalization.

2. We show one step of this calculation and comment on the overall result of an exhaustive calculation.

Consider the input:

```
1 0 0
0 1 0
0 0 1
```

This has a Hamming distance of 4 from the T pattern and 4 from H hence the difference between the two is 0.

The response is F1,F2,F3 = 010 which has a Hamming distance of 2 from the response to T and 1 from the response to H hence a difference of 1 between the two. (Suggestion: give $ the value of one half in the output measurement.) There will be many responses for the same difference Hamming distances of inputs, and it may be best to average these before they are plotted.

On the whole, it will be found that with the firing rule the responses are bunched towards the +3 and −3 values of the output measure whereas without the firing rule the average response follows the input Hamming distance measure much more closely, but with a much greater spread of output measures.

So, again, the firing rule is seen to cause the system to generalize.

3. In broad terms, what the net is doing when starting in patterns close in Hamming distance to one of the prototypes, is to end in a stable cycle of the appropriate prototype itself. Starting in states that are equidistant from the prototypes, on average ends in cycles such as in fig. 1.7(a).

4. Clamping F22 to 1 leaves the net as if unclamped, as F22 outputs 1 for any state. Clamping F22 to 0 causes the net to enter cycles around the prototypes, with F22 modified. For example the following cycle occurs around the T prototype:

```
1 0 1   1 1 1   1 0 1   1 1 1
0 0 0   0 0 0   0 0 0   0 0 0
0 1 0   0 1 0   0 0 0   0 0 0
```

while the following single-state cycle is possible for starting patterns close in Hamming distance to H

```
1 0 1
1 0 1
1 0 1
```

5. In conventional computing, the prototype patterns would be stored in the computer memory as, say, pattern T and pattern H. The algorithm would be something like:

Read unknown pattern U.
Measure the Hamming distance between U and T, let it be UT.
Measure the Hamming distance between U and T, let it be UH.
Find the least of the above measurements, let it be UX.
Output X as the matching pattern.

In some ways this seems simple enough to make neural approaches unnecessary. However, the algorithm implies the built-in ability to perform quite complex arithmetic tasks (. . . calculate the Hamming distance . . .) and ordering tasks (. . . find the lowest of the above measurements . . .). The point that is stressed in neural net science is that the ability to find the nearest pattern is emergent from the structure of the net. This makes it worthy of further consideration.

Chapter 2

1. All except F4 are achievable. The best way of arriving at this conclusion is to visualize the three-dimensional representation in fig. 2.4. Then, for F1, it is seen that the three vertices of the cube at 1 are 000, 001 and 101. The first and third of these are adjacent to the second on the 'floor' of the cube. Therefore a plane can be found that separates them from the rest of the points. For F2, a similar conclusion can be reached by looking at the 0s in the function. F3, on the other hand, represents the 'front face' of the cube and, consequently, can be separated off by a plane. F4, however, contains diagonally disposed 1s on this front face together with 0s placed in the other two corners which cannot be separated by a straight line and, hence no plane can be found to do the separation.
2. The dividing line starts swinging about increasingly without finding a solution.
3. The errors are not cleared. The last two examples simply stress the fact that the selection of parameters d and e is a matter for experimentation, and successful training may depend on whether the correct values have been found.
4. Good convergence takes place, there are fewer overshoots in the movement of the dividing line. Improving the learning rule is a suitable area for investigation.
5. The association rules are at fault, they cannot distinguish between the outer edges of the two patterns. Their function needs to be changed to an AND.

Chapter 3

1. A perceptron of order 1, in this case, is merely a 4-input MCP node. Letting X1 and X4 be 0 and concentrating on the X2,X3 'face' of the

hypercube, we note that the system has to perform the inverse of the parity function, that is, separate linearly 00 and 11 from 01 and 10, which it cannot do.

2. Assume A1 is a parity association unit connected to X1 and X4 and A2 is a parity association unit connected to X2 and X3. They will both output 0 when symmetry is present, hence the MCP part of the perceptron needs merely to find the linear separation that isolates the all-zero vertex of its 2-input cube (rectangle). This result is generally true provided that the association units are connected to the appropriate pairs of the input vector.

3. One solution is to connect two MCP nodes to each corresponding pair of the input (like X1 and X4 in exercise 2). One of this pair of nodes fires when the inputs are 10 and the other when they are 01. Then if any nodes fires there is no parity, and this can be detected by the output OR gate. This solution requires V, 2-input, MCP nodes for a V-input pattern. Other solutions may be found.

4. For 2-input MCP nodes the weights must provide at least 14 different functions (as seen in Chapter 2). These must be found from weight combinations. So 14 distinct weight combinations are required. Roughly four distinct values of each weight will give this as 4×4 covers 14. The total number of weights is 6, so the total number of possible weight combinations is $4^6 = 4096$. This is not a useful way of dealing with larger systems as this number of combinations grows alarmingly with the size of the MCPs.

5. Not a great deal is known of this, but it is in this area of neurophysiology that major discoveries remain to be made.

Chapter 4

1. See the discussion on question 4, Chapter 3, for the answer to the accuracy of weights required for a 2-input MCP model. This number turns out to be 14 positions of the hyperplane which requires two bits per weight. A 3-input MCP model has 108 possible positions of the hyperplane, and a 4-input one about 1000. As this number seems to grow roughly as a power of the number of inputs, it suggests that the number of bits per weight could remain constant at about 2. However, in practice this would be far too little as it would lead to too rough a placement of the hyperplane during training.

2. Not all hyperplanes may be achieved. With an N-input MCP model with two inputs only 4 out of the 14 functions may be achieved. To be precise, letting the weights have values of $+1$ and -1, with the threshold set to 0 (note, the threshold must be exceeded, not just equalled), the functions are (for inputs labelled X1 and X2): X1 OR X2; X1; X2 and the 'always zero'. For N inputs only 2^N functions

can be obtained, meaning 8 instead of 108 for $N = 3$, 16 instead of 1000 for $N = 4$, and so on.

3. Much of the work on optical neural nets is of an exploratory kind. Much depends on the development of highly accurate spatial light modulators. It is, at the time of writing, easier to implement large digital nets in electronics, but optical systems may have an interesting future in applications where very high processing speeds are required and for which the learning has been done off-line.

4. The steps of an assembly-language-like program may be something like (say for a 16-input neuron):

    Allow 16 consecutive locations in memory
    P points to the first of these
    Label A   Store input vector at Q
    Set (counter) C to 0
    Label B   Increment C
    If C < 17 skip next line
    Jump to label A
    Rotate Q
    If RH bit of Q = 1 skip next line
    Jump to label B
    Address P + C to Accumulator
    If interrupted, Halt
    Jump to label B.

5. This article by Mostafa and Psaltis was widely read and drew the attention of many scientists to the fact that neural computing may be an important application area for optical systems. However, the complexity of the apparatus and the rather limited amount of content-addressable storage achieved with it suggests that there is scope for further development before practically useful systems can be built.

Chapter 5

1. A shortcut to the answer is to work out the most likely distribution of 0s as follows. Take the first RAM. The most likely number of 0s at its input is $Q1 = $ the nearest integer to $4.Z/16$.
   Take the second RAM. The most likely number of 0s at its input is $Q2 = $ the nearest integer to $4.(Z - Q1)/(16 - 4)$.
   In this way the most likely distribution of 0s among the RAMs can be calculated. For $Z = 3$, for example, and $Z = 4$ the most likely distribution turns out to be 1, 1, 0 in each RAM leading to a $4/4$ response. For $Z = 5$ the distribution turns out to be: 1,1,1,2, giving a

response of 3/4, for Z = 6, 2/4, for Z = 7, between 1/4 and 2/4. For Z = 8 the most likely response drops to 0/4.

2. Using (5.2) is cumbersome for this type of example, but the principles that go into deriving (5.2) can be applied directly. To calculate the probability of a particular RAM firing, one calculates first the probability of the RAM having all four inputs in the 1 area of the input pattern. This is $((16 - Z)/16)^4$ $(= P(\text{all} -1))$. Then one calculates the probability of precisely one of the four inputs of a RAM being in the 0 area with the other 3 in the 1 area. This is $4 \times (Z/16) \times ((16 - Z)/16)^3$ $(= P(\text{one} -0))$. The overall firing probability is then $P(1) = P(\text{all} - 1) + P(\text{one} -0)$. From this the most likely number of RAMs firing may be given from the nearest integer to $4 \times P(1)$. The results are:

$$
\begin{aligned}
&Z = 1 \quad \text{No. of RAMs firing} = 4 \\
&Z = 2 \quad \text{No. of RAMs firing} = 4 \\
&Z = 3 \quad \text{No. of RAMs firing} = 4/3 \\
&Z = 4 \quad \text{No. of RAMs firing} = 3 \\
&Z = 5 \quad \text{No. of RAMs firing} = 3/2 \\
&Z = 6 \quad \text{No. of RAMs firing} = 2 \\
&Z = 7 \quad \text{No. of RAMs firing} = 2/1 \\
&Z = 8 \quad \text{No. of RAMs firing} = 1 \\
&Z = 9 \quad \text{No. of RAMs firing} = 1 \\
&Z = 10 \quad \text{No. of RAMs firing} = 1/0 \\
&Z = 11 \quad \text{No. of RAMs firing} = 1/0 \\
&Z = 12 \quad \text{No. of RAMs firing} = 0
\end{aligned}
$$

These predictions are lower than those in exercise 1 and are less accurate because of the assumption that each RAM has the same probability of connecting to the input pattern. The larger the input vector with respect to the size of the RAM input, the lower will this discrepancy be.

3. The two are similar to the extent that the WISARD is a perceptron with variable-logic association units, instead of variable weights. This means that it has the same hard-learning limitations. A major difference lies in the speed of learning in the WISARD with respect to the slow rate of Widrow-Hoff type algorithms in perceptrons. The ease with which WISARD can be implemented using RAM technology rather than variable weights, also constitutes an important difference.

4. For a line at 45° the response for both the discriminators should be the same and therefore the value of relative confidence will be zero (from (5.3) in which D becomes zero). At such balance, the overlap area in each discriminator is three-quarters and the response of each

discriminator is $(0.75)^N$. It may be shown that the change in area dA due to an error of e degrees is given by:

$$dA = \sqrt{0.5} \, Sin\,(e)/2 \, Cos\,(45 - e)$$

Then the percentage value of relative confidence is given by

$$100 \times [(0.75 + dA)^N - (0.75 - dA)^N]/(0.75 + dA)^N$$

An error of three degrees has dA of 6.4% hence $N = 1$ will satisfy the requirement. In fact, $N = 8$ will give a confidence of 41.2%. But the power of the WISARD method may be seen for errors of, say, 0.1 degrees which have dA of 0.23%. Setting N to 8 gives a relative confidence of 1.8% and for $N = 16$ the confidence is 3.65%.

5. $N = 4$ will satisfy the first requirement. In the trained position the relative confidence is 47.3%. Half way between the two trained positions the system still indicates the presence of the intruder but with a confidence of 39% (disc 1 responds 48%, disc 2 80%).

Chapter 6

1. As all the V_j and V_i terms are zero all parts of equation (6.3) evaluate to zero, the energy is zero. For the all -0 state not to be an energy minimum at least one node must change from 0 to 1 as there is to be an energy state below 0. Equation (6.2) implies that at least one U_i must therefore be negative.
2. Each of the nodes is required to perform a parity function on the output of the other two, which is impossible.
3. The system becomes deterministic. 010 and 011 are still stable states but 111 has no entry from any other state, while 010 has entries from states 000, 001 and 010. There is a spurious stable state, 011. This has entries from states 100 and 101.
4. A suitable set of values is:

$$T12 = T13 = T23 = -0.2$$
$$T14 = T24 = T34 = -0.4$$
$$U1 = U2 = U3 = -0.3$$
$$U4 = -0.1$$

This result will be used in the next chapter to get over the parity problem precisely by using the fourth unit as an auxiliary neuron.

The exercises in Chapters 7 and 8 are there for the reader to flex his muscles in writing Markov chains on spreadsheets or some other form.

Chapter 9

1. After training on both 'environment' patterns and taking the focus for the first environment as 14 the responses become: Neuron number: 0 1 2 3 4 5 6 7 8 9 10 11 12 13 14 15; Resp. to 001:3 2 2 0 1 1 1 2 2 0 2 0 1 2 3 2; Resp. to 111:1 2 2 2 3 3 3 2 0 2 0 2 2 2 1 2. Hence the net has 'reserved' the area around 14 to signify a recognition of environment 001 and the area around neuron 4 for the recognition of 111. Despite the difference in the initial choice, the two areas are well separated.

2. After training once on 1100 and twice on 0011 (as in the text) the division of input patterns is:

Indeterminate	A Stronger	B Stronger
0000	0100	0001
1111	1011	0101
	1100	0010
	1001	0110
	1101	0011
	1010	0111
	1110	1011

This is a similar division to that obtained in the text except that fewer patterns are in the indeterminate class and the A and B roles have been interchanged. After training on 0110 twice, pattern 0100 swaps from the A to the B class making the presence of the first 1 a discriminatory feature (with the exception of 1011). This confirms that although the overall behaviour of the system remains determined by the training set, some of the details depend on the original weight settings.

3. 'Clearly defined' means that every item in a training set carries either an identification label (as in character recognition, say), or is in itself a prototype that represents others similar to it (in pattern reconstruction where, say, a trace of distorted fingerprint has to be associated with its original). 'Badly defined' refers to data for which no clear labels are known (say, price variations on the stock exchange) or for which it is difficult to provide the labels even if they are known (say, speech, where learning has to take place from continuous spoken language). Perceptron-like systems are useful where clear labels exist, Boltzmann machines where reconstruction of prototypes is required and competitive learning for data that is 'badly defined'.

4. Note that the system is not entirely 'safe'. For example, an upright H can cause the T output neuron to fire when the left or right twist neurons are firing. A upside-down T can never cause an output

neuron to fire as it energizes one middle-layer neuron only in each of the H and T groups.

Chapter 10

1. For the synchronous case, the only stable states are 3, 5 and 6 as trained. Their probabilities are (assuming equal starting probabilities) 0.75, 0.125 and 0.125, respectively. The respective energies are: −1.13, 1.89 and 1.89, all the others being 5.0. For the synchronous case, again all states except the trained ones have zero final probability. The respective final probabilities for 3, 5 and 6 are: 0.382, 0.309 and 0.309, with respective energies: 0.46, 0.46 and 0.78, all the others being at 5.0.

2. To make sense of this question it is best to assume that the initial state of all the memories is 'd'. In both the synchronous and the asynchronous cases only the trained states become stable in the state diagram. The results may be tabulated:

Type	State	Probability	Energy
Synch	3	0.305	0.79
	5	0.347	0.6
	6	0.347	0.6
Asynch	3	0.333	0.67
	5	0.333	0.67
	6	0.333	0.67

Comparing this with the RAM case confirms that training of PLNs leads to a better distribution of energies, which is a reason for using PLNs in the first place.

3. This destroys the previously learnt stable states as a different output is required for the same input in each RAM. The consequences of this, due to the fact that the elements are not connected to themselves, are that patterns differing by just one bit cannot be made stable, as some RAM will need to have the same input for two outputs.

4. By looking at the final value of the stores of fig. 10.7 the response of the PLNs may be obtained. For the first pattern, for example, the response of the PLNs is PLN1:0, PLN2:1, PLN3:d which means that PLN4 receives inputs 011 and 010 with equal probability. For the first of these it responds with a 1 and for the second with d, that is, 0 and 1 with equal probability. On the whole, therefore, it responds 75% of

the time, with a 1 and 25% with a 0. For the second pattern the response is 25% 1, for the third pattern the response is 0 all the time, for the fourth pattern, is 67.5% 1. The pyramid responds roughly to the horizontal/vertical difference. The last result, above, is biased towards the horizontal, as the single centre 1 in PLN2 is recognized as a horizontal pattern.

5. The desired task can be achieved as each PLN can respond with a 1 to a 111 input, with a 0 to 011, 101 and 110 inputs, and, finally with a 1 to the 000 input (only the first-layer PLNs need have the last response). The function is not linearly separable and therefore cannot be achieved with a McCulloch and Pitts node.

6. The main reason for this exercise is to give the reader experience in the writing of simulations of networks and large Markov chains. There are no particular answers to be provided.

References

Aleksander, I. (1965) Fused logic element which learns by example. *Electron. Lett.*, 1 (6) 173–7.

Aleksander, I. (1978) Pattern recognition with networks of memory elements in *Pattern Recognition, Ideas in Practice* (ed. B. G. Batchelor), Plenum, London.

Aleksander, I. (1983) Emergent properties of progressively structured pattern recognition nets. *Pattern Recogn. Lett.*, **3**, 375–84.

Alcksander, I. (1988) The logic of connectionist systems in *Neural Computing Architectures* (ed. I. Aleksander), MIT Press, Massachusetts.

Aleksander, I. and Hanna, F. K. (1978) *Automata Theory: An Engineering Approach*, Edward Arnold, London.

Aleksander, I., Thomas, W. and Bowden, P. (1984) WISARD, a radical new step forward in image recognition. *Sensor Rev.*, 120–4.

Aleksander, I. and Wilson, M. J. D. (1985) Adaptive windows for image processing. *Proc. IEE, Lond.* **132**, 233–45.

Almeida, L. B. (1988) Backpropagation in non-feedforward networks in *Neural Computing Architectures* (ed. I. Aleksander), MIT Press, Massachusetts.

Arthurs, A. M. (1965) Probability theory, *Library of Mathematics*, Routledge and Kegan Paul, London.

Ballard, D., Hinton, G. E. and Sejnowski, T. J. (1983) Parallel visual computation, *Nature*, **306** (21), 26.

Burks, A. W. and Von Neumann, J. (1966) *Theory of Self-Reproducing Automata*, University of Illinois Press, Urbana.

Crick, F. and Asanuma, C. (1986) Certain aspects of the anatomy and physiology of the cerebral cortex in *Parallel Distributed Processing vol 1 and 2* (eds D. E. Rumelhart and J. L. McClelland), MIT Press, Massachusetts.

Fukushima, K. (1975) Cognitron: a self-organising multilayered neural network. *Biol. Cybern.*, **23**, 121–34.

Fukushima, K. (1988a) Neocognitron: a hierarchical neural network capable of visual pattern recognition. *Neur. Net.*, 1 (2), 119–30.

Fukushima, K. (1988b) A hierarchical neural network model for selective attention in *Neural Computers* (eds R. Eckmiller and C. Von der Malsburg), Springer-Verlag, Heidelberg.

Fulcher, E. (1989) BARNABUS: a neural net which learns sequences by a bidirectional chaining of events. *Neural Systems Engineering Internal Report*, Imperial College EF1/89.

Galambos, J. A. and Rips, L. J. (1982) Memory for routines. *J. Verbal Learning and Verbal Behaviour*, **21**, 260–81.

Garth, S. (1988) A dedicated computer for simulation of large systems of neural nets in *Neural Computers* (eds R. Eckmiller and C. Von der Malsburg), Springer-Verlag, Heidelberg, pp. 435–44.

Grossberg, S. (1976) Adaptive pattern recognition and universal recoding: Part I, parallel development and coding of neural feature detectors. *Biol. Cybern.*, **23**, 121–34.

Hebb, D. O. (1949) *The Organization of Behaviour*, Wiley, New York.

Hinton, G. E. (1981) A parallel computation that assigns object-based frames of reference. *Proc. 7th Int. Joint Conf. on Artificial Intelligence*.

Hinton, G. E., Sejnowski, T. J. and Ackley, D. (1984) *Boltzmann Machines: Constraint Satisfaction Networks that Learn*. Tech. Rep. CMU CS 84, 111, Carnegie-Mellon University, Pittsburg.

Hinton, G. E. and Sejnowski, T. J. (1986) Learning and relearning in Boltzmann machines in *Parallel Distributed Processing vol 1 and 2*, MIT Press, Massachusetts.

Hopfield, J. J. (1982) Neural networks and physical systems with emergent collective properties. *Proc. Nat. Acad. Sci. USA*, **79**, 2554–8.

Hubel, D. H. and Wiesel, T. N. (1962) Receptive fields, binocular interaction and functional architecture in the cat's visual cortex. *J. Physiol.*, **160**, 106–54.

Kelly, G. (1955) *An Introduction to the Theory of Personal Constructs*, Norton, New York.

Kirkpatrick, S., Gelatt, C. D. Jr. and Vecchi, M. P. (1983) Optimization by simulated annealing. *Science*, **220**, 671–80.

Kohonen, T. (1984/1988) *Self-Organization and Associative Memory*, 2nd edn, Springer-Verlag, Heidelberg.

Kohonen, T. (1989) Speech recognition based on topology-preserving neural maps in *Neural Computing Architectures* (ed. I. Aleksander), MIT Press, Massachusetts.

Lea, M. L. (1984) Microcircuits for associative memory in *Advanced Digital Information Systems* (ed. I. Aleksander), Prentice-Hall, Englewood Cliffs.

Lighthill, J. (1973) *A Report on Artificial Intelligence*, UK Science and Engineering Research Council.

Mackie, S., Graf, H. P. and Schwartz, D. B. (1988) Implementations of neural networks in silicon in *Neural Computers* (eds. R. Eckmiller and C. Von der Malsburg), Springer-Verlag, Heidelberg, pp. 467–76.

Marr, D. (1982) *Vision*, W. H. Freeman, San Francisco.

May, D. and Shepherd, R. (1988) Implementations of neural networks in silicon in *Neural Computers* (eds. R. Eckmiller and C. Von der Malsburg), Springer-Verlag, Heidelberg, pp. 477–86.

McClelland, J. L. and Elman, H. (1986) in *Parallel Distributed Processing vol 1 and 2*, MIT Press, Massachusetts.

Mead, C. (1989) *Analog VLSI for Neural Systems*, Addison-Wesley, New York.

Minsky, M and Papert, S. (1969) *Perceptrons: an Introduction to Computational Geometry*, MIT Press, Massachusetts.

Reece, M. and Treleavan, P. C. (1988) Implementations of neural networks in silicon in *Neural Computers* (eds R. Eckmiller and C. Von der Malsburg), Springer-Verlag, Heidelberg, pp. 487–95.

Rosenblatt, F. (1962) *Principles of Neurodynamics: Perceptrons and the Theory of Brain Mechanisms*, Spartan Books, New York.

Rumelhart, D. E., Hinton, G. E. and Williams, R. J. (1986) Learning internal representations by error propagation in *Parallel Distributed Processing vol 1 and 2* (eds D. E. Rumelhart and J. L. McClelland), MIT Press, Massachusetts.

Rumelhart, D. E. and Zipser, D. (1986) Feature discovery by competitive learning in *Parallel Distributed Processing vol 1 and 2* (eds D. E. Rumelhart and J. L. McClelland), MIT Press, Massachusetts.

Schank, R. C. and Abelson, R. P. (1977) *Scripts, Plans, Goals and Understanding*, Lawrence Erlbaum, New York.

Sharkey, N. E. (1988) A PDP approach to natural language understanding in *Neural Computing Architectures* (ed. I. Aleksander), MIT Press, Massachusetts.

Stonham, T. J. (1987) *Digital Logic Techniques: Principles and Practice*, 2nd edn, Van Nostrand Reinhold, Wokingham.

Sutton, R. S. and Barto, A. G. (1981) Towards a modern theory of adaptive networks: expectation and prediction. *Psychological Rev.*, **88**, 135–70.

Taylor, W. K. (1959) Pattern recognition by means of analogous automatic apparatus. *Proc. IEE, Lond.*, **106B**, 168–72.

Turing, A. M. (1936) Computing machinery and intelligence (see reprint in Hofstadter and Dennett *The Mind's I*) Basic Books, New York, and Harvester Press, Brighton (1981)

Von der Malsberg, C (1973) Self-organizing of orientation sensitive cells in the striate cortex. *Kybernetik*, **14**, 85–100.

Widrow, B. (1962) Generalization and information storage in networks

of ADALINE neurons in *Self-Organizing Systems* (ed. G. T. Yovits), Spartan Books, New York.
Wiener, N. (1986) *Cybernetics*, MIT Press, Massachusetts.

Index